# Toward a Healthier Contextualization among Muslims

# Toward a Healthier Contextualization among Muslims

A Biblical Theological Evaluation of
the Insider Movement and Its Lessons

WONJOO HWANG

Foreword by Keith E. Eitel

⁌PICKWICK *Publications* · Eugene, Oregon

TOWARD A HEALTHIER CONTEXTUALIZATION AMONG MUSLIMS
A Biblical Theological Evaluation of the Insider Movement and Its Lessons

Copyright © 2019 Wonjoo Hwang. All rights reserved. Except for brief quotations in critical publications or reviews, no part of this book may be reproduced in any manner without prior written permission from the publisher. Write: Permissions, Wipf and Stock Publishers, 199 W. 8th Ave., Suite 3, Eugene, OR 97401.

Pickwick Publications
An Imprint of Wipf and Stock Publishers
199 W. 8th Ave., Suite 3
Eugene, OR 97401

www.wipfandstock.com

PAPERBACK ISBN: 978-1-5326-4711-6
HARDCOVER ISBN: 978-1-5326-4712-3
EBOOK ISBN: 978-1-5326-4713-0

*Cataloging-in-Publication data:*

Names: Hwang, Wonjoo, author

Title: Toward a healthier contextualization among Muslims : a biblical theological evaluation of the insider movement and its lessons / by Wonjoo Hwang.

Description: Eugene, OR : Pickwick Publications, 2019 | Includes bibliographical references and index.

Identifiers: ISBN 978-1-5326-4711-6 (paperback) | ISBN 978-1-5326-4712-3 (hardcover) | ISBN 978-1-5326-4713-0 (ebook)

Subjects: LCSH: Insider movements. | Christian converts from Islam. | Missions.

Classification: LCC BR128.I57 H85 2019 (print) | LCC BR128.I57 (ebook)

Manufactured in the U.S.A.                                01/22/19

Unless otherwise indicated, all Scripture quotations are from The ESV® Bible (The Holy Bible, English Standard Version®), copyright © 2001 by Crossway, a publishing ministry of Good News Publishers. Used by permission. All rights reserved.

# Contents

*Foreword by Keith E. Eitel* | vii
*Preface* | ix
*Acknowledgments* | xi
*Abbreviations* | xiii

1 Introduction | 1
2 Historical Developments of Muslim Evangelism and the Insider Movement | 18
3 An Analytical Framework for Contextualization among Muslims | 59
4 An Evaluation of the Biblical Interpretations of Insider Movement Advocates | 106
5 An Evaluation of the Insider Movement through an Analytical Framework | 148
6 Conclusion | 202

*Appendix: Comparison of Muslim Evangelism Models* | 211

*Bibliography* | 217

# Foreword

VOLUMES SPEAK, AND YET experience speaks volumes. In *Toward a Healthier Contextualization among Muslims: A Biblical Theological Evaluation of the Insider Movement and Its Lessons*, Wonjoo Hwang does both. He brings academic acumen to bear with years of experience living and working face-to-face with peoples of various Islamic persuasions in several settings. He successfully accomplishes a clear critique of the ongoing problem of contextualizing the Christian gospel in such settings. A prominent technique is advocating the so-called "insider movement" whereby new believing Muslims are encouraged to stay inside their Islamic socioreligious contexts by continuing Islamic religious practices while affirming the prophet Isa or Jesus with varying degrees of openness. The author of this book lays out the developments of Christian outreach to Muslims, especially in more contemporary times, and then analyzes the relatively recent phenomenon of these types of Christian movements inside Islam.

This is a certain read for anyone engaged in or advocating Christian work among Muslims worldwide. Students, pastors of sending churches, faculty, and doctoral students will all benefit from different aspects of this work. Even believing former Muslims perhaps locked within an insider movement may gain confidence in stepping on out of the system and coming out for Christ more openly.

If indeed experience speaks, this book speaks volumes in terms of its quality and the contribution it makes to a conversation so easily controlled by only one set of voices these days. His voice speaks loudly and clearly. We all do well to hear him.

Keith E. Eitel, DMiss., DTheol.
Dean, The Roy Fish School of Theology and Missions
Southwestern Baptist Theological Seminary
Fort Worth, Texas

# Preface

THE MOST INFLUENTIAL TEACHING during my early Christian life was the biblical foundation of missions. This class opened my eyes to understand God's love for all nations and his desire to restore them into his Kingdom. It was through this teaching that God called me into his Kingdom ministry among the nations. As I understood the Father's unceasing love, especially for the unreached Muslim nations, my passion continued to grow to serve his divine purpose among those who have not heard the Gospel of the Savior.

Since then the primary interest of my missiological thinking has been involved in how to serve Muslim nations effectively in view of leading them to Christ. After having served in a Muslim nation for ten years, I felt a strong need for a further study on contextualization among Muslims. During my biblical and theological studies at the seminary, my encounter with the debates surrounding the Insider Movement compelled me to investigate into the validity of this approach with the genuine desire of searching more effective, yet biblically sound, ministries among Muslim nations. The current work is my doctoral dissertation that was completed in December 2012 under the title, *A Critical Evaluation of the Insider Movement as a Contextualization Model among Muslims*. The findings of my research led me to conclude that we must have concerns about the biblical and theological foundations of the Insider Movement proponents although there are positive lessons to be learned from this ministry approach.

Discussions on the Insider Movement may continue among evangelical missiologists and missionaries for the goal of developing more effective contextualization approaches among Muslims. Nevertheless, it must be emphasized that a sound biblical theological foundation should guide this process of searching for a healthier contextualization. This is because as much as missions starts with the biblical mandate, so must missions strategies stand upon the sound biblical grounds. My humble desire is that this book will add another perspective to enrich the ongoing discussion for this purpose, and serve those who are committed to develop an approach to Muslim nations that is both biblically authentic and culturally relevant.

Wonjoo Hwang
The Middle East
February 2018

# Acknowledgments

But by the grace of God I am what I am, and his grace toward me was not in vain. On the contrary, I worked harder than any of them, though it was not I, but the grace of God that is with me. (1 Cor 15:10)

I praise the Lord for his abundant grace in my life, both in saving me and calling me. I am especially thankful for the people whom God has surrounded me with; without their presence I would not have been who I am today. My parents raised me with deep commitment and sacrifice, through which I have inherited such great values in life. The constant caring hearts of my parents-in-law have been so essential for my entire family.

I am grateful for Dr. Keith Eitel for his academic excellence and missionary zeal for the nations. His mentoring and friendship have been an invaluable support for my academics as well as for my spiritual life. Dr. Tony Maalouf has taught me great insights for ministries to Muslims. I am honored to witness his love for the Muslim souls; it has inspired me to grow more passionate about sharing the gospel with Muslims. Dr. George Klein, my supervisor in the Old Testament Studies, opened his office to my frequent visits with warm welcomes and heartfelt handshakes and has always been a great source of encouragement. The Lord has used many professors at Southwestern Baptist Theological Seminary to shape my biblical-theological understanding, and I am grateful for their deep commitment to the Lord and scriptural authority.

I am considered a part of the first generation lay missionary movement in Korea which started in the early 1990s. One of the few pastors who initially implemented this paradigm of sending lay people for missions was the late Rev. Yong-Jo Ha, through whom I found wonderful spiritual nourishment and the vision for the Kingdom. Over the years, many more lay missionaries from Korea have obeyed God's calling to take the Gospel to the unreached peoples. I cannot thank enough my brothers, Luke Joo and Mark Kim, who have walked closely with me and exemplified such deep passion for the Lord and compassion for the nations. I consider it a special privilege to serve the Lord with many mission-minded Christian communities and churches throughout my Christian life. I am deeply indebted to them for their partnership in the Gospel. May the Lord greatly reward them for their faithful services for his Kingdom.

I am thankful for my wife, Jaehee, who loves the Lord and serves him so faithfully. Over the years, we have shared both joys and hardships of life together. Yet, she has not lost her true beauty in her loving smile and warm embrace for people. I admire her for such mature character and a serving heart. I am also thankful to my two sons, Dabin and Siyoung, especially for patiently bearing with my absence during my doctoral study. They have grown to be such wonderful men of God that they are the source of my joy and happiness. It has been a privilege to mentor them as my fellow workers for the Kingdom, and I look forward to seeing even greater works of the Lord in their lives. Glory be to God!

# Abbreviations

| | |
|---|---|
| BDAG | Walter Bauer, Frederick William Danker, William F. Arndt, and F. Wilbur Gingrich, *A Greek-English Lexicon of the New Testament and Other Early Christian Literature.* |
| *BibSac* | *Bibliotheca Sacra* |
| CPMs | Church Planting Movements |
| *CT* | *Christianity Today* |
| *EMQ* | *Evangelical Missions Quarterly* |
| *IBMR* | *International Bulletin of Missionary Research* |
| ICBI | International Council on Biblical Inerrancy |
| *IJFM* | *International Journal of Frontier Missions* |
| IM | Insider Movement |
| IMB | International Mission Board |
| ISFM | International Society of Frontier Missiology |
| *JAM* | *Journal of Asian Mission* |
| *JETS* | *Journal of Evangelical Theological Society* |
| MBB | Muslim Background Believer |
| *MF* | *Mission Frontiers* |
| *Missiology* | *International Review of Missiology* |
| *MW* | *Muslim World (Moslem World)* |
| *SFM* | *St. Francis Magazine* |
| SPCK | Society for Promoting Christian Knowledge |
| *WTJ* | *Westminster Theological Journal* |

## SCRIPTURE ABBREVIATIONS

### Old Testament

| | |
|---|---|
| Gen | Genesis |
| Deut | Deuteronomy |
| 1–2 Kgs | 1–2 Kings |
| Jonah | Jonah |

### New Testament

| | |
|---|---|
| Matt | Matthew |
| Mark | Mark |
| Luke | Luke |
| John | John |
| Acts | Acts |
| Rom | Romans |
| 1–2 Cor | 1–2 Corinthians |
| Gal | Galatians |
| Eph | Ephesians |
| 1–2 Thess | 1–2 Thessalonians |
| 1–2 Tim | 1–2 Timothy |
| Titus | Titus |
| Heb | Hebrews |
| 1–2 Pet | 1–2 Peter |
| 1–2–3 John | 1–2–3 John |
| Jude | Jude |

# 1

# Introduction

THE INTERNATIONAL SOCIETY OF Frontier Missiology (ISFM) organized a conference titled "The Jerusalem Council Applied: Apostolic Insights into Today's Insider Movement" in Atlanta in September 2006. The theme of this conference was the Insider Movement (IM), which from thence onward has become one of the most debated missiological issues among those involved in ministries to Muslims.[1] This conference was a pivotal moment in the academic discussion because it set up a public platform for evaluating critically the IM among evangelical scholars.

The IM was little known to missionaries and missiologists before this conference, although some of its early proponents had been experimenting with this ministry approach for a significant number of years.[2] As these early proponents became convinced that it is not only a biblically-theologically valid model for ministry to Muslims but also an effective approach bearing much fruit, they proposed it for an objective evaluation among evangelical missionaries and missiologists with the hopes that the new movement would be used in different parts of the Muslim world. These early proponents suggested that the basic principle of the Jerusalem Council in Acts 15 be applied to the issue of the IM in that the early church made a key

---

1 The IM is a generic term to designate a ministry approach that can be used in all religious groups including Hinduism, Buddhism, and Islam. This study, however, limits its scope to the IM among Muslims. Details and characteristics of this term appear herein later.

2 Due to security reasons, a limited amount of information is available concerning the initial formulation and implementation of the IM. It is estimated that the earliest experimentation had started at least two decades before the Atlanta Conference in 2006.

missiological decision for the Gospel ministry to the Gentiles in the Council as an ecclesiological body.³

Since the 2006 conference, many more have joined in the discussion with differing views, and a significant number of academic writings have appeared.⁴ During the course of discussion, interaction between IM advocates and IM critics has enabled both sides to elaborate on the central issues of the IM more precisely. In this regard, the very purpose of the 2006 Conference was accomplished. A decisive conclusion, however, is yet to be reached among evangelicals because some doubts on the validity of this missiological approach have not been completely resolved.

While most discussions on the IM have been confined to a limited number of components, the lack of a comprehensive analysis has caused more confusion than clarification among evangelicals. The lack of objective criteria for evaluating contextualization models has left evangelicals defenseless against many radical assertions based on pragmatic reasoning in favor of the IM. It is within this context that this study develops an alternative and unexplored method to evaluate the IM by employing an analytical framework that will yield comprehensive evaluation grids and play the role of objective criteria derived from a sound biblical and theological foundation.

## BACKGROUND

### Early Developments of the Insider Movement

The first academic discussion on the IM appeared in *Evangelical Missions Quarterly* in 1998, where two prominent missionary scholars provided contrasting viewpoints.⁵ John Travis introduced a spectrum of six

---

3 One may wonder in what sense the Jerusalem Council can be applied to the contemporary IM issue. As the study proceeds, it will become clearer to see how IM advocates use the Jerusalem Council for their biblical validation of the IM.

4 The primary literary platform for this issue has been *International Journal of Frontier Mission*, but a wider academic platform has become available for the discussion, including *Evangelical Missions Quarterly*, *Mission Frontiers*, and *St. Francis Magazine*. It is worthwhile to mention one valuable online platform, www.biblicalmissiology.org, because it has facilitated useful discussions about various issues specifically related to Muslim contextualization among missiologists and field practitioners.

5 Parshall, "Danger!" 404-6, 409-10; Travis, "C1 to C6 Spectrum," 407-8; Travis, "Must All Muslims," 411-15. Scholars use several terms to designate this new contextualization model in the literature, including Messianic Muslims (John Travis), Islamicized contextualization (Don Eenigenburg), or dynamic equivalence model (Sam Schlorff). Gary Corwin interchangeably uses the two terms, C5 and the Insider

"Christ-centered communities" that were found in the Muslim world.[6] The debate arose when Travis claimed C5 to be a valid and viable Christ-centered community. Phil Parshall saw danger in this claim; it was "going too far" in Muslim contextualization.[7] Although such a notion of C5 was not new in Muslim evangelism, Travis and IM advocates were probably the first to elaborate the notion of C5 in a consistent way and make it an applicable contextualization model.[8]

In his original formulation of the C-spectrum, Travis distinguishes six types of Christ-centered communities through the criteria of "language, culture, worship forms, degree of freedom to worship with others, and religious identity."[9] The IM is the C5 type of Christ-centered communities that consist of "'Messianic Muslims' who have accepted Jesus as Lord and Savior."[10] Travis describes C5 as follows:

> C5 believers remain legally and socially within the community of Islam. Somewhat similar to the Messianic Jewish movement [sic]. Aspects of Islamic theology which are incompatible with the Bible are rejected, or reinterpreted if possible. Participation in corporate Islamic worship varies from person to person and group to group. C5 believers meet regularly with other C5 believers and share their faith with unsaved Muslims. Unsaved Muslims may see C5 believers as theologically deviant and may eventually expel them from the community of Islam. Where entire villages accept Christ, C5 may result in "Messianic Mosques." C5 believers are viewed as Muslims by the Muslim community and refer to themselves as Muslims who follow Isa the Messiah.[11]

---

Movement, and most IM advocates seem to prefer to use the IM. This writer will use these two terms interchangeably, but the primary term will be the IM. See Eenigenburg, "Pros and Cons," 310–15; Schlorff, "Translational Model," 305–27; Corwin, "Humble Appeal," 5–21.

6 Travis, "C1 to C6 Spectrum," 407–8. Travis emphasizes that C does not refer to contextualization, but to "Christ-centered communities."

7 Parshall, "Danger!" 404–6, 409–10.

8 For some earlier innovative thoughts that can be considered as a precursor of the IM, see Anderson, "Missionary Approach," 285–300; McCurry, "Cross-Cultural Models," 267–83; Wilder, "Some Reflections," 301–20; Conn, "Muslim Convert," 97–113; Kraft, "Dynamic Equivalence Churches," 114–28. These early thinkers proposed several creative thoughts concerning a radical form of Muslim contextualization model.

9 Travis, "C1 to C6 Spectrum," 407.

10 Travis, "C1 to C6 Spectrum," 408.

11 Travis, "C1 to C6 Spectrum," 408.

One of the key notions of C5 is that Muslim followers of Jesus do not leave the Islamic community even after believing in Jesus as Lord, but remain within it as Muslim Insiders. In the process, they maintain their socioreligious identity as Muslims, and continue to participate in most of the Islamic religious practices as long as they perceive them compatible with biblical truth. According to Travis, the primary reason to remain within the Islamic community and maintain Muslim identity is for the sake of Gospel witness through the existing social networks.

Travis originally intended C-spectrum to be a descriptive tool to label existing Christ-centered communities rather than a prescriptive tool to promote various types of Muslim contextualization models including C5. Descriptively speaking of the current state of affairs, there are Muslim followers of Jesus who believe in Jesus as Lord and gather for fellowship and Bible studies with like-minded Muslims while remaining in the Islamic community and continuing to observe Islamic religious practices.[12] Although they came to faith in Jesus in a number of variegated ways, the presence of Muslim followers of Jesus within the Islamic community is an undeniable reality.[13]

As the IM developed, however, IM advocates changed the descriptive notion into the prescriptive assertion when they began to prescriptively contend that the IM was a biblically-theologically permissible approach to contextualization and that it was a new effective way to evangelize the Muslim world based upon their own fruitful ministry results. The IM became favored by field missionaries and mission organizations that it was adopted as the major missionary approach of some organizations.[14] The nature of the IM has changed from a descriptive to a prescriptive model in that it is claimed to be a valid, effective, and commendable strategy for evangelical ministries to Muslims.[15]

---

12 IM advocates report stories and testimonies of Muslim followers of Jesus in their writings to point out that these are what God is doing among Muslims. They contend that the life transformation of many Muslim Insiders is sure evidence for the work of the Holy Spirit within this movement. For examples, see Travis, "Messianic Muslim," 53–59.

13 For various ways whereby the Muslim converts have come to the faith, see Woodberry et al., "Why Muslims Follow Jesus," 80–85.

14 John Travis and Anna Travis introduce an ethos of one new mission agency in "Contextualization among Muslims," 15. There are field missionaries who become interested in the IM, and this writer has personally encountered several field missionaries who have adopted this approach in their ministry contexts. Marc Coleman reports some Seventh-day Adventist missionaries who have adopted the IM principles in his thesis. Coleman, "Seventy-day Adventist," 30.

15 John Travis first acknowledged in 2000 that "C5 was never intended to be

There are critical differences between the IM's descriptive and prescriptive natures. When the IM is taken as a descriptive phenomenon, it is normally viewed as a temporary matter that is gradually disjointed by a normative response to two conflicting allegiances. There is a normative anticipation for Muslim followers of Jesus to leave Islam after realizing the incompatibility between their faith in Jesus and their former faith in Islam. When the IM is taken as a prescriptive model for contextualization, Muslim Insiders are expected to remain within their Islamic community and continue their Islamic religious practices within a biblically permissible boundary. Missionaries will also leave them as Muslims and let them follow Christ within the Islamic community. There is a prescriptive and strategic notion in this approach. IM advocates are contending for this approach and practicing it in various Muslim contexts. This subtle line is where IM advocates have crossed over from a descriptive concept into a prescriptive one.[16]

## Definition of the Insider Movement

Though the first explicit idea of the IM appeared in Travis' C-spectrum, its definition has changed over time as IM advocates have endeavored to make more precise arguments in support of the IM. The essence of the IM, however, has remained intact throughout their writings. A leading advocate, Kevin Higgins, proposed a definition of the IM as follows:

> A growing number of families, individuals, clans, and/or friendship-webs becoming faithful disciples of Jesus within the culture

a 'missionary approach,' but rather to describe how some MBBs live out their faith in Christ." See Travis, "Messianic Muslim," 55. His view, however, has significantly changed since then as he states in another article, "We believe God has called us to help 'birth a C5 movement' in our context." See Travis and Travis, "Contextualization," 12. He is not only approving the IM as a valid way of living out biblical faith for MBBs, but also contending for the need to help the birth of the IM. According to the latter, he makes the IM a prescriptive missionary approach.

16 Another related issue is whether the IM should be taken as a contextualization model. Some IM advocates hesitate to accept that the IM is a contextualization model or a strategy. Joshua Massey, for example, contends that "C5 is not a *strategy* to reach Muslims, it is a *reality* effected [sic] by the Holy Spirit among numerous Muslim peoples." See Massey, "Misunderstanding C5," 299. Rebecca Lewis seems to agree when she states, "Insider movements are not primarily about becoming more 'contextualized.'" See Lewis, "Sharing the Gospel," 22. Rick Brown, on the contrary, clearly sees the IM as a contextualization model in his discussion on contextualization: "Contextualization without Syncretism," 130–31. Also see Brown et al., "Movements and Contextualization," 21–23. Although IM advocates have different views on this matter, they cannot deny the fact that they promote this approach as a ministry model among Muslims. It is, therefore, valid to evaluate the IM as a contextualization model in this study.

of their people group, including their religious culture [sic]. This faithful discipleship will express itself in culturally appropriate communities of believers who will also continue to live within as much of their culture, including the religious life of the culture, as is biblically faithful. The Holy Spirit, through the Word and through His people, will also begin to transform His people and their culture, religious life, and worldview.[17]

Higgins identifies the main idea of the IM as remaining within the cultural and religious communities to which believers belong. Like Higgins, most IM advocates desire to make the IM idea a more generic term which can be applied to other religious contexts.[18] Rebecca Lewis provides a similar generic definition as follows:

> An "Insider Movement" is any movement to faith in Christ where a) the gospel flows through pre-existing communities and social networks, and where b) believing families, as valid expression of the Body of Christ, remain inside their socioreligious communities, retaining their identity as members of that community while living under the Lordship of Jesus Christ and the authority of the Bible.[19]

The definition of the IM in this study, however, is confined to the original concept of C5 within a Muslim context, as initially suggested by Travis. This study, therefore, uses the definition of Travis as a starting point while some generic aspects of the IM definition are taken into account whenever necessary:

> "Messianic Muslims" follow Christ but remain within the Muslim community. These Messianic Muslims reject or modify unbiblical Islamic teachings (e.g., they insist Jesus did die on the cross), yet still see most aspects of their lives woven together by the social fabric of Islam. They are not silent about their faith in Jesus, though they are discerning about when and where to share. They strive to form groups with other like-minded Muslim followers of Jesus to study the Bible, pray for each other, and fellowship in Christ. Yet, they do not view or call themselves "Christians."[20]

---

17 Higgins, "Key to Insider Movements," 156.

18 For the IM in the Hindu context, see Hoefer, "Proclaiming a 'Theologyless' Christ," 97–100. For a case of the Buddhist context, see Deneui, "Typology of Approaches," 415–36.

19 Lewis, "Promoting Movements to Christ," 75.

20 Travis, "Messianic Muslim," 53.

According to this definition, there are commendable aspects of the IM such as the emphasis on evangelism and forming believers' community within Islamic societies. On the other hand, concerns and doubts are unavoidable about this approach when one considers clearly conflicting teachings between Christianity and Islam and the exclusive truth claim of the Bible. Pros and cons have prevailed among evangelicals, and various reasoning has been proposed in favor of or against the IM. Up to date, there is a lack of objective and comprehensive evaluation grids to evaluate the IM. It is imperative, therefore, to investigate the IM through a comprehensive analytical framework which incorporates an examining tool for underlying biblical, theological, and missiological assumptions in regards to Muslim contextualization from a biblical perspective.

## Main Features of the Insider Movement

The best way to analyze the main characteristics of the IM is to compare it with the C4 contextualization model of Parshall, since a wider evangelical community accepts the C4 model as a valid contextualization approach.[21] As Travis distinguishes C5 from C4 on the C-scale, the IM (C5) can be viewed as a Muslim contextualization model which moves one step away from C4 in the C-continuum. One of the major distinctions between C4 and C5 is in the matter of maintaining former religious identity as Muslims. In the C4 model, Muslim background believers (MBBs) are eventually not capable of remaining within the Islamic community after being identified as non-Muslims, despite their intention to remain within the sociocultural community. The unwanted outcome is the loss of an evangelistic momentum through a preexisting social network. In the C5 model, on the other hand, Muslim followers of Jesus remain within the Islamic community because they maintain their identity as Muslims and continue to participate in Islamic religious practices as before. The primary reason to keep Muslim identity is, according to Travis, to have an evangelistic momentum "for the sake of the lost."[22]

Several foundational assumptions or contentions are commonly held by IM advocates. First, they contend that the greatest hindrance in Muslim evangelism is "not theological, but one of culture and religious identity."[23]

---

21 International Mission Board (IMB) recently expressed the official position that it would go as far as C4 in the C-spectrum of Muslim contextualization when describing general principles of contextualization. See Graham, "IMB Trustees Adopt Guidelines."

22 Travis, "Must All Muslims," 411.

23 Travis, "Must All Muslims," 414–15.

They contend that Muslim Insiders should be able to maintain their Muslim identity by practicing most Islamic cultural and religious practices because "being a Muslim" is perceived as a cultural term in the minds of Muslim Insiders.[24] This implies that missionaries should find a way to allow or encourage Muslim followers of Jesus to remain as Muslims within the Islamic socioreligious community.

Second, IM advocates argue that Muslim evangelism should not aim at Muslims' changing their religion from Islam to Christianity. They argue that it is simply unthinkable for Muslims to change their religion not only because Christianity carries such a negative connotation in Muslims' mindset, but also because Muslims live in a tightly linked socioreligious community.[25] Therefore, maintaining Muslim identity becomes a necessity for the effective promotion of the Gospel among Muslims in the logical claims of IM advocates.

Third, since the only way for these Muslim Insiders to remain within the Islamic community is to practice all the Islamic religious practices and use Islamic ritual forms except in the matters explicitly incompatible with biblical teaching, Muslim Insiders follow normative Muslim religious life in the Islamic community. In the process, they either reinterpret some of the major Islamic doctrines or privately modify them. The Islamic confession (*Shahada*) is one such case. Travis asserts that Muslim Insiders may confess the *Shahada* without the inner agreement or change it slightly by removing the part on the prophethood of Muhammad so that their conscience may remain free of guilt.[26] Other IM advocates contend that even the prophethood of Muhammad can be acknowledged, not in an orthodox Islamic theological sense, but in the sense that he was a messenger from God to accomplish a social reform among Arabs by transforming pagan Arab tribal society into a monotheistic Islamic society.[27]

---

24  Brown, for example, contends that asking Muslim Insiders to quit being Muslims is like asking someone to "quit being Jewish or Hispanic." See his response in Corwin, "Humble Appeal," 12.

25  Muslims in general have a negative perception about Christianity as a religion. Also, no one will deny the fact that missionaries should not make efforts to convert Muslims to Christianity simply by changing religious affiliation without experiencing the genuine spiritual transformation in Christ. Their reasoning does not seem fair because their presentation of the word "Christianity" is more Islamic than "genuinely Christian or biblical." IM advocates tend to stress Muslims' negative attitude toward the term "Christianity" because they take it as "religion," not in the true biblical faith in Jesus.

26  Travis, "Messianic Muslim," 56.

27  Higgins describes one way of Muslim Insiders' approval of the prophethood of Muhammad: "I can accept and affirm all of the teaching of Muhammad as I find it in

Fourth, IM advocates place a great emphasis on the work of the Holy Spirit in the life and ministry of Muslim Insiders. They contend that the most fruitful field results reveal clear evidence of life transformation among Muslim Insiders, and that this evidence itself is a strong indication of Muslim Insiders being under the guidance of the Holy Spirit. Even in the process of discipleship, IM advocates contend that outsiders, either missionaries or national leaders who are not Muslim Insiders, should leave Muslim Insiders in such a way that they can grow in the Word of God under the guidance of the Holy Spirit.[28]

Fifth, the way Muslim Insiders can remain as Muslims relies on the assumption that the term "Muslim" is considered a "cultural term."[29] IM advocates argue that there is no ethical problem for Muslim Insiders to claim to be Muslims because there is a wide spectrum of Muslims in the world, from fundamentalist groups to nominal groups.[30] They contend that it is not a problem for Muslim Insiders to practice the Islamic religious forms because these practices are mostly cultural in the minds of Muslims. Even in the religious components the Islamic meanings are altered or reinterpreted so that their consciences are not violated. They contend that Muslim Insiders will be perceived by other Muslims as a strange subgroup within a wide variety of Muslim groups.

Lastly, IM advocates claim that it has been proven to be a fruitful approach in various Muslim countries, especially in South Asian countries. John and Anna Travis state, "It would appear that the largest movement to Christ among Muslims in the world today is C5 in nature, occurring in Asia."[31] Based on a recent field-based survey among experienced missionaries, it is asserted that a strong correlation exists between active Gospel movements and contextualization approaches including the IM.[32] According to this survey, it is implied that a significant portion of missionary teams are actually using the IM as a key strategy and that they have produced

the Qur'an, and can say honestly that he had a prophetic role in calling Arab, Christian, and Jewish people of his time to repent. I can call him a prophet. I can say the shahada with integrity because I believe Muhammad was called by God to a prophetic role." Higgins, "Identity," 121.

28 Travis says, "The interaction of C5 believers with outside Christians and theologians is very limited. They rely heavily on the Word of God and the Holy Spirit. We must pray for these groups and trust the Holy Spirit will give them supernatural wisdom to respond to the inherent religious and social tensions that arise in their families and communities." Travis, "Messianic Muslim," 56; See also Higgins, "Acts 15," 34–35.

29 Massey, "Misunderstanding C5," 9–10.

30 Massey, "God's Amazing Diversity," 11–12.

31 Travis and Travis, "Maximizing the Bible," 22.

32 Brown et al., "Movements and Contextualization," 21–23.

10    Toward a Healthier Contextualization among Muslims

better results in the fields for the Gospel movement. As IM advocates actively promote the IM to other mission fields, the IM seems to increasingly attract more interest from field-based missionaries while well-informed missiologists and sending churches remain deeply concerned about the IM.

## Recent Developments on the Insider Movement Debates

During the period between the *EMQ* issue in 1998 and the Atlanta ISFM Conference in 2006, both IM advocates and IM critics have continued the discussion by developing their respective arguments with a more carefully articulated reasoning.[33] IM advocates have rightly taken the burden of proof on their shoulders and have provided their biblical and theological validation for the IM. Some of the major proponents include John Travis, Joshua Massey, Rick Brown, and Kevin Higgins.[34] While emphasizing the effectiveness in field ministries among several Muslim nations, these major advocates have made cases for validating the IM by using a few selective biblical passages. In this process, it has explicated some important facets of missiological thinking of IM advocates and the IM theology of mission, such as hidden assumptions, theological methods, and exegetical methods of these IM advocates.

On the other hand, IM critics have provided several evaluations on the IM and tried to warn the evangelical community to become aware of the dangers of this new proposal.[35] Timothy Tennent points out one methodological weakness of IM advocates in that their argumentations have been mostly ad hoc without comprehensive validation:

> Most of the argumentation in favor of C-5 is decidedly ad hoc and is developed as a reaction against criticism which has been posed, rather than an independent case which biblically, theologically, historically and contextually sets forth the necessary

---

33  Several papers presented in the ISFM conference in 2006 were published in *IJFM*. Tennent, "Followers of Jesus," 101–15; Higgins, "Identity," 117–23; Travis et al., "Four Responses," 124–26.

34  Travis, "C1 to C6 Spectrum," 407–8; Travis, "Must All Muslims," 411–15; Travis, "Messianic Muslim," 55–59; Travis and Travis, "Maximizing the Bible," 21–22; Massey, "God's Amazing Diversity," 5–14; Massey, "Misunderstanding C5," 1–18; Higgins, "Key to Insider Movements," 155–65; Brown, "Son of God," 41–52; Brown, "What Must One Believe," 13–21; Brown, "Contextualization without Syncretism," 127–33. See the bibliography for a comprehensive list.

35  Schlorff, "Translational Model," 305–27; Woods, "Biblical Look," 188–95; Williams, "Aspects of High-Spectrum," 75–91; Nikides, "Evaluating 'Insider Movements,'" 1–15. See the bibliography for a comprehensive list.

arguments. There is currently no single source where a reader can find a complete case for C-5 which sets forth all of the evidence which is found in the literature.[36]

With thanks to several evangelical critics of the IM, a carefully delineated discussion on the IM has been prompted and the central issues are better identified. This process has enabled both IM advocates and IM critics to move to a constructive direction to bring forth a carefully elaborated evaluation of the IM from an evangelical perspective.

Since the ISFM Conference in Atlanta, several changes began to appear on the part of IM advocates. First, the writings of IM advocates seem to reflect more precise arguments and solid theological reasoning than before. The major players have strengthened their cases for the IM through more clarified arguments from a variety of perspectives.[37] Second, some of these ideas became hastily publicized and uncritically promoted in the public platforms. For example, this IM notion became a main driving force of an international consultation where many experienced evangelical missionaries and missiologists participated in the discussion to search for fruitful practices in ministries to Muslims.[38] The IM was simply assumed as a normative evangelical approach to Muslims. The IM paradigm was also incorporated as one major component in the proceeding publication from this consultation.[39] This can seriously mislead field missionaries who are not aware of the current debate within the evangelical community. This

---

36 Tennent, "Followers of Jesus," 104. Tennent also points out that missiological models are sometimes developed in a field context first and that the biblical and theological considerations come later. By noting that the IM case follows this typical pattern, Tennent contends that IM advocates have a weak standing in establishing a biblical theological foundation for the IM.

37 Some representative works include: Higgins, "Acts 15," 29–40; Higgins, "Inside What," 74–91; Woodberry, "To the Muslim," 23–28; Lewis, "Promoting Movements," 75–76; Lewis, "Insider Movements," 16–19; Lewis, "Integrity of the Gospel," 41–48; Travis and Woodberry, "When God's Kingdom," 24–30; Kraft, "Contextualization of Essential Christianity," 80–86.

38 The Vision 5/9 Global Consultation for Muslim Evangelism in 2007 drew many experienced field missionaries among Muslims and missiologists with the purpose of accelerating the evangelization of Muslim nations through partnership and cooperation. One special attempt was to identify fruitful practices, and the IM was implicitly assumed to be the central thrust of this collaboration while not many field missionaries were keenly aware of its essential nature and the dangers involved.

39 The findings from this consultation were published as a book, *From Seed to Fruit*, edited by Woodberry. This writer was personally present in this Consultation in 2007 when a letter from one Muslim Insider was read in a plenary session appealing that the global evangelical Christian community would accept Muslim Insiders as part of the body of Christ.

writer finds this approach of IM advocates unwarranted because this debate is still ongoing and far from reaching a consensus within the evangelical community.

## Recent Studies on the Insider Movement

No comprehensive study dealing with the IM or the IM theology of mission has been published at the time of writing this dissertation, and most of IM advocates have publicized their views in the form of journal articles. This phenomenon is the same with IM critics because they deal with certain components of the IM and publish their works in journals or internet websites.[40] Two recent doctoral dissertations offer an in-depth study of the IM. Doug Coleman evaluates the IM from four selective perspectives while Henry Wolfe treats the IM from intensely biblical-theological and missiological perspectives.[41] They reach similar conclusions that the IM stands upon a tenuous theological foundation.

Both dissertations, however, contain certain limitations because each study focuses on certain aspects of the IM and thus is lacking in its comprehensiveness. This current study differs from these two works in that it provides a comprehensive evaluation of the IM through an elaborated analytical framework of contextualization. Second, since their treatment of the IM is rather generic, not specific to the Islamic context, the treatment on Islam and the theological discussion on using Islamic religious forms for Christian witness are not sufficiently evaluated in either work. Third, the two works pay little attention to the theoretical foundation of the IM theology of mission. This study, however, carefully configures a connection between the missiological framework of Charles H. Kraft and the IM theology of missions, and pays special attention to the underlying presuppositions behind the IM. Last, the treatment of the IM as a contextualization model is not explicitly developed in either dissertation. This study emphasizes the importance of formulating an analytical framework for Muslim contextualization by considering various missiological grids before applying this framework to evaluate the IM.

---

40 *IJFM* and *SFM* have been the most widely utilized literary platform for the debates. Two recent edited works are helpful for a further discussion on the IM: Lingel et al., *Chrislam*; Nichols and Corwin, *Envisioning Effective Ministry*.

41 Wolfe, "Insider Movements"; and Coleman, "Theological Analysis."

## STATEMENT OF THE PROBLEM

An evangelical evaluation of the IM is still ongoing, and a consensus is yet to be reached. Further dialogue among evangelical scholars and missionaries would advance this discussion by addressing all related issues to the IM. While a comprehensive evaluation is desirable, the IM as a contextualization model is subject to at least two tests. One test is biblical-theoretical in nature, and the other is a test of field-oriented effectiveness. The first test is fundamentally more important than the second because there is no use of having effective ministry models that do not stand on a sound biblical-theological foundation. For this reason, it is necessary to pay careful attention to the biblical and theological foundation of the IM which can be gleaned from the writings of IM advocates. There exists a sufficiently congruent theology of mission among IM advocates so that it is possible to call it the IM theology of missions.

Second, solid field research is necessary since any missiological model is supposed to secure its effectiveness and relevancy through various field experiments. Although IM advocates claim that the IM has been fruitful, the reports available are either limited in scope or debatable. One most quoted survey is the "Islampur case" where "72 key people of influence" within this C5 movement participated in the survey in 1995. Based upon the survey results, Parshall expressed a serious concern about the IM because of a strong indication of theological syncretism among Muslim Insiders.[42] The lack of other field reports makes it difficult to understand the real picture of the IM in the fields. This study, therefore, will have a limited source in terms of field survey, other than some references to testimonies of Muslim Insiders in the writings of IM advocates.[43] It is hoped that both IM advocates and IM critics cooperate for a rigid field survey in multiple Muslim lands as long as the security issue is resolved.[44]

---

42 Parshall, "Danger!" 406. The Islampur case as a C5 experiment had started in the early 1980s and had been going on for around thirteen years at the time of Parshall's article in 1998. This field survey contains probably the most concrete survey result available at the time of writing this dissertation.

43 Some stories and testimonies of Muslim Insiders can be found in Travis, "Messianic Muslim," 56–58; Travis and Travis, "Maximizing the Bible," 21–22; Travis and Woodberry, "When God's Kingdom," 24–25; Jameson and Scalevich, "First-Century Jews," 35–38; Brown, "Brother Jacob," 41–42. The life testimony of Mazhar Mallouhi, who promotes and practices the IM in his ministry, is published in Chandler, *Pilgrims of Christ*.

44 Higgins suggests a low-key event where evangelicals who hold different views on the IM meet face-to-face to have better dialogue and mutual understanding. He does not, however, propose cooperative work between the two sides in implementing various field surveys to gather more precise field reports. Security concerns would be

## PURPOSE STATEMENT

The purpose of this dissertation is to provide a critical evaluation of the IM as a contextualization model by evaluating the biblical interpretations of IM advocates in their validation of the IM and by utilizing a comprehensive analytical framework for assessing Muslim contextualization models. The analytical framework used in this study comes from the generic analytical framework proposed by David Hesselgrave and Edward Rommen, which consists of five perspectives that involve contextualization: epistemological, theological, anthropological, hermeneutical, and communicational.[45] This analytical framework is modified in order to incorporate contextualization issues related to the Islamic context so that it is applied to the critical evaluation of the IM.

## METHODOLOGY AND LIMITATIONS

The major method of evaluating the IM as a contextualization model, first, is to analyze the writings of IM advocates because the real picture of various IM cases in the Muslim world is not directly available. Nevertheless, all the writings of IM advocates provide sufficient materials to understand the theological framework of this new movement and the specific views of Muslim contextualization. In this regard, this study is a critical evaluation of the IM theology of mission as reflected in the writings of IM advocates. Second, it is noteworthy to mention that there had been early thinkers of this radical form of Muslim contextualization even though it might have been only a theoretical or hypothetical proposal in the past.[46] This writer finds a certain connection between these theoretical models of the early thinkers and IM advocates. Especially the IM theology of mission is influenced by the academic works of Charles H. Kraft, whose background is anthropology in his missiological approach. This study will assess the theoretical foundation behind the IM theology of mission by examining the influence of Kraft's missiological model on the IM. While analyzing the theoretical foundation, this study will critically evaluate the core factors behind the IM and the IM advocates' theology of mission.

---

the major issue, but it seems inevitable for them to open up the IM fields for a more objective evaluation. Higgins, "Speaking the Truth," 86.

45 Hesselgrave and Rommen, *Contextualization*, 127–96.

46 For these early innovative thinkers who had thought of various radical forms of contextualization models, see footnote 8 in this chapter. As will be discussed later, Charles Kraft has been a key missiologist who has played such an important role in the development of the IM.

There are several limitations in the scope of this study. First, this study is limited to the IM among Muslims. Second, no field survey is utilized to evaluate the IM because there is a very limited source available for evaluating various field experiments. Third, the views of major IM advocates will be taken into account although the views of IM advocates are not always homogeneous in details.[47] Nevertheless, this is reasonable because there is sufficient agreement on the main components of the IM theology. Fourth, since some of the most recent discussions and materials on the IM appear as internet sources, they will be selectively used for more updated discussions.

## KEY ASSUMPTIONS AND DEFINITIONS

Several assumptions are laid as a foundation for this study. First, this study acknowledges that IM advocates have a genuine desire to see Muslims coming to know the Lord and entering into the Kingdom of God. The intention of this study is not to criticize or to judge these IM advocates, but to genuinely seek for a true path of evangelizing Muslims more effectively. This writer affirms that the tenor of this study lies in "speaking the truth in love" (Eph 4:15) as a biblical act of loving others. It is vital for the evangelical church to test whether the IM is an acceptable Muslim contextualization model because missionaries may mislead Muslims with eternal consequence while they seek to be creative and culturally relevant. This study, therefore, bears significance in directing the evangelical community to a biblically authentic and culturally relevant contextualization model.

Second, this study begins with an assumption that it is essential for any missiological model to stand upon a sound biblical-theological foundation. Every contextualization model has to be evaluated and judged by the biblical guidelines under the authority of Scripture. In this regard, almost all IM advocates will agree. The problem arises, however, in more delicate areas, such as differing views on biblical interpretation, the authority of Scripture, the relationship between culture and the Bible, etc. This writer will pay close attention to these subtle differences behind commonly accepted theological statements.

Third, the major evaluation of the IM is based upon the IM theology of missions which is reflected in the writings of IM advocates. While

---

47 For example, concerning how to interpret the prophethood of Muhammad, some are willing to admit his prophethood as social reformer while others go beyond to admit him as a religious prophet sent to Arab people from God. In the latter case, too much of the Islamic view is incorporated in the IM discussion. See Higgins, "Identity," 117–23.

IM advocates are evangelical Christians who believe in the authority of Scripture, the major controversy over the IM involves a more foundational biblical-theological discussion. Therefore, it is important to define several key theological terms and identify the theological stance of this writer before evaluating the IM theology of mission.

Evangelicalism: While the term, evangelical, is difficult to define precisely because of its diversity and changing nature over time, it is reasonably accurate to characterize an evangelical by "a passion for the gospel of Jesus Christ, by a deep commitment to biblical truth, by a sense of urgency to see lost persons hear the gospel, and by a commitment to personal holiness and the local church."[48] Nevertheless, a more subtle confusion has risen in recent decades among evangelicals concerning the different views of essential components of evangelicalism so that it has become necessary to qualify commonly agreed essential components in a more specific manner.[49] R. Albert Mohler's "confessional evangelicalism" expresses well the core spirit of biblical and historical evangelicalism in contrast to various modern theological challenges. This encompasses "the trustworthiness and truthfulness of Scripture" especially in terms of biblical inerrancy, "the exclusivity of the gospel" in contrast to inclusivism, "the integrity of theism" in contrast to open theism, and the nature of justification and the atonement."[50]

This writer takes confessional evangelicalism as orthodox evangelical theology because it derives its origin both from the authority of Scripture and from the church history. Within confessional evangelicalism, scriptural authority is highly respected and historical Christian faith is well preserved by acknowledging the historic creeds or confessions. The notion of theological orthodoxy plays a crucial role in discerning subtle digressions in these foundational theological underpinnings. Therefore, this study will take the Lausanne Covenant, the Chicago Statement of Biblical Inerrancy, and the Baptist Faith and Message 2000, as the foundational theological stance because they reflect the orthodox evangelical theology.[51]

---

48 Mohler, "Confessional Evangelicalism," 69.

49 In the past David Bebbington's quadrilateral characteristics of evangelicals were well accepted: conversionism, activism, Biblicism, and crucicentrism. See Bebbington, *Evangelicalism*, 5–17. However, due to ongoing historical evolution of theological notions, each element has to be redefined with more elaboration to encounter digressing theological challenges. Mohler, for example, underscores the need for this task to encounter a revisionist challenge. See Mohler, "Confessional Evangelicalism," 86–96.

50 Mohler, "Confessional Evangelicalism," 89–94.

51 Lausanne Movement, "Lausanne Covenant"; ICBI, "Chicago Statement"; Blount and Wooddell, *Baptist Faith*.

## OUTLINE OF THE STUDY

After this introduction, chapter 2 provides a historical review of various approaches to Muslim evangelism that have been employed historically. Four major Muslim evangelism approaches are comparatively evaluated in order to identify some of the crucial issues in the Muslim contextualization model. The findings from this analysis will be utilized to delineate the major characteristics of the IM in terms of the continuity and discontinuity from other Muslim evangelism approaches.

Chapter 3 develops an analytical framework for Muslim contextualization by using a generic framework of Hesselgrave and Rommen as a benchmark. Five analytical perspectives of their framework are further elaborated in order to incorporate critical issues in the contemporary contextualization debates and, more specifically, special issues pertinent to Islamic context. After providing an evangelical definition of contextualization, this chapter identifies biblically permissible boundaries for parameters of contextualization within each perspective before its use for a comprehensive evaluation of the IM. The same analytical framework is employed to evaluate Kraft's missiological model because his model has influenced the missiological thinking of IM advocates and shaped the foundation of the IM theology of mission.

Chapter 4 provides a critical evaluation of the biblical interpretation of key passages that IM advocates use as a biblical basis for validating the IM. The exegetical conclusions and the theological assertions of IM advocates will be critically examined. Since the hermeneutical process and the application play a central role in the IM discussion, it is important to pay close attention to how IM advocates draw their conclusions from the biblical interpretations of key passages.

Chapter 5 provides a critical evaluation of the IM by using the five perspectives in the analytical work developed in chapter 3. The five perspectives provide a well-balanced, comprehensive evaluation of the IM and enable to make a cumulative case for or against it. Special attention will be paid to various features of Islam and Islamic religious components in the contextualization process. Chapter 6 summarizes the research findings and proposes a direction for further research areas in Muslim contextualization.

# 2

# Historical Developments of Muslim Evangelism and the Insider Movement

IN THE HISTORY OF reaching out to Muslim nations with the Gospel, missionaries and mission agencies have made efforts to find more effective missionary approaches by asking: What is the best approach to Muslim evangelism? What are the best practices? What methods would produce fruitful results in certain parts of Muslim lands? These questions have occupied many strategic discussions and conferences as the major theme among evangelicals.[1]

The evangelical church has developed and utilized many different avenues to reach out to Muslim nations, as George W. Peters rightly points out concerning the creative and diverse nature of Muslim evangelism in the lives of missionaries: "Their degree of adaptability and ingenuity is marvelous. Their goals were fixed, though not their approaches and methods."[2] A study of historical developments of Muslim evangelism helps to understand the nature of contemporary approaches such as the IM from a historical perspective.

This chapter provides a typological survey of the historical developments of Muslim evangelism, and delineates critical issues and the evangelical responses to them so that they might be used as building blocks in the formulation of an analytical framework for Muslim contextualization in

---

1 The Vision 5/9 Global Consultation for Muslim Evangelization in 2007 is such an example.

2. Peters, "Overview," 391.

chapter 3.³ In the meantime, the comparative, critical appraisal of the historical models brings to light many valuable lessons and guiding principles for effective Muslim evangelism by identifying strengths and weaknesses of various approaches from the past.

## STUDIES ON THE HISTORY OF MUSLIM EVANGELISM

In endeavoring to evaluate various historical approaches to Muslim evangelism, several authors have proposed different categorizations.⁴ Peters, for example, identifies three major approaches in Muslim evangelism: direct, comprehensive, and indirect or infiltration.⁵ Peters favors the indirect/infiltration approach as the most adequate, yet he finds the direct approach an essential foundation to sharing the Gospel with Muslims. He warns, however, against using controversy in direct evangelism and using polemic literature against Islam. Overall, his categories are too simple and do not include recent models, such as the dialogical and contextual models.

John Mark Terry classifies Muslim evangelism into five categories: confrontational, traditional-evangelical, institutional, dialogical, and contextualization.⁶ His categories are more updated and his analysis of each model is more elaborate than Peters's analysis. Yet, several limitations exist. First, there is a lack of historical dimension in his evaluation. Although he organizes them chronologically, Terry does not consider the historical background of each model and thus fails to reveal the overall trend in Muslim evangelism.⁷ Second, his presentation of individual models is limited to one key proponent so that the depth is still in want. In the end of his study, Terry favors the contextualization model and provides several guidelines for its strategy. His analysis of contextualization, however, is too brief in that it

---

3 The earlier version of this chapter was presented at the Evangelical Missiological Society regional meeting: Hwang, "Historical Development."

4 The earlier attempt to present various Muslim evangelism approaches is Werff, *Christian Mission*. His work only covers Anglican and Reformed approaches during the period of 1800–1938. Due to the limitedness in its scope his work is not considered in this study.

5 Peters, "Overview," 392–99. All the names referring to different approaches or models are the individual authors' choice rather than universally agreed-upon terms.

6 Terry, "Approaches," 167–73. While he uses the term "traditional-evangelical model," it does not mean that this is the only evangelical model. All the models discussed in this chapter can be considered as evangelical models in different degrees, which evangelical missionaries have actually used in their ministries.

7 This writer intentionally uses a historical dimension of Muslim evangelism in order to identify shifts in the overall trend. This also provides a comprehensive frame of reference for evaluating the IM.

cannot provide a way to distinguish a radical form, such as the IM, from adequate evangelical contextualization models.

A recent study on this topic is done by Sam Schlorff, a longtime missionary of Arab World Ministries and an expert missiologist. Schlorff identifies six significant Muslim evangelism models: nineteenth-century imperial, direct, indirect or fulfillment, dialectical, dialogical, and dynamic equivalence or translational.[8] His appraisal of the nineteenth-century imperial model is thorough. Since a historical dimension is incorporated into his analysis, one can see how Muslim evangelism has evolved throughout the nineteenth and the twentieth centuries. His comparative evaluation through analytical grids is insightful to highlight the peculiarities of each model.[9]

His work contains several weaknesses. First, Schlorff's goal of writing this book is to evaluate critically "the Islamicized contextual model," and to propose his own biblical-theological model called "the betrothal model."[10] Since his main focus is to critique the IM, there is no equally comprehensive treatment of other models, such as the dialogical or the contextual. Second, some models are more theoretical than practical in that they do not hold as much significance as the other field-oriented models. The dialectical model represented by Hendrick Kraemer is such an example with little usefulness and applicability for field missionaries. Moreover, it is not so different from the direct approach in Schlorff's analysis. Third, his presentation of the contextualization model is rather insufficient to represent its varieties as it is promoted and used by contemporary field missionaries. This weakness comes from the fact that Schlorff singles out the dynamic equivalence/translational method as if it represents the entire contextualization model. It is, however, necessary to distinguish adequate contextualization models from inadequate ones within a larger spectrum of the contextual model.

## THE ANALYTICAL METHOD

Among the many models in Muslim evangelism, only four representative models are chosen for analysis for several reasons. First, they are the most

---

8  Schlorff, *Missiological Models*, 3–27.

9  Schlorff, *Missiological Models*, 3–27. The criteria Schlorff uses include the objective of mission, theology of non-Christian religion, contextual approach, church strategy, hermeneutics, strengths, weaknesses, and the current model.

10  Schlorff, *Missiological Models*, 79–89. Schlorff refers to the IM as "Islamicized contextualization model." He is also critical about Parshall's contextual model, although he himself admits the need for a certain degree of contextualization. In order to distinguish his model from Parshall's, this writer categorizes Schlorff as a proponent of the traditional-theological model even though he calls his own "the betrothal model."

widely used approach in history in many Muslim lands, and are still in use in contemporary ministries. These models have made the most distinctive contribution to the evangelical church's understanding of Muslim evangelism. It is, therefore, significant to assess the historical models for the purpose of this study—namely, a critical evaluation of the IM. They also reveal either clearly contrasting features or striking continuity in their relationship with the IM. The four models are referred to as confrontational, traditional-theological, dialogical, and contextual.[11]

Several aspects of this evaluation deserve attention. First, each model is introduced in terms of major proponents, main characteristics, and evaluation of strengths and weaknesses. Since differing views exist on certain details within each model, this evaluation will pay attention to a spectrum of views by considering multiple proponents. Nevertheless, this kind of categorization inevitably has to use a certain degree of generalization. Second, all of these models are still effectively in use either in original form or with modification. Some contemporary practices will be discussed to emphasize their continuous influence. Third, as a result of this historical analysis, a certain characteristic trend will be identified in the development of Muslim evangelism. Fourth, in the process of evaluating individual models, the main focus is given to delineating factors that play a significant role in Muslim contextualization. These factors will be used to compare and contrast each model through analytical grids for a comprehensive assessment.[12]

## THE CONFRONTATIONAL MODEL

### Major Proponents

The confrontational model was called a polemic approach, and its modern equivalence is an apologetical approach.[13] During the colonial period in

---

[11] These references are this writer's own choice after considering other categorizations of the previous studies. It is important to recognize that this classification may not be clear-cut because some practical models may belong to more than one category. Therefore, the models described here need to be taken as generic in nature because the distinction is more to do with the emphasis rather than to do with clear-cut distinction of individual models.

[12] The comparative overview of the four models is presented in a chart in the Appendix according to delineating factors, including major proponents, evangelism, use of the Qur'an, attitude to Islam, prophethood of Muhammad, converts, worship and church forms, theology of religions, view of culture, and contribution to Muslim evangelism.

[13] Strictly speaking, polemics is distinguished from apologetics since the former deals with "the defense of Christian truth from objections and attacks within

the nineteenth century, missionaries had confidence in the superiority of western civilization over the Islamic world. Their missionary approaches reflected this mindset, and thus they assumed the victory of Christianity over Islam through logical reasoning and public debates. Many of these polemicists went to public platforms to argue with Muslims, and wrote tracts against Islam to prove the superiority of Christianity and to defend Christian truth.

One of the earliest proponents of this model is Henry Martyn (1781–1812), who was a missionary in India and Persia. Three polemical tracts he wrote for his debate against a Persian Muslim are known as "the first Protestant writings addressed to Muslims."[14] Other proponents include Karl Pfander (1803–1866), Sir William Muir (1819–1905), and W. St. Clair Tisdall (1859–1928).[15] They wrote prolifically both in defense of Christianity and in making unreserved attacks against Islam and Islamic sources.

## Main Characteristics

Polemicists approached Muslim evangelism with the basic assumption that they could win Muslims to Christ by exposing the serious flaws of Islam, answering the popular objections of Muslims against Christian truths, and demonstrating the superiority of Christianity over Islam through rational debate. Tisdall identified three major obstacles that hindered Muslims from being convinced of the Gospel, and he believed it was possible to remove these obstacles by logical explanation.[16] He also categorized popular Muslim objections against the Christian faith under six headings and attempted to provide logical answers to each, with the desire to lead Muslims to faith in Christ.[17]

Christianity" and the latter deals with "the defense from outside of Christianity." In this study, however, both terms are interchangeably used because the early polemists defended the Christian truths from Islam in the apologetical sense. Philip and Cherian, "Introduction to Integrated Christian Apologetics."

14 Schlorff, *Missiological Models*, 3. These three tracts appear in Lee, *Controversial Tracts*, 80–160.

15 Some of the representative writings are Pfander, *Balance of Truth*; Muir, *Coran*; Muir, *Rise and Decline of Islam*; Muir, *Mahomet and Islam*; Tisdall, *Religion of the Crescent*; Tisdall, *Manual of the Leading Muhammedan Objections*; Tisdall, *Original Sources*.

16 Tisdall, *Christian Reply*, 26–27. This work is a reprint of *Manual of the Leading Muhammedan Objections*. The three obstacles include: Muslims' misunderstanding of the Christian doctrines, their knowledge of "the corruptions of certain forms of Christianity," and their "ignorance of the facts of Muhammad's life and the teachings of the Qur'an."

17 Tisdall categorized the Muslim objections against Christianity under six

Since Tisdall and other polemicists believed that giving reasonable answers to Muslim objections was both possible and necessary, their works focused on not only proving the truthfulness of the Christian faith and the Bible but also the falsity of the Qur'an and the prophet Muhammad. Pfander also thought that Muslims would "automatically acknowledge 'Christian truth and superiority' and would abandon Islam as incapable of removing the burden of sin," if only they could read the New Testament in their own languages.[18] These men firmly believed that leading Muslims to the Bible was the key to their conversion, so they relentlessly translated the Bible and polemic literature into vernacular languages.

The logical reasoning of the polemicists generally took the following procedure. First, they endeavored to establish the authenticity of the Bible as a firm foundation in encountering Muslim objections. Many Qur'anic verses were used for the goal of proving that the Old and New Testaments were neither corrupted nor abrogated. Tisdall claimed that using the Qur'an, the Hadith, or even Muslim commentaries was necessary because one had to "argue from facts which the Muslim deems incontrovertible."[19] He clearly emphasized, however, that using the Qur'an did not accepting its authority by stating, "The line of argument which a missionary has to use, therefore, must be accommodated to the limits of his opponent's knowledge or comprehension."[20] This may be called simply a receptor-oriented approach in modern communication terminology.

The second step, only after establishing the biblical authority, was to answer common Muslim objections against the essential Christian doctrines, such as the Trinity, the deity of Christ, his death, atonement, and resurrection. Contradictions between the Qur'an and the Bible were explicitly pointed out to stress that both could not be simultaneously true. In this process, it was usually demonstrated that the Qur'an contradicted itself by

---

headings: "I. Objections against the genuineness of the Bible as it now exists. II. Objections against the present authority of the Bible, regarded as annulled by the Qur'an. III. Objections against certain leading Christian doctrines as alleged to be taught in the Bible, on the ground that they are contrary to Reason and the Qur'an; e.g., the doctrine of Trinity. IV. Objections against the doctrine of Atonement of Christ. V. Objections against Christianity on the ground of Muhammad's Divine mission, as asserted to be proved by prophecies in the Bible. VI. Miscellaneous Objections." Tisdall, *Christian Reply*, 26.

18 Pfander to Basel Mission, September 1, 1831, cited in "The Late Rev. Dr. Charles Gottlieb Pfander, D.D.," 98. Requoted from Bennett, "Legacy of Karl Gottlieb Pfander," 77. Some of the earliest Bible translations were initiated by these polemicists due to this conviction.

19 Tisdall, *Christian Reply*, 23.

20 Tisdall, *Christian Reply*, 28.

pointing out various inconsistencies within it.[21] Historical critical study of the Qur'an and the historical facts of Islam were discussed in the process.

The polemicists generally had a negative attitude toward Islam because they believed that it was a false religion and that Muslims became blind to the truth due to Islamic distortions. Their reference to Islam as "Muhammadanism" was a way of undermining Islam and its validity.[22] Moreover, they did not hesitate to attack Islam, the Qur'an, and Muhammad's prophethood. For example, they unreservedly pointed out "reasons why the Qur'an was not considered to be the Word of God" by giving evidences such as its apparent mistakes, erroneous geography, immoral criteria, support for violence, and seclusion of women.[23]

Concerning Muhammad, most rejected his prophethood for several reasons, including the quality of his personal life and a biblical and theological basis. Only a small number of people attempted to appreciate his role from a historical-political perspective, and perceived him as a political leader with "much of religious fervour, much of patriotism blended with political ambition."[24] This kind of reasoning, however, was taken to be purely speculative and was not shared by the majority of the polemicists. After a thorough presentation of the Qur'an and Muhammad's life from the original sources, Muir summarizes the person of Muhammad as follows:

> Mahomet sought power; he fought against those who denied his claims; he put a whole tribe to the sword; he filled his harem

---

21 Tisdall, for example, argued against the Muslim's claim for the sinlessness of the prophets as follows: "Do not therefore accuse us of altering the Bible by inserting accusations against the prophets. Your own Qur'an does this; and if we agree with the Qur'an in holding that the prophets were sinners who repented, what is there against reason in the belief?" Tisdall, *Christian Reply*, 23.

22 J. N. D. Anderson argued that the word "Muhammedanism" should be replaced by the word Islam because it gave an implication that Muslims were simply followers of Muhammad rather than the people of the religion of Islam. Committee of Evangelical Missionaries to Islam, *Report of Conference*, 10.

23 Muir, "Koran Examined," 12–43.

24 Dale, *Contrast*, 33. One anonymous writer asserts, "Muhammad's giving himself out as a prophet of God was at first sincere. He supposed himself to be called upon by God to speak for Him and introduce a better religion. Gradually, however, he began to insist quite as much as on men's accepting him as a prophet as on accepting the great truth which he first proclaimed. His creed now became, 'There is no god but God: Muhammad is the Apostle of God.' He aspired to become the ruler as well [sic] the spiritual guide of his countrymen, and through them of the world." See Christian Literature Society for India, *Papers for Thoughtful Muslims*, No. 3, 28. This positive view of Muhammad is taken up in the dialogical and contextual models to promote peaceful dialogue and mutual respect. Even some IM advocates incorporate this notion for their attempt to validate the Muslim Insiders' use of the *Shahada*. Higgins, "Identity," 120–21.

with women, bond and free; he cast aside, when they had served his purpose, the Jewish and Christian Scriptures; and he engrafted his faith on the local superstition of his birthplace. He did all these things under cover of an alleged divine authority, but he did no miracle.[25]

## Evaluation

The confrontational model has several commendable features. First, it uses logical reasoning as an important tool for leading Muslims to Christ. It appeals to Muslim minds more than their hearts or feelings. For this purpose, the polemicists were well trained in Islamics and had incredible minds in the areas of linguistics and religion. The succinct observation of Peters is valid: "Their apologetic was keen and sharp while their heart was warm and tender."[26] Based upon a biblical goal of leading Muslims to Christ, the apologists relied on sharpened reasoning to appeal to the minds of Muslims.

Second, the polemicists' writings were powerful instruments in enlightening the critical minds of both Muslims and Christians. Many works were translated into different languages and published for wide distribution.[27] Although debates prevailed concerning whether this kind of literature was effective in preaching the Gospel, it certainly helped to clarify Christian responses to Muslim objections in the context of evangelism. Even today some of these materials are reprinted and read as valuable equipping tools for missionaries. Their in-depth analysis of the history of Islam and of the Qur'an still provides a valuable source for contemporary missionaries and missiologists.

Third, the confrontational model can be useful in certain contexts. For example, one may use the logical reasoning promoted in this model in equipping MBBs to have a deeper understanding of theological differences between Islam and Christianity. A clear presentation of the Christian reply to Muslim objections, used in conjunction with solid biblical-theological teachings, can strengthen the theological foundation of MBBs. When there is an opportunity to defend the Christian faith against the wrong accusations of Muslims, one can wisely employ this model.

Fourth, this model emphasizes the publication and wide distribution of the Bible and Christian literature. The polemicists firmly believed that it

---

25 Muir, *Mahomet and Islam*, 249.

26 Peters, "Overview," 392.

27 Pfander's *Balance of Truth* was already translated into five languages in 1910. Zwemer, "Karl Gottlieb Pfander," 222.

was ultimately the Bible, especially the New Testament, which would lead Muslims to faith in Jesus Christ. Their zeal for the translation of the Bible into the vernacular and their efforts toward wide distribution of Christian literature are surely laudable.[28]

There are, however, several critical issues that deserve careful evaluation. The polemicists were partly influenced by Western colonialism in their missionary thinking and evangelistic approach.[29] Their boldness in standing in public arenas to preach the Gospel is commendable, but that might have been possible simply because of colonial protection from western political powers. Some missionaries, in fact, expected to be protected under the Western colonial government, and others had close ties to civil authorities.[30] This connection between polemical missionaries and colonial power, whether intended or unintended, engraved a deep impression upon the minds of Muslims to perceive missionaries as part of Western colonialism, which is still one of the most serious hindrances to Muslim evangelism.[31]

Second, most polemicists extensively used the Qur'an to dispute objections because they had a good command of the original Islamic sources, whether it was the Qur'an, the traditions, or Islamic commentaries. The problem is how this process of using the Qur'an can be justified. The polemicists did not accept the Qur'an as God's revelation; they used it to defeat Muslim objections against Christianity based upon authoritative sources Muslims would acknowledge. Schlorff argues that there is a matter of inconsistency in their approach. On the one hand, they attempt to undermine

---

28 Martyn showed his strong desire to translate the Bible into Arabic in his diary entries dated September 8 and 9, 1810: "Arabia shall hide me till I come forth with an approved New Testament in Arabic. . . . Will government let me go away for three years before the time of my furlough arrives? If not I must quit the service, and I cannot devote my life to a more important work than that of preparing the Arabic Bible." Zwemer, *Arabia*, 319.

29 Western triumphalism played a certain role in shaping the polemicists' thinking. Muir, for example, after giving the reason why Islam would not expand any further beyond the Middle East from a theological, moral, and social perspective, argued that the current political dominance by the West was evidence of the depression of Islam and the ascendancy of Christianity. Muir, *The Rise and Decline of Islam*; Muir, *Mohammedan Controversy*, 100.

30 Pfander, for example, was supported favorably by Colonel Edwardes, who said, "The civil government will protect the missionary who goes forth to preach the Gospel." Zwemer, "Karl Gottlieb Pfander," 222.

31 After historically tracing how modern Arabic Islamist writers have developed such a strong antagonistic reaction against Christianity, Heather J. Sharkey contends that the hostility displayed by these Islamist writers of anti-missionary treatises fundamentally derives from the "humiliation that Western dominance has entailed in the modern Arab world" in the nineteenth and early twentieth centuries. Sharkey, "Arabic Antimissionary Treatises," 98–102.

Islam by criticizing its foundational claims and the authority of Islamic sources. On the other hand, they use the Qur'an to establish Christian truth by the "positive uses of the 'truths' of Islam."[32] Schlorff sees this as a serious weakness of the polemical approach. It might be inevitable that missionaries mention the Qur'an or quote it in evangelistic dialogue. The real questions are, rather, "What is the right use of the Qur'an?" and "On what basis can this use be validated?" It becomes a complicated matter in the later development of Muslim evangelism, and many diverse views have arisen since the polemicists first wielded it. This issue will play a crucial role in the Muslim contextualization discussion, especially concerning the IM.

Third, and most importantly, many have doubted the effectiveness of the confrontational model because of the questionable results of the use of debate and controversy. Some argued that it provoked anti-Christian sentiment among Muslims and that it did more harm than good.[33] The critics of this approach thought that negative reactions of Muslims far outweighed any positive impact. They attributed the unfruitfulness of the polemicists during the nineteenth and early twentieth centuries to the ineffectiveness of this method. Walter Fairman, a missionary in Egypt in the early twentieth century, cried out:

> For many years I used this method, and many others have done the same and are still doing it. . . . But what has been gained? Our opponents have been beaten in argument, *but they have not been won for Christ*. . . . I am convinced that they will never be won for Christ in this way, or by the means of public discussion, however, or whomsoever, conducted. Destructive criticism never yet won a soul for Christ.[34]

Christy Wilson is also critical of the confrontational model, which he refers to as "the Great Moslem Controversy," in a similar tone: "The simple fact is that in the vast majority of cases this method did not succeed. . . . The

---

32 Schlorff, *Missiological Models*, 6–7. Schlorff provides an excellent analysis on this topic over four chapters in his book, chapters 3–6.

33 Lewis Bevan Jones, for example, was critical about Pfander's books and his approach. Jones, *People of the Mosque*, 248. Bennett notes the impact of Pfander's writings: "The bitterly anti-Christian literature that Pfander's books provoked still colors some Muslim polemic today, for example, the work of Ahmed Deedat." Bennett, "Legacy of Karl Gottlieb Pfander," 80. The Christian Literature for Moslems Committee made a decision in Lahore, India, in 1935 that, "in view of the undesirability of circulating literature which contains attacks on the Muslim prophet, Muhammad, it was voted to . . . consider the immediate suspension of the sale of such literature." Requoted from Peters, "Overview," 392.

34 Fairman, "Approach to Moslems," 274 (emphasis in the original).

Christians may have won the argument, but they failed to win their men."[35] The effectiveness of controversy was clearly challenged due to its provocative nature in the hearts of Muslims.

Although there is a certain degree of validity in these criticisms, several qualifying comments are necessary for a more objective evaluation. First, it is inaccurate to suggest a simplistic connection between the unfruitfulness during the colonial era and the effectiveness of the model because there could have been so many other factors involved in the barrenness.[36] Moreover, up until today no methods or approaches have been claimed to be so effective in producing major breakthroughs among Muslim nations, such as people movements and church planting movements (CPMs). In fact, polemicists knew that debate might not be the best way to lead Muslims to Christ, and they were keenly aware of its proper role and its limitations. Tisdall states:

> Remember that our aim is not to silence our opponent, nor to gain a merely logical victory, but *to win souls to Christ*. Hence, in argument, we should endeavor to remove misconceptions which hinder Muslims from giving careful attention to the Gospel message. The object that we have in view in *controversy* is chiefly to remove stumbling-blocks. We must not expect it to convert a soul. That is the work of the Holy Spirit, whose aid must at every step be prayerfully and believingly invoked.[37]

Tisdall, possibly the latest among the polemicists, modified the earlier approach on account of unproductive field results and new political and social circumstances in Muslim lands. He clearly emphasizes the right use of controversy and its limitations. Therefore, it is an unfair judgment to consider debate as completely useless or counterproductive in Muslim evangelism.

The correct use of logical reasoning is not only necessary but also profitable for certain purposes in Muslim evangelism. A well-reasoned debate is necessary to defend Christian truths against Muslim objections or attacks. When Muslims challenge the Bible's authority or the doctrine of the Trinity, missionaries should be able to defend these basic tenets of biblical truth. It may be necessary to point out discrepancies between the Qur'an and the Bible or differences between the Islamic and Christian theology when it is

---

35 Wilson, *Christian Message to Islam*, 40.

36 Some possible factors behind the slow pace in Muslim evangelism may include: a small number of missionaries, a short history of ministries to Muslims, western prejudice against Muslim nations, Muslim antagonism against western Christianity, and Islamic oppression against conversion.

37 Tisdall, *Christian Reply*, 13–14 (emphasis in the original).

proper. Another case is a public forum for open debate between Muslims and Christians. Objective questions and critical comments are allowed in such a context, so apologetics or the proper use of logic with evidence is critical in presenting and defending the Gospel. This can be useful in discipleship training for the MBBs.

Nevertheless, it may not be wise to use debates in circumstances where they lead to unprofitable and emotionally charged disputes. It is generally advisable not to attack Islam or Muhammad in Muslim evangelism because that does not foster good relationships. At the same time, such an approach is considered as culturally insensitive to Muslims who highly esteem honor and shame. The contemporary use of this confrontation model is employed by apologetic scholars such as Normal Geisler, Jay Smith, John Gilchrist, and Nabeel Qureshi.[38] If one follows Mark Hana's definition of apologetics, "a systematic response of the reflective and culturally informed Christian to attacks that inevitably come upon the truth claims of the Christian faith," there seems to be no way to avoid getting involved in Christian apologetics in Muslim evangelism.[39] Harold Netland asserts that properly conducted apologetics can play a vital role in Christian witness because it involves claiming the propositional truths of Christianity.[40] Jay Smith, one of the most upfront confrontational apologists, concurs with Netland at this point when he contends that Christians should publicly proclaim the propositional truth without hesitation, so that Muslims can pay due respect for the Christian faith.[41]

---

38 Geisler and Saleeb, *Answering Islam*; Smith, "Courage in Our Convictions," 28–35. Smith regularly goes to a public park in London to witness to Muslims. John Gilchrist is an active apologist who is involved in answering Muslim objections against Christianity through web-based apologetics in www.answering-islam.org. Some of his writings include: Gilchrist, *Qur'an*; Gilchrist, *Christian Witness*; and Gilchrist, *Muhammad and the Religion*. Nabeel Qureshi provides wonderful resources to defend the biblical truth by cautiously hiring sound theological reasonings as well as objectively examining historical evidences on Christianity and Islam. The uniqueness of his approach is found in the good combination of "telling the truth in love." His deep compassion is clearly revealed in narrating his own personal journey to find Christ. All his three books deserve careful reading for anyone who is involved in Muslim evangelism. Qureshi, *Seeking Allah*; Qureshi, *No God But One*; and Qureshi, *Answering Jihad*.

39 Hana, *Crucial Questions*, 63.

40 Netland, "Evaluating Truth Claims," 91.

41 Smith asserts that argument should not be taken as negative because it is a biblical concept of dialogue appearing in the New Testament. For example, Paul sought to prove what he said by providing evidences (Acts 17:3). Smith even uses a historical-critical approach to the Qur'an to argue against its validity: "New historical evidence points to many impurities in the Qur'an. It brings into question whether the Qur'an was written or even existed at the time of Muhammad. News like this must be communicated. In fact, I consider it unloving not to do so." Smith, "Courage in Our Convictions,"

It is, therefore, wrong to shun the confrontational model completely, but rather necessary to appreciate its worth and maximally employ it in a wise manner. First and foremost, this model has biblical support because the Bible encourages Christians to do apologetics in a proper manner, namely "with gentleness and respect" (1 Pet 3:15). A more pertinent question in using confrontation is how and under what circumstances one can practice it. This is why Netland emphasizes the importance of sensitivity and creativity in cross-cultural Christian witness.[42] In the end, one must remember that the ultimate goal of confrontation is not to win arguments, but to win Muslims to Christ.

## THE TRADITIONAL-THEOLOGICAL MODEL

### Major Proponents

Partly due to dissatisfaction with the general results of the old polemic model and its unintended adversative effects, and partly due to the changing political circumstance, several evangelical missionaries developed a conversational approach based on orthodox Christian theology.[43] In 1924, John Mott observed the significant change from the confrontational model to the conversational as follows: "The positive, constructive, irenic and sympathetic approach, method and spirit now largely prevail in Christian work among Moslems, as contrasted with the negative, destructive, polemic and unappreciative."[44] This approach is referred to as the traditional-theological model in this study since it has been the predominant evangelism approach among missionaries in the twentieth century.

The most representative proponent of this model is Samuel Zwemer (1867–1952), who laid a tremendous foundation for Christian missions among Muslims for the twentieth century. He, both as a field missionary and as an academician, continued to study Islam like the former polemicists. What distinguished him from other polemicists was the fact that he

---

28–31. Netland, at the same time, emphasizes "the need for sensitivity and creativity when doing apologetics in different cultural contexts." Netland, "Evaluating Truth Claims," 91.

42 Netland, "Evaluating Truth Claims," 91.

43 Another important factor that necessitated a new approach in Muslim evangelism was the changing political circumstances, namely the end of the colonial era after World War I. Clayton P. Cloer points out that Zwemer experienced a transition in his view of Muslim evangelism from the old polemicists' method to a more conversational model partly because of this political change. Cloer, "Samuel Zwemer," 52–53.

44 Mott, *Outlook in the Moslem World*, 10.

did not use his extensive knowledge on Islam for controversy, but for personal conversation in evangelism.

Since Zwemer promoted this model, it has become the most traditional evangelical missionary approach to Muslims throughout the twentieth century. Christy Wilson (1891–1973) favored this model in comparison to the controversial approach of the polemicists.[45] Martin Goldsmith and Sam Schlorff are the contemporary proponents while the majority of evangelical missionaries still use this model as their primary approach to ministries among Muslims.[46]

## Main Characteristics

The first main characteristic of the traditional-theological model is its theological emphasis in Muslim evangelism. This model takes special note of the theological differences and discontinuity between Islam and Christianity. For example, based upon his extensive knowledge and historical research, Zwemer explicitly says of Islam that *"this religion was in no sense a preparation for Christianity, but was a retrogression."*[47] He stressed the theological disparity between Christianity and Islam by commenting that "at first glance, the two religions may seem to have much in common, but upon closer examination, they differ in every detail."[48] This model assumes that missionaries develop a deeper understanding of Islam and the Qur'an, and are thus able to point out the many contradictions between Islam and Christianity; this aspect is also emphasized and practiced by the polemicists in the confrontational model.

Key distinctions of the traditional-theological model from the former confrontational model, however, are made in at least two ways. First, the deep knowledge of Islam and the Qur'an is not used to make a direct attack or initiate controversies. Its primary application is to clarify the theological distinctiveness of Christianity and to expose the discontinuity between the two religions. Zwemer emphasized a thorough study of Islam and the

---

45 Wilson argued for the ending of "the Great Moslem Controversy" in the following words: "These are monuments of a system that is past; they may still be of use today, after a man has come far along the Christian path and has the love of Christ in his heart. They may serve to drive out vestiges of Islam, but they are no longer examples of the line of approach we should follow in presenting Christ to the Moslem heart. 'The Great Moslem Controversy' has gone into the limbo of things that are past." Wilson, "Presenting Christ to Moslems," 336.

46 Goldsmith, *Islam and Christian Witness*; Schlorff, *Missiological Models*.

47 Zwemer, *Cross Above the Crescent*, 3 (emphasis in the original).

48 Zwemer, *Cross Above the Crescent*, 36.

Muslim mindset, but he did not recommend using this knowledge to confront Muslims argumentatively. Wilson stressed that a missionary should become "an expert in avoiding argument," which he considered as a difficult task because most Muslims enjoy arguments over religious matters whether they are devout or nominal, well-versed or illiterate.[49]

The second distinction is that the assessment of Islam and Muhammad is made from a purely biblical and theological perspective in this model. Scripture plays an exceedingly important role, as it is the ultimate criteria to judge Islamic doctrine and theology within the context of a biblical theology of religions.[50] In his evaluation of Islam, Zwemer points out its faults from a biblical standpoint without attacking Islam like the former polemicists. He states, "The great failure of Islam, however, has been its spiritual failure. It stands out among all the non-Christian religions as the religion which has blindfolded Christ and for thirteen centuries has raised the cry: 'Not this man, but Barabbas.'"[51] On the question of "what think ye of Mohammed?" Zwemer simply provides several biblical passages by saying, "according to the testimony of the Scriptures (Deut 13:1–6; Matt 7:15–20; 24:24; 1 John 4:1–4)," so that readers and Muslims might come to their own conclusion based on Scripture.[52]

The second characteristic of the traditional-theological model lies in its emphasis on personal conversation over group controversy. The proponents stress that there should be no mention or little use of the Qur'an or Islamic sources because it automatically provokes Muslim emotions and prevents evangelists from sharing Christ. Zwemer takes the primary goal in evangelism to be "preaching the Christ crucified" so that his method is referred to as the Christological approach.[53] Direct friendship evangelism in personal conversations is strongly recommended.[54] In describing evangelism, Zwemer stresses the importance of authentic Christian witness among Muslims through revealing Christ's life: "After forty years' experience—sometimes heart-breaking experience, of sowing on rocks and of watching the birds pick away the seed to the last grain—I am convinced that the nearest way to the Moslem heart is the way of God's love, the way of the Cross."[55] Wilson

---

49 Wilson, *Christian Message to Islam*, 42.

50 Schlorff, "Theological and Apologetical Dimensions," 337. This factor becomes an important issue in establishing an evangelical theology of religions.

51 Zwemer, *Cross Above the Crescent*, 53.

52 Zwemer, *Cross Above the Crescent*, 71.

53 Zwemer, *Cross Above the Crescent*, 233–34 and 257–68.

54 Wilson, *Christian Message to Islam*, 46.

55 Zwemer, *Cross Above the Crescent*, 245–50.

emphatically contends for the life witness of a godly Christian in Muslim evangelism:

> If we are determined to avoid argument, what should be our method of approach to the Mohammedan? It may be remarked in the beginning that whatever we say can be answered; but to a holy life, filled with the spirit and love of Christ, there is no answer. We are not, however, holding ourselves up before our friends, but asking them to look with us at Christ.[56]

The translation and distribution of the Bible occupies a special place in this model because the proponents believe that the Bible is the most effective missionary in the Muslim world.[57] Wilson shares the same conviction when he states, "In a great number of instances those who have become Christians attribute their first real knowledge of Christ and their conversion to reading of the Bible or hearing it read. Bible distribution is an old method in the world of Islam but it should be continued and increased in every possible way."[58] Some helpful literatures are advised to be used for carefully scrutinized purposes. Wilson proposes a wise use of literatures in Muslim evangelism by categorizing them into four classes: "(1) for the first approach, (2) for follow-up work, (3) to bring conviction to the reader, (4) to build up in the faith."[59] Polemic literatures, however, are discouraged to be used in evangelism.

Both Zwemer and Wilson are opposed to the idea that a convert can remain within a former Muslim community by keeping silent about new faith in Christ. Because of the discontinuity and theological incompatibility

---

56  Wilson, *Christian Message to Islam*, 45.

57  Zwemer, "Chasm," 113. He says, "At all of these points the missionary is to bridge the chasm with courage and tact, by the manifestation of the truth in love. The distribution of the Word of God always holds the first place. It has always proved its power." Also see Zwemer, *Evangelism Today*, 96–97.

58  Wilson, "Moslem Converts," 177.

59  Wilson, *Christian Message to Islam*, 52. He gives an example of a "Guide to Christian Literature in Persian," which provides field missionaries with the most up-to-date information on literatures with "a short resume of the contents of the book or tract and suggestions as to its use." In this model, controversial Christian literatures of the polemicists are advised to be avoided, though they can be used for certain people in some situations. For instance, if a Muslim is genuinely seeking truth, Wilson recommends a missionary to give a literature to answer his struggle or objections just for his own reading. He does not, however, recommend a personal debate or discussion on the material. Schlorff holds a similar viewpoint and contends that when Islamic sources are inevitably used, it can be helpful to point out the distinctiveness of Christianity and to vindicate the supremacy of the biblical revelation. Schlorff, "Muslim Ideology," 173–85; Schlorff, "Theological and Apologetical Dimensions," 337.

between Islam and Christianity, they contend that new converts should make a clean break by separating themselves from the Islamic community. Zwemer boldly states:

> Unless we ask the Moslem enquirer to make a clear-cut decision, to break with his past to accept a new way of life in Christ, we are really doing him an injustice. The easy way is not the way of the Gospel. A friendlier attitude toward Christ and Christianity is not enough. The way of the Cross means crucifixion, not inoculation.[60]

Conversion is understood as a separation from previous religious affiliation and the practices of Islam. New Muslim converts are expected not to remain silent about their beliefs, but are encouraged to join a church for public confession of their new faith. Zwemer thinks that only those who remain faithful in spite of persecutions and sufferings will become the foundation for the church established in Muslim lands, and that this body of believers will have permanence.[61] Even though Muslim converts may wish to stay within their social network, persecutions or social oppositions will force them to leave, especially because of the Islamic doctrine of apostasy and the tightly-knit nature of the Islamic community.[62] Wilson explains this as a common phenomenon in Muslim lands and stresses it as a necessary step toward seeing a MBBs church:

> It is interesting to note that many of those who accepted the Christian faith at first made an earnest effort to live with their own families and in their Moslem environment. The decision is fraught with suffering and torment of soul, but it seems that only through such travail can the new man in Christ be born

---

60 Zwemer, *Cross Above the Crescent*, 261.

61 Wilson, *Christian Message to Islam*, 173. Wilson solemnly states, "Above all else, we believe that the encouragement to remain silent about Christian faith is not Scriptural. Though we should change our missionary methods to meet altered conditions, the New Testament must remain our guide and standard and the words of Christ and the apostles have divine authority. In the New Testament times churches were founded only on persecution, on sacrifice and suffering and travail, and we doubt that an easier method can be discovered. There is no 'twilight sleep' procedure for the birth of the churches."

62 Goldsmith, "Community and Controversy," 318. Zwemer, *Law of Apostasy*. Though Islamic scholars claim that Islam is a religion of peace and tolerance, Zwemer convincingly argues against their claim by noting not only all relevant Islamic sources but also the actual practices of the Islamic societies in his day and time.

out of Islam and the foundation stones of the Church be laid in Moslem lands.[63]

As a result, new converts are encouraged to join the existing churches, however few they may be in certain countries. Churches are expected to play an important role by providing these new converts with an alternative community for their spiritual nurturing and discipleship. When there is no existing church, group conversion is recommended as an ideal alternative.[64] Whether it is a foreign, historic minority, or MBB church, its presence in Muslim lands is considered an essential foundation for evangelizing the whole Muslim nations in the traditional-theological model.

## Evaluation

The strength of this model lies in its emphasis on a clear presentation of the Gospel based on Scripture and an orthodox theological foundation. This is the most traditional method being utilized by missionaries and MBBs. The proponents of this model are ready to distinguish Christianity from Islam and to point out the faulty aspects of Islam from a biblical theological foundation whenever necessary. To a certain degree they share the same view of Islam with the polemicists. Peters describes the common viewpoint on Islam between the confrontational and the traditional-theological model:

> I am inclined to stand in line with such men as Pfander, Zwemer, Freytag and others who see in Islam a "supra-humanly designed" anti-Christian religious movement to offset and oppose the gospel of our Lord Jesus Christ. It is the only religion which explicitly in its original sources plainly contradicts and denies the very foundation stones of Christianity—the reliability of the Book, the Fatherhood of God, the Sonship of Christ, the atoning necessity and sufficiency of the death of Christ, the justifying resurrection of Christ. It is *the Great Controversy of Christianity* and the gospel of our salvation. Not Christianity but Islam is the great Controverter.[65]

It is certainly commendable to focus on a clear presentation of the Gospel and Christ crucified while wisely avoiding counterproductive controversies. In doing so, a constant use of Scripture is emphasized as the

---

63  Wilson, *Christian Message to Islam*, 109–10.

64  Goldsmith, "Community and Controversy," 319.

65  Peters, "Overview," 401 (emphasis in the original). This view of Islam is commonly shared in both the confrontational and the traditional-theological model.

supreme authority. This is a significant improvement from the confrontational model because it promotes the teaching of the Christian truth in a straightforward manner while wisely avoiding controversies in the evangelistic conversations with Muslims.

This model has a strong advantage in promoting conversational evangelism through friendship. Personal relationship is a ground for the Christian witnesses to share the love of Christ through a Bible-based exemplary lifestyle. This has been proven to be the most effective principle used by many evangelical missionaries throughout the twentieth century. In a recent survey among MBBs asking about why Muslims follow Jesus, respondents ranked the lifestyle of Christians as the most important influence in their decision to follow Christ.[66]

In emphasizing personal friendship as a facilitator to the Gospel presentation, another significant improvement is found in this model. Zwemer, for example, stressed the need to distinguish Muslims as people of genuine religious pursuit from Islam as a religious system; he demanded that missionaries make a careful study of Muslims as people through observing their mystic religious practices in order to better understand their felt-needs.[67] In this regard, Clayton Cloer's observation is correct when he says that Zwemer integrated an anthropological insight into his missiological paradigm even though his major emphasis was on a theological approach.[68]

There are, nevertheless, several limitations in this model. First, the tendency of separating converts from the Islamic community has led to a counterproductive practice of extraction evangelism. While persecution may have made such separation inevitable, this model seems to encourage new converts to leave the Islamic community too quickly. When new believers, after having been separated from the Islamic society, gather into the church, Muslims develop a negative perception of the Christian church for converting their people into a foreign religion. If new believers remain within their social network to initiate evangelistic momentum among their own people, group conversion can be a possibility in the long run. Extraction of converts, whether intentional or unintentional, has become one of the biggest limitations and liabilities of this model.

---

66 Woodberry et al., "Why Muslims Follow Jesus," 80–85 (emphasis in the original).

67 Zwemer, *Studies in Popular Islam*, viii. Zwemer states, "A knowledge of Mohammedan mysticism, its vocabulary, its aims and its organization would prove the key to the hearts of the masses in nearly every part of India." Also see Zwemer, "Diversity of Islam in India," 120.

68 Cloer, "Samuel Zwemer," 56–59.

Second, there is a lack of emphasis on cultural sensitivity compared to the following models. The proponents did not differentiate cultural elements from religious ones in Muslim society, and missionaries were too cautious about using cultural factors for innovative expression of the Gospel in indigenous cultural terms. While a theological emphasis certainly takes precedence in Muslim evangelism, it is essential for missionaries to consider accommodating various indigenous cultural aspects that are not against the biblical teachings for a more effective Gospel communication. Otherwise, the church and Christian practices, as fruits of Christian missions, would become so foreign to Muslims that there will be no real impact of the Gospel.

Some who are critical of the traditional-theological model for its ineffectiveness may characterize the twentieth-century missions to Muslims as "faithful sowing without seeing much fruits." There are potential areas of improvement to increase its effectiveness. Nevertheless, one cannot deny the fact that a positive trend of evangelization among Muslim nations in the last century is a product of the majority of missionaries and national Christians who have employed this model as a primary approach. It is in this sense that this model has been a foundational evangelical approach to Muslims throughout the last century. Starting from this model, some missionaries have innovatively developed other approaches, such as the following two models.[69]

## THE DIALOGICAL MODEL

### Major Proponents

While the traditional-theological model emphasizes differences between Islam and Christianity, the dialogical model begins with similarities or commonalities between the two. This model begins by noting positive aspects of Islam and Muslims, and promotes peaceful dialogue with Muslims.[70] Ray

---

69 There exists a certain degree of continuity between the traditional-theological model and the alternatives, so it is valid to consider it as the foundational evangelical model in Muslim evangelism. The contextual model of Parshall, in particular, can be viewed as an extension of the traditional-theological model. Parshall himself asserts that he basically follows Zwemer's approach with "the added dimension of exploring relatively untried and untested methodological options for communicating Christ in an Islamic cultural and religious milieu." Parshall, *Muslim Evangelism*, 23. The dialogical model also shares some commonalities with the traditional-theological model, but makes a significant departure in some critical areas as will be elaborated in the following section.

70 Interfaith dialogue can occur on different levels: high-official level, community level, and personal level. The major proponents of high-official interfaith dialogue are

G. Register and Fouad E. Accad have proposed evangelistic models through personal-level dialogue by appreciating common human pursuits and religious desires for God in the hearts of Muslims.[71]

## Main Characteristics

The dialogical model is critical about the confrontational argumentative approach for the same reason mentioned in the traditional-theological model. Furthermore, the proponents of the dialogical model are skeptical about the traditional-theological model because the traditional view of Islam in this model does not allow for effective penetration of the Gospel into the Islamic world. Accad describes the fundamental weakness of the traditional-theological model in the following words:

> One of the foundation stones of Samuel Zwemer's ministry was that he wanted Muslims to understand there is another way. This concept does not translate well to a Muslim, however, because a Muslim says there is only one way, *God's* way. If you advocate anything else, that's blasphemy. This is all the more reason why you have to go side by side with a Muslim, communicating with him through his own religious book, in his way.[72]

The best way to understand the dialogical model is to know its departure from the traditional-theological method. First of all, this model asserts that a genuine personal dialogue is a prerequisite for effective preaching of the Gospel to Muslims. Dialogue is an attempt to "know life through

---

Kenneth Cragg and W. Montgomery Watt, and their approach is rather philosophical without proposing a concrete evangelistic model; therefore, it is not discussed in detail in this section. They are sometimes mentioned because some of Cragg and Watt's proposals have influenced the dialogical model presented in this section. Some of their representative works of influence include: Cragg, *Sandals at the Mosque*; Cragg, *Call of the Minaret*; Watt, *Islam and Christianity Today*. Moreover, a high-official level of dialogue is promoted in some ecumenical movements, and many evangelical theologians have been skeptical about this, especially because of the theological compromise that interfaith dialogue may entail. It is worthwhile to note that some features of the missions theology of Cragg and Watt are criticized by conservative evangelicals. For example, George Braswell makes a critique of Cragg's theology in that his view of revelation is closer to Karl Rahner, who holds an openness view to other faiths with the "anonymous Christianity" idea, than to Hendrick Kraemer, who holds an absolutist view of revelation. Braswell, "Encounter of Christianity and Islam," 117–27. For a historical sketch of how interfaith dialogue evolved, see Register, *Dialogue and Interfaith Witness*, 10–12; Schlorff, *Missiological Models*, 19–23.

71 Register, *Dialogue and Interfaith Witness*; Accad, *Building Bridges*.
72 Accad, *Building Bridges*, 54.

## Historical Developments of Muslim Evangelism and the Insider Movement 39

the other person" by getting to know Muslims in their own sociocultural and religious contexts. Dialogue breaks down communication barriers in the relationship between Christians and Muslims.[73] While the goal of interfaith dialogue is defined as bringing reconciliation between Christians and Muslims in the spirit of incarnation, Register carefully differentiates the biblical notion of interfaith dialogue from an ecumenical concept popularly promoted among non-evangelicals:

> Dialogue, for the Christian, should not be a compromising of his faith, but an attempt to understand the other person as a human being in the spirit of the Incarnation. It allows each to maintain his personhood, while granting the opportunity to share his faith. Interfaith witness is an integral part of the Christian-Muslim dialogue.[74]

Register believes that conversing with Muslims opens the door for an objective sharing of Christian truth while acknowledging the differences between the two religions. The goal is to motivate Muslims to study the Bible through the "Scripture to Scripture" approach, because the dialogue should stand on the original sources as its ultimate authority.[75]

Although conversation based on friendship is emphasized in the traditional-theological method, there are several differences between conversation in the traditional-theological model and dialogue in the dialogical model. Dialogue starts with a positive attitude to Islam whereas conversation relies on a didactic approach by assuming that there is no need for Christians to learn additional truth from Islam. In the conversation of the traditional-theological model, the Christian witness builds personal relationships and shares the Gospel without necessarily getting into discussion on Islam or Islamic sources. Use of the Islamic sources is not encouraged for the Christian witness. Instead, the Christian witness is encouraged to share the Gospel in a straightforward manner by relying on scriptural authority.

In the dialogue of the dialogical model, the Christian witness is willing to allow Muslim friends to share their beliefs from Islamic sources, but also he is encouraged to use Islamic sources to defend or explain the Christian truths. The proponents believe that only this kind of sincere dialogue with open-mindedness on both sides can break down barriers between Christians and Muslims and create a genuine openness in the hearts and minds

---

73 Register, *Dialogue and Interfaith Witness*, 5.

74 Register, *Dialogue and Interfaith Witness*, 9.

75 Register, *Dialogue and Interfaith Witness*, viii. Register provides a practical guide for dialogue with Muslims and for answering popular questions encountered in the process. See chapters 3 and 4 of his book.

of Muslims. Register refers to the conversation of the traditional-theological model as "two-sided monologue," and argues that it does not have the same degree of impact on Muslim evangelism as the genuine "two-sided dialogue" in the dialogical model might have.[76]

Second, the central contention of the dialogical model is to build bridges through establishing common ground, so that one may gain the listening ears and the receptive hearts of Muslims. In contrast, the traditional-theological model emphasizes the uniqueness of Christ and the radical discontinuity between Christianity and Islam. Concerning some similarities observed in the two religions, they are only viewed as points of contact in the Gospel presentation, not common ground which the dialogical model promotes.[77] While criticizing the traditional-theological approach for its main focus on the discontinuities between Christians and Muslims, Accad contends that it builds up more barriers than bridges. He instead proposes a bridge-building approach to Muslims based upon the notion of common ground. By taking note of the commonality between the two religions, new possibilities can be available to facilitate an effective Gospel communication.[78] In explaining the need and usefulness of Christians' learning about the Qur'an, Register says, "You will be surprised to learn how much Christians have in common with Muslims. You will also note the crucial differences. By accepting positive contributions of Islam, you will gain the respect and friendship of the Muslim."[79] He emphasizes the importance of focusing on Christ in his "virgin birth, miracles, and ascension" as the common ground between Muslims and Christians for an effective Gospel presentation.[80]

76 Register, *Dialogue and Interfaith Witness*, xii.

77 The two terms, "common ground" and "points of contact," bear significantly distinctive meanings in the contextualization discussion. The detailed distinctions will be elaborated in formulating the analytical framework of contextualization in chapter 3. One prior warning is in order. Since the two terms are customarily used in the writings without much detailed explanations, one has to discern how writers use each term. The notion of points of contact in the dialogical model is equivalent to the term "common ground" in the analytical framework of this study.

78 Accad, *Building Bridges*, 10–11. He mentions using the Qur'an as a bridge to the Bible in chapter 2 and contends for using it as common ground in evangelism in chapter 3.

79 Register, *Dialogue and Interfaith Witness*, 18.

80 Register, *Dialogue and Interfaith Witness*, 19. Accad, however, adds the death of Christ in this list because he relies on a different interpretation of certain verses of the Qur'an from traditional Islamic interpretations. Accad, *Building Bridges*, 10–11. Cragg similarly stresses the use of common human religious experiences for building bridges that are to do with the divine relation to the human situation, such as "prophecy, worship, prayer, mercy, law, scripture, patriarchs, God's design in nature, creation and sin."

## Historical Developments of Muslim Evangelism and the Insider Movement 41

The most striking peculiarity of this model is the active use of the Qur'an in the dialogue. The polemicists used the Qur'an to defeat common Muslim objections against Christian Scripture and truths, but its use in the dialogical model is positive or affirmative in that selective verses of the Qur'an are used to affirm some key biblical truths.[81] Although quite a few missionaries support the idea of using the Qur'an in Muslim evangelism, not many of them demonstrate how this method can be validated. Since Accad provides the most explicit explanation for validation, his approach and arguments are examined here.

Accad validates the use of the Qur'an in Muslim evangelism by showing the biblical examples of Acts 17.[82] He identifies the different evangelism methods in Paul's ministry. Paul, while preaching to the Jews, begins with the concept of Christ (the Messiah) and their own scripture (the Old Testament) before he introduces Jesus Christ. Accad compares Paul's use of the Old Testament with Christians' use of the Qur'an as a starting point.[83] Another validating argument for using the Qur'an is found when Paul makes "a reference to the Athenians' philosophers and poets as a bridge to introduce them to a few quotations from the Old Testament about God."[84] Based on such interpretation of Acts 17, Accad explicitly affirms the validity of using the Qur'an:

> It is worth noting that Paul did not hesitate to mention Greek poets in his declaration, though he was perfectly aware that these poets had been inspired by sister goddesses named Muse. It is worth noting that the Spirit of God, who inspired the writer of the book of Acts, did not hesitate to include a statement from one of Greek poets in the content of the Bible. It is in this light that the Christian can skillfully share truth from the Qur'an with his Muslim friend. If he does so, both will be surprised and edified by what it says about Christ as the Word of God who took

---

Cragg, *Sandals at the Mosque*, 74–75.

81 For a helpful critique of different uses of the Qur'an, see Schlorff, *Missiological Models*, 31–78.

82 Accad, *Building Bridges*, 12–33.

83 Accad states, "Using Paul's method, we can introduce accurate verses about Christ from the Qur'an to Muslims, which will naturally arouse their respect for what Muhammad has brought them and at the same time open a door of curiosity about the full deity of Jesus Christ. But we must first reinforce their comfort zone with truth from the Qur'an before we try to expose them to the fuller truth from the Bible." Accad, *Building Bridges*, 16.

84 Accad, *Building Bridges*, 22. This passage is extensively used by IM advocates; there will be a more detailed exegetical analysis of this passage in the biblical theological evaluation of this study.

a body like ours, although without sin, and became the son of Mary and the Savior of the world.[85]

Accad asserts that it is possible to bring Muslims to a realization of the superiority of Christ through a new interpretation of the Qur'an. This depends on the assumption that the Qur'an needs to be reinterpreted in light of Christ, which produces a radically different perspective of Jesus from the popular Muslim interpretations. If this new interpretation is properly applied to the Qur'an, Accad believes that one can affirm that "Muhammad did *not* in any way intend for the Qur'an to be anti-Christ or an anti-Christian document."[86] He summarizes his contention on this issue:

> Because of the largely pro-Christian attitude in the Qur'an, it seems just as legitimate to use it in our witnessing as to use a pro-Christian quote from any other respected book or leader. God wants us to know His truth. Because of the complexity of cultural circumstances in this world, it is reasonable—indeed, it is a necessity!—that we exercise the same kind of wisdom demonstrated by the writers of the books of the Bible in order to establish common ground with people who otherwise would probably never be open to hearing the gospel message.[87]

Another notable feature in the dialogical model is that new converts are encouraged to remain within an Islamic community and continue to witness to Muslims through their social networks. Accad argues that "following Christ should not—and need not—bring out persecution and blame from other Muslims, since Christ is considered one of the greatest prophets in the Qur'an."[88] The reason converts should be allowed to remain within the Islamic community lies in the assumption that they do not consider themselves as "Christians," but as "genuine Muslims," in the sense that "they have surrendered to God."[89] This means that Muslim converts would remain

---

85 Accad, *Building Bridges*, 22–23. Accad also makes his case by arguing that the New Testament biblical writers used "terminology and ideas from nonbiblical sources, often quoting directly." See chapter 3, "A Case for Common Ground," in the same book, 25–29.

86 Accad, *Building Bridges*, 28.

87 Accad, *Building Bridges*, 28–29. See also Accad, "Qur'an," 331–42.

88 Accad, *Building Bridges*, 8.

89 Accad, *Building Bridges*, 8. Accad asserts that "these new believers in Christ are reading the Bible with their Muslim friends, and no one has kicked them out of their homes and communities, for they are not viewed as traitors." It seems that new converts call themselves either "Muslim" or "follower of Isa" while avoiding the term "Christian." This idea becomes important in the discussion of the IM.

within their former Muslim community to become living witnesses to Christ, and that they should be encouraged to do so.

Since this model promotes peaceful dialogue and open sharing based on friendship, cultural sensitivity is all the more emphasized. Most Islamic religious terms are extensively employed to express the Christian message based upon the communication principle of "meet them where they are!" A better acquaintance of Islam and the Muslim mindset is necessary for Christians to discern what Muslims would understand by various religious terms and how they should be correctly approached in dialogue.

Accad contends that the effectiveness of the dialogical model can be verified through successful field reports: "In fact, we have found that 60 percent of Muslims who are approached with the method explained in this book put their trust in Christ—and all who do, do so without becoming detestable to their own communities."[90] It is rather unfortunate that he does not provide a more detailed report to support his claim. He claims that peaceful dialogue produces a better communication of the Gospel than other previous models because of their respective drawbacks: the confrontational model for being argumentative, and the traditional-theological model for being two-way monologue instead of genuine two-way dialogue.

## Evaluation

There are several commendable features in the dialogical model, including the emphasis on peaceful dialogue based on personal friendship, a positive attitude to Muslims as religious people, due respect for the Muslim scripture, cultural sensitivity in personal dialogue, seemingly positive fruitful results in the field experience, and the emphasis on a fuller understanding of Islam and the Muslim mindset for an effective communication of the Gospel. In a sense, this model is an attempt to overcome some of the weaknesses of the traditional-theological model. Although it may simply be a matter of difference of degree in some areas, such as friendship, positive attitude to Muslims as religious people, or cultural sensitivity, this model adds significant contributions to the development of Muslim evangelism by overcoming some of the weaknesses of the traditional-theological model.

The dialogical model, however, presents some problematic matters in the Muslim evangelism discussion, some of which being implicit and unnoticeable. While certain practical suggestions of this model seem reasonable, there are subtle problems behind those explicit assertions. First, the dialogical model assumes that one can start with a positive view of both Muslims

90  Accad, *Building Bridges*, 10.

and Islam. Its proponents claim that this positive view is not only profitable but necessary to build bridges to create peaceful dialogue, and to produce an effective communication of the Gospel. Accad's assertion that the Qur'an is pro-Christ and pro-Christianity represents one example of their positive view of Islam.

Zwemer seems to agree on the need for a sympathetic outlook on Muslims as people who have devout religious pursuit.[91] Zwemer, however, would never endorse Islam or Islamic sources (the Qur'an and the Traditions) as a valid foundation to discuss and teach God's truth. While bluntly proclaiming that "Islam is in its spirit anti-Christian," Zwemer emphasizes the importance of pointing out the distinctiveness of Christian truth from Islamic doctrines and the superiority of Christ over Muhammad.[92] In this regard, the proponents of the dialogical model stand in opposition to Zwemer and the traditional theological view of Islam. The main reason for their positive outlook on Islam comes from the assertion that Islam portrays Christ in a genuinely honorable way if rightly understood, and that the Qur'an contains many parcels of truth about Jesus Christ that can be used for Christian witness.

While leaving an in-depth treatment of these issues for later chapters, suffice it to say that some theological problems are pertinent to this positive view of Islam and the Qur'an. This problem directly involves theology of religions and the following questions should be addressed: When the proponents of this model look at Islam from a positive light, what is the biblical foundation for this position? What about some contradictory teachings of Islam against biblical truth? Can anyone approach Islam from a positive outlook by using selective elements of Islam that seem to be more compatible with Christian truth? One should ask what the Bible says about other religions, especially concerning Islam. Without examining a proper understanding of biblical theology of religions, promoting a sentimentally positive approach to Islam based on seemingly common elements in the two religions can be misleading. The unequivocal assumption of the dialogical model to the validity of Islam and the Qur'an, therefore, demands much deeper biblical and theological assessments.

---

91 Zwemer says, "We must become Moslems to the Moslem if we could gain them for Christ. We must do this in the Pauline sense, without compromise, but with self-sacrificing sympathy and unselfish love. . . . The barrier may be in the heart of the missionary as well as in the heart of the Moslem. He should cultivate sympathy to the highest degree and an appreciation of all the great fundamental truths which we hold in common with Moslems." Zwemer, *Moslem Christ*, 183.

92 Zwemer, *Moslem Christ*, 182–85.

## Historical Developments of Muslim Evangelism and the Insider Movement 45

The second problem, which is closely related to the first, involves the validity of the Qur'an in revealing God's truth. While using it as a source for corroborating or supporting biblical truth, does one accept that the Qur'an is inspired by God or that the Qur'an itself contains God's revelation in part? Accad denies that the Qur'an is the inspired Word of God when he says, "When Christians quote from other books while witnessing, they are by no means stating that everything in them is true or that those books are divinely inspired."[93] Nevertheless, he gives a high status to the Qur'an and appreciates the significant role of Muhammad in bringing the Qur'an to Arabs from a historical perspective:

> In the seventh century, the Scriptures had not yet been translated into Arabic. Jews and Christians from non-Arab cultures living in Arabia had the Word of God in their languages, but the Arabs did not have Scriptures in Arabic. . . . The historical perspective of the Arabs is that God remedied this situation by appointing Muhammad to communicate to them in their own language. . . . In light of this passage from the Qur'an [Sura 5:68], it seems that Muhammad saw himself as a 'warner' who was bringing the Qur'an in a clear Arabic tongue in order to fill this literary vacuum within the Arab religious culture and to help turn the Arabs from idolatry to worship of the one true God.[94]

Accad holds a positive outlook on Islam and the Qur'an because he accepts too much of the Islamic historical interpretation in his attempt to validate the Qur'an as an authentic source for preaching Christ through new interpretations. Moreover, by using the Qur'an to declare Christian truth to Muslims, Accad actually gives far greater authority to the Qur'an than can be justified for the sake of peaceful dialogue. The imperative line of questioning stands: What is the biblical-theological evaluation of the other religious sources? Does the Bible approve their use in the Gospel proclamation? If so, what are the biblical guidelines and specific limitations for using sources from other religions? All of this remains unanswered behind the assumptions of the dialogical model. This topic is one of the most controversial issues in the Muslim contextualization debates, and it demands a carefully articulated treatment in the critical evaluation of the IM.

The third problem involves a question of whether it is valid to reinterpret the Qur'an by applying Christian hermeneutics. The practical method of the dialogical model relies on a Christianized reinterpretation of the Qur'an, so that the life, death, and resurrection of Jesus can be affirmed

---

93 Accad, *Building Bridges*, 26.
94 Accad, *Building Bridges*, 36–37.

by the Qur'an. Concerning the hermeneutical method in interpreting the Qur'an, Donald Rickards makes a distinction between Qur'anic hermeneutics and Muslim hermeneutics.[95] The former traces the original meaning of the Qur'anic verses within the original context, and its hermeneutical conclusions can be different from the popular Islamic teachings, which is the result of the Muslim hermeneutics.

For example, when the Qur'anic hermeneutics is applied to the topic of the Trinity, the proponents of the dialogical model argue that one can prove that Muhammad must have known about the Trinity. They contend that Muhammad did not attack the doctrine of the Trinity. What Muhammad attacked was actually heretical trinitarian beliefs of his days.[96] All of these conclusions, however, heavily depend upon the validity of the Christianized interpretation of the Qur'an or the Qur'anic hermeneutic, which is significantly different from orthodox Islamic theology. Arguable questions arise: With what authority can anyone make such reinterpretations of the Qur'an? Whose interpretation is more correct, Islamic theologians' or the Christian missionaries'? What about the explicitly contradicting verses in the Qur'an against the biblical truth about Christ?[97] While the answers to these questions are dependent on a foundational assumption of the dialogical model, its proponents have not sufficiently addressed this issue in a rigorous manner. They simply assert the usefulness and the effectiveness of the approach from a pragmatic perspective without making necessary biblical and theological evaluations.

Another question lingers: Can and should new converts remain within the Islamic community?[98] Although the proponents of this model argue that it is not only possible but also necessary for new converts to stay within their social networks, there is much doubt about the possibility of this prac-

---

95 Donald R. Rickards asserts, "The distinction must be made between a Qur'anic hermeneutic and a Muslim hermeneutic. To accept what Muslims have written about the Qur'anic passages involved and to analyze their literature about their standpoint would constitute a Muslim hermeneutic, not a Qur'anic hermeneutic. Such a Muslim hermeneutic would be of little or no value to the convert from Islam." Rickards, *Contextualization of the Gospel*, 48–68.

96 Rickards, *Contextualization of the Gospel*, 58.

97 Some of these questions will be discussed in the analytical framework of Muslim contextualization, with reference to theology of religions, hermeneutics, and epistemology.

98 The idea of new converts remaining within the Islamic community had existed in the history of Muslim evangelism even before the dialogical model. The argument for "secret believers" in Muslim lands was an issue during the colonial era, when the law of apostasy was practiced in a harsh manner. Most evangelical missionaries of that era, however, rejected this notion of secret believers, based on their conviction that Christians should stand for the Gospel in spite of sufferings and oppositions.

tice. The Islamic community is so tightly knit that it is hardly plausible for new converts to hide their faith in Christ when they begin to live according to the biblical teaching. Persecution and expulsion will occur when their new faith is recognized by other Muslims.

When new converts continue to practice Islamic religious practices after confessing faith in Christ, there is also an ethical issue. Some people are critical of this idea of maintaining dual religious loyalty because it involves intentionally deceiving others.[99] One way of remaining within an Islamic community is to privately redefine the term, Muslim, as "one who surrenders to God" and continue to follow Islamic religious practices based upon the notion of "surrendering to God as revealed in the Bible." The issue of religious identity, however, is not so simple and it demands further elaboration in the contextualization discussion.

The dialogical model emphasizes peaceful, friendly dialogue with Muslims and takes into consideration the Islamic cultural and religious forms. The proponents of this model, Accad and Register, confirm the notion that the ultimate goal of dialogue must be to evoke faith in Jesus Christ, which Arthur Glasser calls "authentic dialogue."[100] This is the most important distinction that separates this model from the ecumenical movement, which tends to lead to a theologically compromising situation in the context of interfaith dialogue.[101] The dialogical model has developed innovative thinking into a practical method and is claimed to have produced fruitful results in field experiments. In spite of creative attempts, it stands upon several problematic assumptions demands a critical examination of the foundational issues from a biblical and theological perspective.

---

99 Parshall is but one example who gives a critical assessment on maintaining dual religious identity because of its deceitful, unethical nature. Parshall, "Danger!" 404–6, 409–10.

100 Glasser, "Friendly Dialogue," 265. Glasser asserts that dialogue itself is not sufficient because the biblical concept of evangelism is characterized as didactic in essence, including the notion of persuasion and proclamation. Gordon D. Nickel also stresses that Christians should express the truth claims with conviction in the midst of peaceful dialogue. Nickel, *Peaceable Witness*, 75–77.

101 Some evangelicals see certain usefulness of high-official dialogue because it can create a positive impact on evangelical work among Muslims. Woodberry, for example, argues that dialogue with Muslim authorities may provide an opportunity to hear their concerns and to express a "Christian desire for greater religious freedom" in Muslim lands. Woodberry, "Can We Dialogue," 108. Schlorff, on the other hand, expresses a pessimistic view of interfaith dialogue, asserting that the majority of Muslims would not be willing to take part in it with Christians.

## THE CONTEXTUAL MODEL

### Major Proponents

The contextual model starts with the assumption that the insensitive treatment of the cultural and religious factors of Muslims on the part of Christian communicators has seriously hindered the cross-cultural communication of the Gospel with Muslims. It is, therefore, imperative for missionaries to start with a deeper understanding of and genuine engagement with the Muslim context in terms of its culture, religious rituals, social practices, and worldviews.[102] The major proponent of the contextual model is Phil Parshall, a long time missionary and an academic writer. He innovatively developed his contextual model and practiced it among several Asian Muslim nations. According to Parshall, the result was more than encouraging, so that he has become the most outspoken statesman of the contextual approach.[103]

Although Parshall is known as the major pioneering formulator, his contextualization attempts were not completely new. Earlier thinkers had already suggested creative proposals of Muslim contextualization, although most of their ideas had not been tried or tested in the field.[104] Parshall's notable contribution is the comprehensive presentation of the contextual model by incorporating both practical and theoretical elements. When he made his first proposal a quarter century ago, he was much criticized by some conservative evangelical scholars because of the unconventional practices and the thought-provoking approaches to Muslim evangelism. Today, however, most of his ideas are well received by the majority of evangelical

---

102 Some proponents of the dialogical model, such as Accad, take into account Islamic cultural and religious factors, but there is a significant difference between their model and the contextual model, as will be explored in this section.

103 Parshall and his team began to apply this new contextual model in 1975 and reportedly experienced significant progress in reaping a large number of converts. He reports, "some thirty-seven Muslims... accepted Christ in the two years," preceding his writing, "Evangelizing Muslims" 28–29.

104 Some earlier thinkers of similar views can be found in McCurry, *Gospel and Islam*; Shumaker, *Report of Conference*; and eight articles in a special issue of *Missiology* 6 (1976) 259–372.

missionaries.[105] Timothy Tennant, among many evangelical missiologists, endorses Parshall's contextualization model.[106]

## Main Characteristics

The contextual model agrees with the traditional-theological in its orthodox theological stance, but is critical of the latter's ineffectiveness in Muslim lands. The main cause of its ineffectiveness, according to the proponents of the contextual model, is the lack of cultural sensitivity and the practice of extraction of converts. Parshall formulates his model by taking into account an Islamic cultural and religious milieu to explore relatively untried and untested methodological options for communicating Christ.[107] The contextual model, therefore, takes the traditional-theological model a step further by innovatively incorporating the cultural and religious elements of Muslims for a more effective presentation of the Gospel.

First, it is assumed that a real and formidable barrier in Muslim evangelism is the foreignness of the Christian church and of its practices in the minds of Muslims. Parshall stresses the importance of recognizing the prevalent chasm between Muslim and Christian minds concerning Christian religious forms and practices.[108] Parshall contends that some western-

---

[105] The first comprehensive proposal appears in Parshall's *New Paths*, which contains several tentative contextualization ideas. In 2003, he published the revised edition, *Muslim Evangelism*, where he provides concrete conclusions on certain proposals of the first edition after many years of experiments. One fundamental notion of Parshall's missiological model derives from his conviction that evangelical missionaries should not remain "content with a methodology that has proven to be ineffective in bringing Muslims to our Lord." He also challenges evangelicals to "proceed with careful and sensitive experimentation" for developing innovative contextualization models. Parshall, *Muslim Evangelism*, 22.

[106] Tennent, "Followers of Jesus," 101–15.

[107] Parshall, *Muslim Evangelism*, 23. Parshall is correct in stating that, although Zwemer had suggested the importance of cultural sensitivity in Muslim evangelism, he had not experimented much in his field of ministry. Parshall's contribution lies in his innovative implementation of the foundational suggestion of Zwemer in the contemporary Muslim contexts.

[108] Parshall, *Muslim Evangelism*, 63–68. Parshall introduces his daughter's essay on how a typical Muslim experiences cultural hindrances in his perception of Christian practices in the church. Typical Muslims, for example, feel embarrassed when they see Christians not remove their shoes inside the church. Since this is simply a cultural matter that does not essentially involve the core of the Gospel, some missionaries and MBB churches in Muslim lands practice taking off shoes inside the church. Some of the westernized forms of Christian practices are being replaced by those with which Muslims would feel more comfortable. These factors are simply a matter of cultural relevance that have nothing to do with the essence of the Gospel.

ized cultural forms of Christianity should be removed or radically modified in the Gospel proclamation among Muslims. He claims that Muslims are hindered from approaching Christ simply because the western forms and practices provoke Muslims to look negatively on Christianity before they can even hear the Gospel. It is also strongly recommended that missionaries use local cultural elements for the expression of Christian truth as long as they do not violate biblical teaching. Local customs, music, poetry, and literature can become important instruments of Gospel communication. The fundamental idea is to remove cultural foreignness of Christianity in the expressions of the Christian Gospel by indigenizing biblical truth.

In addition to using Muslim cultural practices, Parshall's contextual model moves further into cautious use of the religious forms of Muslims. He asserts that some of the Islamic forms can be used for the Christian church and for the communication of the Gospel by making sure that their biblical meanings are carefully preserved. Several examples include fasting in Muslim ways, praying in Muslim forms, or using religious chanting in Christian worship.[109] While missionaries tend to agree on incorporating certain cultural forms, some of them become rather uneasy with the notion of borrowing religious forms because "they [traditional missionaries] have strongly advocated a total break with all that is Islamic" under the traditional-theological model.[110] This issue deserves a careful evaluation from a practical and biblical-theological level.

Concerning the attitude towards Islam, the contextual model is in closer proximity to the traditional-theological model. There is no blindly positive evaluation of Islam; rather, a critical biblical evaluation is emphasized. Parshall is willing to "appreciate the good in Islam and affirm the theology which agrees with the Bible," while emphasizing the presentation of the distinctive Christian theological teachings in a culturally sensitive manner and "undeservedly loving individual Muslims."[111] Parshall, like Zwemer, stresses the importance of a deeper understanding of ordinary Muslims by contemplating their hearts and minds.[112] He encourages missionaries to study carefully the traditional Muslim mindset in order to figure out their felt-needs.

The contextual model also fundamentally assumes the discontinuity between Islam and Christianity, whether it is in the comparison of similar religious concepts or in theological discussions. On the other hand, it

---

109 Parshall, *Muslim Evangelism*, 211–21.
110 Parshall, *Muslim Evangelism*, 211.
111 Parshall, "Lessons Learned," 261.
112 Parshall, *Cross and the Crescent*.

moves more progressively than the traditional-theological model to build common theological bridges for communication of the Gospel. Parshall provides various examples of potential bridges, such as scriptural authority, Old Testament prophets, Jesus in the Qur'an, the concept of God, sacrificial festivals, and supernatural experiences in Sufism.[113] He refers to the shared concepts or terms between Islam and Christianity as "common ground" upon which various bridges can be built.[114]

In this respect, Parshall's approach seems somewhat similar to Accad's dialogical approach, but at least two critical differences are noteworthy. First, Accad seems to be willing to admit that the Qur'anic witness to Christ is partially true while the presentation of Jesus in the Bible is complete. He also seems to agree on the fulfillment view of other religions, although he does not explicitly mention it.[115] Parshall, on the other hand, simply uses the quotes of the Qur'an in order to introduce Jesus from the Bible. He never sees Islam as an incomplete but true form of God's revelation, and never approves the Qur'an as the revealed Word of God.[116] Second, Accad does not promote the presentation of conflicting biblical truth against the Qur'an or the Muslims' understanding because, in his view, maintaining friendship should take a higher priority. Accad contends that new converts need to remain within the Islamic community by continuing Islamic rituals and practices, which is only possible by reinterpreting them privately from a biblical perspective. Parshall, however, does not see this process as naively as Accad, because Parshall believes that some Islamic religious practices are blatantly against biblical truth and thus cannot be practiced by believers from Muslim background.[117]

The contextual model discourages extraction evangelism, but encourages converts to maintain their social relationship within their former Islamic community for as long as possible.[118] New believers are encouraged

---

113   Parshall, *Muslim Evangelism*, 143–69.

114   Although his definition of this term is not precise, it is proved to be equivalent to "points of contact" in the analytical framework of this study.

115   For the fulfillment view of a Christian theology of religions, see Tennent, *Invitation to World Missions*, 199–203.

116   For this reason, his use of the term "common ground" is equivalent to that of "points of contact" in the analytical framework of this study.

117   Parshall, for example, contends that converts cannot participate in mosque worship because it "is pregnant with Islamic theology." Parshall, "Danger!" 409.

118   The extraction model of Muslim evangelism has been criticized by many. Khair-Ullah, for example, argues against it: "Are we justified in insisting that a person must completely break away from his past, his culture and all that is worth cherishing in life? It is not only linguistic hang-ups that impede communication between us and Muslims—there are social, cultural and psychological hang-ups too." Khair-Ullah,

to exhibit a changed life as a dynamic witness to fellow Muslims, so that evangelistic momentum can continue through the existing social networks. Parshall agrees that it may not be feasible for MBBs to remain within the Islamic community due to persecution and communal expulsion. This, however, must be the last resort rather than a planned or normative decision. The most desirable consequence of the contextual model, in contrast to an extraction model, is its positive results in producing more fruits in terms of planting indigenous churches.[119]

As a solution to the problem of Muslim converts being expelled from the Islamic society, the contextual model promotes the idea of the homogeneous unit principle as a church planting strategy. Parshall sees the value of gathering MBBs into an independent church separate from the existing Christian churches in Muslim nations. Parshall asserts that the MBB church can be contextualized in such a way that Muslims may perceive it as more culturally relevant and less foreign. Parshall, for example, proposes that the Islamic structure of the mosque and its religious leaders may be benchmarked in the formation of the MBB church as long as biblical principles are kept intact.[120]

## Evaluation

The contextual model opens a new horizon in Muslim evangelism in a variety of ways. The removal of cultural and social barriers by adopting local cultural expressions for the Gospel communication has made the MBBs church less foreign. It seems to have produced more fruitful results in the field through the ongoing personal witness of new converts as they continue to remain within the Islamic social networks. Some aspects of this model, nevertheless, arouse some concerns in the evangelical community that demand more careful examination.

First, while a critical and innovative use of Islamic cultural and religious factors for the sake of Gospel communication is understandable, there is a potential danger of confusion because of the arbitrary nature of the contextualization attempts. The real question is how to establish the criteria to determine which Islamic religious forms are permissible and helpful for expressing biblical truths. This task is not easy because it encompasses

---

"Linguistic Hang-ups," 312.

119 Though it is difficult to provide numerical results, Parshall indicates that there have been a greater number of conversions and church plants in several Asian Muslim countries by using this method. Parshall, "Lessons Learned," 264.

120 Parshall, *Muslim Evangelism*, 171–93.

### Historical Developments of Muslim Evangelism and the Insider Movement 53

many different dimensions of the contextualization process. On the one hand, this task must start with laying a well-defined evangelical theology of religions.[121] On the other hand, through the application of various field experiments, one must look into the effectiveness of using Islamic cultural and religious forms to see if the biblical meanings expressed in Islamic religious forms are correctly communicated without distortion.[122]

Second, the contextual model promotes the use of Islamic religious forms as long as the biblical meanings behind these forms are properly communicated. There is an underlying theoretical assumption that forms can be separable from their meanings in the process of communication. Parshall emphasizes the dynamic equivalence principle over formal equivalence in that he assumes the potential possibility to separate meaning from form.[123] This means that Islamic religious forms can be used for transmitting the substance of the Gospel through cautious personal reinterpretation of the message so that the biblical meaning remains intact within the dynamic equivalence framework.

The separation between forms and meanings, however, cannot be made as clearly or as easily as claimed in this model. Islam emphasizes the external forms of religious practices to an exceptional degree, and their theological meanings are so strongly attached to their forms that it is difficult to separate them. When new converts follow the Islamic pattern of fasting, the communicated message might be more Islamic than biblical. Using Islamic forms may cause them to produce syncretistic results in their minds if clear teaching and proper understanding do not take place on a personal level.

---

121 The following questions, for example, need answering: "What is the biblical view of Islam? On what basis can one acknowledge the good of Islam? What is the limitation of viewing Islam from a positive outlook? How much of the Islamic forms can be used for the Gospel communication?"

122 Parshall, for example, has experimented with different forms of baptism due to the fact that traditional Muslims view water baptism in a negative light. According to the survey data collected from the participants of the North American Conference on Muslim Evangelization in Colorado Springs in 1978, baptism was identified as "one of the largest problems confronted in evangelism among Muslims." See Parshall, *Muslim Evangelism*, 204. After his attempts to find an alternative form of baptism, Parshall concludes that water baptism is the only biblical teaching and that it is a "universal, historical practice of the church." See Parshall, "Lessons Learned," 253.

123 Parshall seems to agree with Kraft, who strongly contends for the dynamic equivalence principle: "God seeks to use and to cooperate with human beings in the continued use of relative cultural forms to express absolute supracultural meanings. The forms of culture are important not for their own sake but for the sake of that which they convey." Kraft, *Christianity in Culture*, 78.

Theoretically speaking, it is important to evaluate critically the validity and the limitations of the dynamic equivalence principle. Although it is a popular idea in translation and communication theories, the principle can allow practitioners to make arbitrary applications or invalid claims through subjective abuse. Inserting new meanings into old forms or reinterpreting Islamic religious forms can go askew without an objective guideline.

Third, Parshall's use of the Qur'an in this model can become an issue, although he claims to use it only for finding theological bridges and points of contact. This approach can easily cross a biblically permissible borderline in various contextualization attempts unless a solid biblical and theological basis for using the Qur'an is carefully defined. Some fundamental questions need to be asked and answered in providing a rigid guideline for the proper use of the Qur'an in Muslim evangelism.

Lastly, it is still questionable whether new converts would be allowed to remain within the Islamic community when they reveal the witness of a transformed life and stop participating in the Islamic religious practices. Parshall agrees that Muslims would not allow known converts to remain within their community and that believers will eventually have to leave their community at some point. When this happens, the desired evangelistic momentum may not become a real possibility.

The contextual model has certainly challenged the traditional model of Muslim evangelism and changed the missiological thinking of evangelical missionaries. More creative approaches are being implemented in various mission fields to bring increasing numbers of Muslims to the full knowledge of Christ. As MBBs and their churches in various countries have been growing both in number and maturity, Christian missions is expected to experience a much deeper understanding of how to plant culturally relevant churches among Muslim nations. It seems right to expect that the evangelical missionary movement will take the contextual model seriously and make innovative attempts to develop it for various Muslim contexts. The key question is, "How far is too far in Muslim contextualization?" Developing an objective evangelical guideline of Muslim contextualization based on a sound biblical theological foundation is urgently needed.

## THE INSIDER MOVEMENT FROM A HISTORICAL PERSPECTIVE

The historical developments of Muslim evangelism since the nineteenth century reveal a certain trend although the exact dating of individual models may not be feasible. The confrontational model mainly prevailed during the nineteenth-century colonial era and into the early twentieth century. The traditional-theological model was promoted by Zwemer and other evangelical missionaries in their effort to overcome the weaknesses of the confrontational model. Since its first proposal in the early twentieth century, it has continued to be the most foundational model for evangelical missionaries until now.

Dissatisfied with the ministry results of the traditional method and its heavy emphasis on the theological differences between Islam and Christianity, some felt the need for a new approach. The dialogical model was proposed in the 1950s and 1960s, partly because of the influence of the ecumenical movement and partly because of the wider influence of MBBs who were familiar with the Qur'an and Islamic religious culture.[124] The dialogical model emphasized building friendlier relationships with Muslims through a positive evaluation of Islamic sources and theology. Especially the positive use of the Qur'an has laid a new foundation for the peaceful bridge-building in terms of common ground in Muslim evangelism. The dialogical model can be effective in a religiously pluralistic society where interreligious dialogue is regular social norm.[125]

The contextual model, mainly promoted through new experiments during the 1970s, added more emphasis on the cultural and religious components of Muslim society than the preceding models. Since its first attempts, many more methods and models have been proposed and implemented in various Muslim contexts. The contextual model seems to have gained increasing popularity among evangelical missionaries with a higher expectation for field results. While contextualization is acknowledged as a necessary approach in reaching Muslims, the real question for evangelicals is to determine objective guiding principles and biblical boundaries of Muslim contextualization.

This historical perspective enables one to understand the context behind the birth of the IM as a model of Muslim evangelism. Several points are worth noting. First, the IM is introduced as a radical contextualization model which moves further away from the contextual model of Parshall. Travis benchmarks the C4 model of Parshall's contextualization and identifies

---

124 Schlorff identifies three prominent Arab Christians who promoted the wider use of the Qur'an in Muslim evangelism as Fouad Accad, Michael Youssef, and Abdiyah Akbar 'Abdul-Haqq. Schlorff, *Missiological Models*, 25–26. Their views can be gleaned in their representative works: Accad, *Building Bridges*; Accad, *Have You Ever*; Youssef, *Making Christ Known*; Abdul-Haqq, *Sharing Your Faith*.

125 One effective ministry example in the Western society through dialogue is "Church without Walls" founded by Anees Zaka in 1982. McDowell and Zaka, *Muslims and Christians*. Zaka, "Church without Walls," 47–54. Another example is the ministry of Henry Martyn Institute in India. See D'Souza, "Evangelism, Dialogue," 155–84.

the IM (C5 in the C-scale) as an extension of C4. His intention, although it seems subtle, is to show that the IM remains within a permissible scale of evangelical contextualization. This placement of two contextual models within a spectrum, however, demands careful assessment by the evangelical community. Although C4 and C5 may look similar and their difference seems to be only a matter of degree, there are some indications that they stand on completely different grounds in terms of their presuppositions and theological orientations. This study takes this question to be a starting point and evaluates different facets of the IM by utilizing an analytical framework for Muslim contextualization.

Second, the IM seems to have received the greater influence from the last two models, the dialogical and the contextual. That is, they share more common features with the IM than the first two models. In regards to the dialogical model, commonalities include a positive view of Islam and Muhammad, the positive application of the Qur'an toward discovering and verifying biblical truth, an affirmation of Muhammad as a prophet to Arabic people on a historical ground, the importance of converts' remaining within an Islamic community by continuing Islamic religious practices through a private reinterpretation of their meanings, and the Christianized hermeneutics of the Qur'an and the traditions.

In regards to the contextual model, the common features comprise a more comprehensive contextualization from evangelism to church planting, hiring both cultural and religious factors for the Gospel communication, and the strategic emphasis on the homogeneous group principle and indigenous MBB churches. Although the IM is framed within the Muslim contextualization continuum and shares many common facets with other historical models, one cannot simply assume that various similarities and commonalities make the IM a biblically acceptable contextualization approach. In evaluating the IM as a contextualization model, it is imperative to examine its presuppositions and underlying theories.

## CONCLUSION

Revisiting the historical developments of evangelism to Muslims reveals several important features for the discussion on contextualization among evangelicals. First, the adequate role of theology must be emphatically restored. Historically a significant shift occurred in Muslim evangelism: from the emphasis on theological factors to the emphasis on cultural, religious, and communicational factors. As the notion of contextualization has become popularized among evangelical missionaries, a missiological study is deeply influenced by social sciences, such as anthropology and communication theories. In the meanwhile, the role of theology has significantly decreased in the contextualization discussion. This tendency has become a concern for some evangelical scholars because they believe that contextualization is fundamentally a biblical and theological issue.[126] Edward Rommen, for example, notices the de-theologizing tendency in missiology and calls for re-theologizing in the missiological discussion.[127]

Second, a sound biblical and theological view of other religions, Islam in specific, should become the foundation for evaluating Islam with its cultural and religious factors. When these factors are viewed through the lens of a comparative religions approach in contrast to a biblical theological approach to religions, much confusion prevails among evangelicals concerning what the proper outlook on Islam and Muslim culture should be. While there is an increasing emphasis on a high view of Muslim culture and a greater appreciation of Islam as a religion, a biblical theological assessment of both has been seriously lacking among missiologists. This is an urgently needed area of study in the Muslim contextualization debate.

Third, the use of the Qur'an and other Islamic sources remains an underdeveloped issue in the contextualization discussion. When missionaries and missiologists make assertions and proposals for a positive employment of them, their main reasoning is primarily pragmatic in nature. Although these pragmatically reasoned ministry models and proposals have increasingly gained popularity among missionaries, there is a lack of an in-depth study for such an important missiological issue. The evangelical community needs to establish a firm biblical and theological guideline for proper use of the Qur'an and other Islamic resources in contextualization.[128]

126 This writer addresses this very issue in Hwang, "Concern."

127 Rommen, "De-Theologizing of Missiology," 4. Rommen gives a warning against the de-theologizing tendency of North American missiology: "North American missiology has been subjected to gradual erosion of its theological foundation. Active theologizing has been replaced by business techniques and applied social science. As a result the future development of the discipline is uncertain. It is to this challenge that the next generation of missiologists must rise. Theological skills will have to be recultivated and reasserted in every area of mission. What is now required is nothing short of the re-theologization of North American missiology."

128 Recently, a constructive evangelical discussion on the use of the Qur'an has been promoted because of the "Camel Method," which some IMB missionaries have been using as a ministry approach. It is claimed to have produced remarkable results in some Asian Muslim nations. For the Camel Method, see Greeson, *Camel Training Manual*; Greeson, *Camel: How Muslims are Coming to Faith in Christ*. Some leaders of the Southern Baptist Convention expressed serious concerns about the Camel Method because they believe that it does not pass a biblical theological test for its validity. See Allen, "Baptist Seminary President."

58   Toward a Healthier Contextualization among Muslims

    Incorporating critical issues of Muslim evangelism identified in this historical review, the next chapter will develop an analytical framework for contextualization. Special attention will be given to whether underlying presuppositions and theoretical underpinnings behind five dimensions of contextualization remain within the range of evangelical parameters. This is especially important because these are not explicitly stated in the general contextualization discussion. This framework will be applied to the missiological model of Charles H. Kraft who has been very influential in missiological circles and specifically in the formulation of the IM theology of missions.

# 3

# An Analytical Framework for Contextualization among Muslims

SINCE ITS FIRST CONCEPTUAL introduction in the early 1970s, the term, "contextualization," has drawn the attention of both theologians and field missionaries because of its seemingly favorable dynamic feature of emphasizing contexts and flexibility. The meaning of contextualization, however, has been understood in a variety of ways, and many different models and methods have been proposed within the missiological circle. In spite of a great deal of discussion, confusion continues to prevail concerning related issues of contextualization. One urgent need is to establish a solid biblical and theological foundation from an evangelical perspective in order to construct an objective guideline for evaluating and developing various contextualization models.

Beginning with developing an evangelical definition of contextualization, this chapter introduces an analytical framework by utilizing the generic framework proposed by Hesselgrave and Rommen.[1] Their generic framework is useful because it helps to delineate multi-dimensional features of contextualization for evaluating various practical models by evangelical parameters. Some factors that are specifically related to Islam will be incorporated into this generic framework for the purpose of this study, an evaluation of the IM as a Muslim contextualization model.

---

1 Hesselgrave and Rommen, *Contextualization*, 127–96.

## TOWARD AN EVANGELICAL UNDERSTANDING OF CONTEXTUALIZATION

### Clarifying the Definition of Contextualization

Since the first use of the term, various scholars have proposed diverse definitions to describe the essential meaning of contextualization. Dean Flemming is correct in pointing out the fuzziness of its meaning in the scholarly circles.[2] The major differences essentially arise from varying theological orientations and epistemological presuppositions of individual scholars. Different meanings of contextualization, in turn, produce different methods and models, as Hesselgrave and Rommen imply in the title of their book.[3] Many ministry proposals have flourished under the name of contextualization, but not all of them are legitimate from an evangelical perspective. Timothy Tennent rightly observes the danger of making this term a *shibboleth* in order to freely validate any kind of context-driven ministry models:

> Contextualization sometimes has served as a *shibboleth* "code word," which provides amnesty for any kind of experimentation that helps to identify with the target culture.... Some, for example, have advocated that contextualization in the Islamic context means downplaying the deity of Christ or, among postmoderns, downplaying the doctrine of sin or the call to repentance. However, this demonstrates a denial of Christ, contempt for the gospel, and an insult to the multitude of Christians over the centuries who have given their lives for the faithful proclamation of the gospel.[4]

The prevalent confusion related to the term of contextualization has much to do with its historical origin although its fundamental notion can be traced back to the New Testament era. The term was birthed in the ecumenical movement during the early 1970s when liberal and neo-orthodox theological orientations challenged many facets of the traditional

---

2 Flemming notes this fuzziness of the term when he provides three examples of its definition: 1) "a hermeneutical activity that is virtually equivalent to what has traditionally been thought of as application of Scripture"; 2) "the process of developing local theologies in a context of rapid social and cultural change"; 3) "a missiological activity that involves the cross-cultural communication of the gospel and various other functions of the Christian mission." Flemming, *Contextualization in the New Testament*, 19.

3 Hesselgrave and Rommen, *Contextualization*. Readers might take note of the subtitle of this book, *Meanings, Methods, and Models*. They convincingly demonstrate that the meaning of contextualization is intimately connected to its method and model.

4 Tennent, *Invitation to World Missions*, 351 (emphasis in the original). For a biblical reference to the term *shibboleth* Tennant uses, see Judg 12:6.

evangelical position, especially in regards to the authority of Scripture.[5] Shoki Coe and Aharon Sapsezian, directors of Theological Education Fund (TEF), used this term for the first time in their report, *Ministry in Context*:

> It [contextualization] means all that is implied in the familiar term "indigenization" and yet seeks to press beyond. Contextualization has to do with how we assess the peculiarity of third world contexts. Indigenization tends to be used in the sense of responding to the Gospel in terms of a traditional culture. Contextualization, while not ignoring this, takes into account the process of secularity, technology, and the struggle for human justice, which characterize the historical moment of nations in the Third World.[6]

The key assertion is that human cultural contexts, in addition to Scripture, play an important role in a theologizing process because the traditional approach, dominated by Western Christians, is thought to have lost its effectiveness in the contexts of non-Western nations. Within the TEF paradigm, human contexts are placed alongside Scripture, and theologies are reckoned to be culturally conditioned and relative. As a result, it is claimed that a correct theological method must involve contextual theologizing or context-driven theologizing.[7]

In their attempt to define contextualization from a biblical perspective, Hesselgrave and Rommen identify four major theological orientations that are "profoundly different and universally recognized," and connect them to different meanings of contextualization.[8] According to their categorization, the approach which has produced the TEF definition of contextualization belongs to a neo-orthodox theological orientation. The key distinctiveness

---

5 Two evangelical works provide an extensive treatment of the historical analysis of the term within a larger theological debate, which is then coupled with an insightful evangelical critique on the proponents of contextual theologies. Fleming, *Contextualization of Theology*; Hesselgrave and Rommen, *Contextualization*, 29–31.

6 Coe and Sapsezian, *Ministry in Context*, 20.

7 Various scholars favor this new theological approach. Among Protestant scholars, Kraft agrees with this context-driven theologizing in his article, "Contextualization of Theology," 31–36. Stephen Bevans, a Catholic missiologist, emphasizes the validity of contextual theology and provides a comparative study of different models in his book, *Models of Contextual Theology*. Bevans asserts, "There is no such thing as 'theology'; there is only contextual theology: feminist theology, black theology, liberation theology, Filipino theology, Asian-American theology, African theology, and so forth. . . . The contextualization of theology—the attempt to understand Christian faith in terms of a particular context—is really a theological imperative." Bevans, *Models of Contextual Theology*, 3.

8 Hesselgrave and Rommen, *Contextualization*, 145–57.

of neo-orthodoxy lies in its assertion that, "though the Bible is unique, it is also human and therefore contains the Word of God in imperfect form."[9] Therefore, in addition to the important role that Scripture plays, human cultural factors are also highly regarded.

The traditional evangelical position or an orthodox theological orientation differs from this new approach in several ways. First, belief in the supremacy of scriptural authority is upheld as the foundational source of theology. Human contexts are then taken into account in the process of application or appropriation of biblical theological principles. In other words, orthodoxy declares that theologizing should not be context-driven, but Scripture-driven.[10] Second, evangelical theologians are not willing to approve the relativity notion of neo-orthodoxy that makes all theologies "contextual" and relative. Instead, they contend that there is a unified theology manifested as the overarching truth in Scripture, which is independent of human cultural contexts. The evangelical scholars with an orthodox theological orientation reject the theological presuppositions that are subtly embedded in the notion of contextual theologies.[11] The relativistic assertion of contextual theologies causes a significant departure from the orthodox evangelical theological position.[12]

## An Evangelical Definition of Contextualization

Since the rise of contextual theologies and the term, contextualization, the evangelical community has debated over how to view human cultural contexts in an evangelical theological approach. No final agreement has been reached on this issue among evangelicals, and differing views are still prevalent. For example, diverse views among evangelical scholars prevailed in the Lausanne Consultation on Gospel and Culture in Willowbank in 1978, where evangelical scholars gathered to discuss the Christian view of culture

---

9 Hesselgrave and Rommen, *Contextualization*, 147.

10 William J. Larkin Jr. provides an evangelical treatment of the dynamic relationship between Scripture and Culture in *Culture and Biblical Hermeneutics*.

11 The discussion on the singularity or plurality of biblical theology will be further elaborated in the theological grid of the analytical framework in this chapter.

12 There is an ongoing discussion among evangelical scholars concerning the relationship between the universal nature of theology vs. local theologies. For example, see Ott and Netland, *Globalizing Theology*. These writers following the traditional evangelical view of theology attempt to find biblical theological answers to new challenges in regards to the global theology and local theologies.

in the context of missions. This consultation revealed a surprisingly wide gap in their views which has yet to be narrowed.[13]

Three major responses appeared among evangelical scholars to the new term, contextualization. First, some have rejected it partly because they believed the traditional term (indigenization) was sufficient to describe the necessary meaning, and partly because the term has been deeply immersed into liberal theology. Fleming, for example, refused to use it due to liberal theological influences in its meaning: "Properly speaking, evangelicals do not, and should not, contextualize the gospel. The indigenizing, or more properly, the context-indigenizing of the gospel, should be the method of evangelical work."[14] James O. Buswell III hesitated to borrow this term without qualification and preferred to use it in three categorical meanings: inculturation (contextualization of the witness), indigenization (contextualization of the church and its leadership), and translation or ethnotheology (contextualization of the Word).[15]

Most evangelical scholars, however, have acknowledged its wide use as a given reality, and so endeavored to redefine this term from an evangelical perspective. Bruce Nicholls, David Hesselgrave, and Edward Rommen have made significant contributions to providing a precise evangelical understanding of contextualization.[16] They carefully delineated factors that were not consistent with an evangelical theological viewpoint, and removed any unacceptable presuppositions, so that they could establish the meaning of contextualization within an evangelical biblical theological boundary.

The last group of scholars has absorbed the term, contextualization, with little critical reflection because they agreed on the notion of context-driven or contextual theologies. Some of them favored the idea of contextual theology, and validated it by extensive use of anthropological and communication theories. In the process, several problematic presuppositions were uncritically admitted into their models. Dean Gilliland and Charles H. Kraft belong to this group, as they agree on TEF's concept of contextualization.[17] Gilliland defines "contextualized theology" as "the dynamic reflection carried out by the particular church upon its own life in light of the Word of

---

13 Coote and Stott, *Down to Earth*. The major question of this consultation is how culture relates to the Bible, evangelism, conversion, the church, and ethics.

14 Fleming, *Contextualization of Theology*, 60–67.

15 Buswell, "Contextualization," 90–97.

16 Nicholls, *Contextualization*; Hesselgrave and Rommen, *Contextualization*.

17 Gilliland holds the same view of theology as the contextual theologians. He asserts, "In a very real sense there is no theology that is not a contextual theology." Gilliland, "Contextual Theology," 12.

God and historic Christian truth."[18] This is closer to the concept of contextual theologians because there is no clear precedence of the Word of God over human cultural context.

In considering these differing evangelical responses, there is an urgent need to clarify the meaning of contextualization from an evangelical perspective and qualify it with biblical and theological presuppositions. Byang Kato and Bruce Nicholls are the earliest evangelical scholars to counter the confusion and provide biblically based definitions. Kato takes contextualization to express a deeper concept than indigenization, defining it as "an effort to express the never changing Word of God in ever changing modes for relevance."[19] Nicholls similarly defines it as "the translation of the unchanging content of the Gospel of the Kingdom into verbal form meaningful to peoples in their separate cultures and within their particular existential situations."[20] Both scholars agree that contextualization presumes the unchanging truth of God as independent of culture, and that the central issue is an effective communication of that unchanging Gospel truth within various human contexts.

In the same spirit, Hesselgrave and Rommen define contextualization as "the attempt to communicate the message of the person, works, Word, and will of God in a way that is faithful to God's revelation, especially as it is put forth in the teachings of Holy Scripture, and that is meaningful to respondents in their respective cultural and existential contexts."[21] The key idea, therefore, can be summarized as "being authentic to biblical revelation and being relevant to a particular human context." While both factors are crucial in contextualization, biblical authenticity should always take precedency over cultural relevancy.

## THE FIVE ANALYTICAL PERSPECTIVES

A significant degree of confusion is reduced by refining the evangelical definition of contextualization. In addition, this section establishes an objective

18  Gilliland, "Contextual Theology," 12.

19  Kato, "Gospel," 1217.

20  Nicholls, "Theological Education," 647. Nicholls asserts that the evangelical should start the process of contextualization with the unique and final revelation of God in Christ and the Gospel, which he interprets in the context of his own and the receiving culture, not vice versa. This directly opposes TEF's approach, which considers human contexts an equally important primary source as the Bible in the contextualization process. Nicholls argues that biblical revelation should take the highest precedent and judge all of human culture in theologizing. Nicholls, *Contextualization*, 62.

21  Hesselgrave and Rommen, *Contextualization*, 200.

## An Analytical Framework for Contextualization among Muslims 65

and comprehensive analytical framework to discern biblically permissible contextualization models. This framework can not only play an evaluative role for various practical models, but also provides a normative guideline for formulating innovative contextualization models. Consequently this framework can guard against pragmatic proposals in contextualization by identifying their underlying problems or unacceptable presuppositions behind them.

This framework is required to satisfy several qualifications. First, since contextualization fundamentally involves biblical and theological issues, individual parameters of the analytical framework are to remain within an evangelical boundary of biblical theology. Second, it is required to be general enough to become an evaluative tool for various culture-specific contextualization models with little modification. Third, this framework is well-balanced between two main criteria of contextualization, biblical authenticity and cultural relevancy. Last, it is to be comprehensive so that it incorporates various dimensions of contextualization, not only practical but also theoretical.

In terms of an analytical framework for contextualization models, two works by evangelical scholars deserve mentioning.[22] Fleming suggests an evangelical approach called "context-indigenization," which stands in contrast to the context-driven theology that incorporates more liberal or neo-orthodox concepts.[23] He asserts that contextualization should start with the Word of God as its primary source of theology and provides a useful flow chart to describe the process. According to this chart, the process should follow this order: "the living Triune God, verbally inerrant Bible, historical-grammatical exegesis, Old and New Testament theology, systematic ethno-theology, theology of missions, and mission principles and practices."[24] This framework is useful for clarifying the procedure of contextualization, but it does not go sufficiently in-depth in discussing theological presuppositions and incorporating foundational underpinnings of culture and religions.

The other masterpiece on contextualization by Hesselgrave and Rommen provides a thorough, consistent, and well-balanced framework for

---

22 While many evangelical scholars provide different models of contextualization, most of them do not provide an analytical framework. The most recent work that seems to be relevant for this study is not available at the time of writing. See Moreau, *Contextualization in World Missions*. Moreau provides a comprehensive map of various contextualization models in his essay: "Evangelical Models of Contextualization," 165–93. Although Moreau inclusively treats various contextualization models, not all of them remain within an evangelical boundary according to the criteria of this study.

23 Fleming, *Contextualization of Theology*, 52–76.

24 Fleming, *Contextualization of Theology*, 75.

contextualization.²⁵ This work considers fundamental factors of contextualization from five perspectives and evaluates them by using clearly defined evangelical parameters. The most important contribution of this framework is that it enables one to identify distinctive theoretical foundations and presuppositions behind various features of contextualization models. Therefore, it provides a good generic view for analysis and evaluation. One additional component necessary for the purpose of this study is to consider issues that are involved in Islamic cultural and religious contexts.

## A Philosophical Perspective

The first fundamental analytical grid of contextualization involves genres of revelational epistemology from a philosophical perspective. The foremost question has to do with "how to view the Bible" because contextualization involves theology, theological methods, and hermeneutics for its larger context. Biblical authority and the hermeneutical task lie at the core of the theological orientation of contextualizers which in turn directly influences the meanings, methods, and models of contextualization.

As mentioned above, liberal and neo-orthodox theological components infiltrated the contextualization discussion since the first use of the term so that the traditional evangelical view of Scripture could no longer be assumed in the contextualization debates.²⁶ Nicholls specifically emphasizes four factors that challenge the traditional evangelical stance in regards to the Bible, namely, "critical biblical studies, the new insights gained from the social sciences of cultural anthropology and sociology, the impact of technology and political theory in rapid cultural change and the issues raised by cross-cultural communication on a global scale."²⁷ It is, therefore, no longer possible to assume that all missiologists accept the authority of the Bible in the same sense that the orthodox evangelical community has traditionally affirmed.

---

25 Hesselgrave and Rommen, *Contextualization*, 127–96.

26 The categories, such as orthodox, neo-orthodox, neo-liberal, and liberal are borrowed from the theological continuum of Hesselgrave and Rommen simply for the purpose of distinguishing various theological orientations. They contend that this categorization is universally recognized among scholars.

27 Nicholls, *Contextualization*, 37. Kraft, who has great influence on the missiological model of IM advocates, extensively uses the second and the fourth factors in his model of contextualization. Hesselgrave and Rommen provide various examples of non-orthodox theological contextualization attempts that stand upon a different view of the nature of the biblical authority. See Hesselgrave and Rommen, *Contextualization*, 37–126.

The first analytical foundation involves the nature and role of the Bible in contextualization. The Lausanne Covenant succinctly summarizes the biblical position:

> We affirm the divine inspiration, truthfulness and authority of both Old and New Testament Scriptures in their entirety as the only written word of God, without error in all that it affirms, and the only infallible rule of faith and practice. We also affirm the power of God's word to accomplish his purpose of salvation. The message of the Bible is addressed to all men and women. For God's revelation in Christ and in Scripture is unchangeable. Through it the Holy Spirit still speaks today. He illumines the minds of God's people in every culture to perceive its truth freshly through their own eyes and thus discloses to the whole Church ever more of the many-colored wisdom of God.[28]

The authority of Scripture involves several central themes, such as inspiration, inerrancy, and revelation. A careful clarification of these terms is necessary because even these fundamental concepts are differently understood by some Christians. The traditional evangelical view states that the Bible is God's revelation, indeed His very Word, and that it holds the supreme authority for Christian faith, life, and ministry. The authority of Scripture is proved by the Bible's own witness, as 2 Tim 3:16 clearly states, "All Scripture is *breathed out by God* and is profitable for teaching, for reproof, for correction, and for training in righteousness."[29] An orthodox evangelical understanding of biblical inspiration is that "the Scriptures are a Divine product, without any indication of how God has operated in producing them."[30] At the same time, it affirms the historical role of human authors in communicating God's divine truth (2 Pet 1:21–22). The emphatic focus of biblical inspiration affirms that all the Scriptures are the very Word of God in their entirety in a propositional sense.

---

28 Lausanne Movement, "Lausanne Covenant."

29 ESV is purposefully used here to emphasize the aspect of "God's breathing out" (emphasis added). The Greek term, *theopneustos*, here means "God-breathed" or "breathed out by God." While several Bible translations (NET, NRSV, NASB, NKJV, and NLT) use the concept of "inspiration" for this Greek term, Wayne Grudem rightly points out that it conveys such a weak sense of the authority of Scripture because of its contemporary connotation: "However, the word inspiration has such a weak sense in ordinary usage today (every poet or songwriter claims to be 'inspired' to write, and even athletes are said to give 'inspired' performances) that I have not used it in this text. I have preferred the NIV rendering of 2 Tim 3:16, 'God-breathed,' and have used other expressions to say that the words of Scripture are God's very words." See Grudem, *Systematic Theology*, 75.

30 Warfield, *Inspiration and Authority*.

In addition to inspiration, scriptural inerrancy occupies another component in biblical authority. Inerrancy means "the quality of being free from all falsehood or mistakes," and thus in a religious context it safeguards "the truthfulness and trustworthiness of Scripture in its all assertions."[31] While affirming that the written Word in its entirety is the revelation given by God, the evangelical view denies the notion that "the Bible is a mere witness to revelation, or only becomes revelation in encounter, or depends on the response of men for its validity."[32] Therefore, the evangelical doctrine of the Bible, specifically the authority of Scripture, should be cautiously examined in the analysis of individual contextualization models because this may not be explicitly stated in the discussions.

One dangerous result occurs in the contextualization conversation when biblical revelation is redefined either on a neo-orthodox theological ground or on anthropological and communicational grounds.[33] Though these redefinitions don't seem to move too far away from the evangelical parameters, they cause a significant digression from the orthodox position and eventually can produce bizarre implications in the area of contextualization. Karl Barth, one of the most prominent neo-orthodox theologians, takes God's revelation to be exclusively limited to Jesus Christ because he defines revelation as knowing God "as event, as act, as life."[34] While giving too much emphasis to the event of Christ, Barth perceives the Bible not to be identical with God's revelation, but simply a mere record of it. Consequently, in his eyes, the Bible does not hold absolute authority. At the same time, God's revelation within a neo-orthodox theological framework is no longer propositional but personal or experiential. Revelation continues to occur as long as the Word of God encounters people in a fresh way through the Holy Spirit.[35] That means, God's revelation has not ended with the canonization of Scripture, but is still occurring. The importance of the Bible lies in its nature of witnessing "a transcendent divine confrontation with humanity."[36] While the authority of Scripture is substantially under-

---

31 ICBI, "Chicago Statement."

32 ICBI, "Chicago Statement."

33 Karl Barth's view is the case of redefining revelation theologically, and Kraft's is the case of redefining it from the anthropological and communicational perspective. Since the next section deals with Kraft's redefinition, this section only mentions Barth's.

34 Barth, *Church Dogmatics*, 264.

35 Gerald R. McDermott summarizes Barth's notion as follows: "Just as our relationship to God is never possessed once and for all but is continually established anew by the ongoing activity of grace, so revelation is always an event or happening and never a thing." See McDermott, *Can Evangelicals Learn*, 60.

36 Hesselgrave, *Scripture and Strategy*, 31.

mined to the level of a mere subjective record of past historical encounters, personal experiences in life are elevated to a plane of a significant revelatory nature on par with God's Word. The absolute propositional truth value and the authority of Scripture are jeopardized within a neo-orthodox theology.

Another epistemological issue involves how to understand general and special revelation. General revelation has been a topic for serious theological discourse and has added much confusion to the contextualization debates. One particular question of importance is whether general revelation is salvific or not. When one acknowledges the presence of salvific components in other cultural and religious contexts, some contextualization models can easily move beyond evangelical boundaries. One example is the theological assumption behind the use of redemptive analogy as a Gospel communication tool.[37] Don Richardson argues that general revelation is salvific without an explicit knowledge of Christ and God's redemptive plan. He takes Melchizedek as a paradigmatic model for his assertion. The contention for the salvific nature of general revelation does not find a valid biblical support.

Bruce Demarest and Richard Harpel rightly make a case that Richardson's redemptive analogies are in fact "nonredemptive analogies" because they do not hold intrinsically salvific values. Based upon the exegesis of Rom 1:18–32, Demarest and Harpel state, "Paul concludes that universal general revelation does not save, rather it condemns. Having understood the truth content of general revelation and rejected it, all people are 'without excuse' before the court of divine justice."[38] They assert that these redemptive analogies should be regarded as illustrations or points of contact for the Gospel communication.[39] While the insight gained from Richardson's redemptive analogies is useful, his assertion that they contain salvific value cannot be supported on exegetical and biblical grounds. It is, therefore, important to underscore the biblical understanding of general and special revelation in regards to the doctrine of salvation. The straightforward biblical position is that general revelation alone cannot lead people to the saving grace of God, but that special revelation is necessary.[40]

---

37 The concept of redemptive analogies is first introduced by Don Richardson in *Peace Child*. This concept is later expanded as his missiological model in *Eternity in Their Hearts*.

38 Demarest and Harpel, "Don Richardson's 'Redemptive Analogies,'" 337.

39 Demarest and Harpel, "Don Richardson's 'Redemptive Analogies,'" 336.

40 Grudem, *Systematic Theology*, 123. Thomas C. Oden shows that this evangelical view of general revelation was consistently taught by the ancient church leaders before the Reformation in his article. Oden, "Without Excuse," 55–68.

## A Theological Perspective

Since various theological orientations produce different sets of meanings, methods, and models of contextualization, it is crucial to examine the underlying theological orientation of each contextualizer. Hesselgrave and Rommen demonstrate the connection between one's theological orientation and the resultant contextualization model in their analytical framework. Concerning theological orientations, they develop a useful continuum by identifying four theological categories: orthodox, neo-orthodox, neo-liberal, and liberal.[41] The criterion for classifying these four groups is the comparative weight between supracultural/divine elements and cultural/human elements in understanding biblical revelation. Although this continuum looks simple, it accurately points out the central issue in approaching contextualization from different theological orientations. This study pays special attention to the distinction between orthodoxy and neo-orthodoxy because a neo-orthodox orientation causes more subtle confusion for the evangelical missionaries in their contextualization approach than any other non-orthodox theologies.

The most dangerous challenge from the neo-orthodox camp is the eradication of biblical authority. According to Hesselgrave and Rommen, neo-orthodoxy gives significant weight to human/cultural elements in addition to supracultural/divine elements both in defining biblical revelation and in theologizing. The Bible is taken to be a collection of historically and culturally conditioned human words and thus contains the Word of God in imperfect form.[42] The impact of the lost authority of Scripture in the neo-orthodox view is enormous in the contextualization debates, especially when neo-orthodox theological influence is combined with reasoning from social sciences. As a result, the contextualization approach affected by neo-orthodox theology has notably moved away from fundamental evangelical parameters.

According to the neo-orthodox understanding of divine revelation, contemporary human cultural contexts are claimed to play an important role because God is still doing His divine work in human history. By discerning God's hand in a human cultural context, one can continue to see the revealed will of God and incorporate His revelation in theologizing. Hesselgrave and Rommen refer to this as prophetic contextualization because it "entails entering a cultural context, discerning what God is doing

---

41 Hesselgrave and Rommen, *Contextualization*, 144–57.
42 Hesselgrave and Rommen, *Contextualization*, 147.

in that context, and speaking and working for the needed change."[43] In this approach, both biblical revelation and human contexts become equally indispensable sources. Although biblical revelation in Scripture remains an important guiding principle of contextualization, it does not necessarily occupy the supreme and authoritative source of God's revelation. As contemporary cultural contexts are taken into account in the contextualization model, even the content of the Gospel is affected for the sake of being culturally relevant in the dialectic process between Scripture and human contexts.

Hesselgrave and Rommen note that the two different theological orientations lead to two different contextualization models: "teaching truth" in orthodox theology, and "discovering truth" in neo-orthodox theology. The peculiarity of the neo-orthodox orientation finds the beginning of its faith in "some universally valid and relevant factor that can erase religious, cultural, and political demarcations."[44] The emphasis on human needs and universal human experiences becomes an important basis for theological formulation and also provides a crucial foundation for various contextualization models. Suspect forms of contextualization are the logical consequence of a contextualization model by discovering "truth" in cultural and religious circumstances.[45]

On the contrary, the contextualization model based upon orthodox theology would be "didactic" in essence because the unchanging message revealed in God's Word has been preached to all nations as the biblical and historic Christian truth.[46] The apostles preached the Gospel both by proclamation and by defense (*apologia*), and the same Gospel was proclaimed to the nations in their different cultural religious contexts. The Gospel has maintained the same essence wherever it was preached throughout church history among all the nations. This has been possible because the supreme authority of Scripture has remained unapologetically preserved in every context. The sound exegetical study of the Bible has also played a foundational role in enabling Christian church of every generation to remain faithful to an "apostolic doctrine" in contrast to provisional knowledge or human speculation.[47]

---

43  Hesselgrave and Rommen, *Contextualization*, 150.

44  Hesselgrave and Rommen, *Contextualization*, 154–55. The water buffalo theology of Kosuke Koyama is provided as an example.

45  Hesselgrave and Rommen, *Contextualization*, 154–55.

46  Hesselgrave and Rommen, *Contextualization*, 155.

47  Hesselgrave and Rommen, *Contextualization*, 154–55, 156. Nicholls refers to this approach as "dogmatic contextualization" in contrast to "existential contextualization," which is the product of neo-orthodox theology. Nicholls, *Contextualization*, 24. Although the term "dogmatics" carries a negative connotation in contemporary

In this regard, it is understandable why some contemporary missiologists attempt to minimize the value of historic Christianity in their contextualization approaches and downplay the significance of historic Christian creeds. One should be careful not to place historic creeds above or equal to the authority of Scripture. At the same time, one must not trivialize their worth because they are valuable expressions of absolute biblical truth derived from various historical contexts. Although their expression may have been culturally conditioned within certain historical contexts, it should be emphasized that the essential truth voiced in these creeds is still propositionally right and binding for all Christians in all cultures.

Another notable difference between orthodox and neo-orthodox theology centers on whether one can contend for a single unified biblical theology. Neo-orthodox theologians argue for the plurality of theology for two main reasons.[48] First, real life contexts give different sets of theological questions. Second, different human contexts inevitably affect the cultural and religious conditionings of theologians in their interpretive process. Consequently, no single biblical theology can be claimed to be an objective guide. In a neo-orthodox theological orientation, multiple theologies entailing various contextual issues and culturally conditioned perspectives are acknowledged as valid expressions of theological reasoning. Some evangelical scholars, however, expressed serious concern about such neo-orthodox influence on contextualization. Peters, for example, makes a strong critique against the neo-orthodox influence on the contextualization discussion:

> The concept of "contextualization" however has fallen into evil hands and upon evil soil. As a result we speak of Western theology, Asiatic theology, African theology, Latin American theology. Philosophically and culturally such language is understandable. Biblically and Christian it is unacceptable, there is only one kind of theology for the Christian. It is *biblical* theology. The Bible is the all determining factor and final authority in all matters of faith, practice, purpose, goal and methods of procedure.[49]

Nicholls stands on the same ground when he says, "The unique inspiration of the canonical books, which God caused the church to recognize

---

culture, Nicholls contends that one should not hesitate to use it because its meaning is biblical (1 Tim 4:16; Titus 1:9; 2:1).

48 Different terms have been used to refer to the plurality of theology: "contextual theologies" (Stephen Bevans), "ethnotheologies" (Charles Kraft), "contextualization of theology" (Bruce Fleming), and "contextualizing of theology" (Bruce Nicholls).

49 Peters, "Issues Confronting Evangelical Missions," 169–70 (emphasis in the original).

as such, ensures the essential unity and rationality of the biblical message. It is therefore right to speak of a unitary or undivided biblical theology."[50] Evangelical scholars are willing to admit different cultural expressions of the central biblical doctrines, but they contend that the variety of cultural expressions is fundamentally grounded on a single divinely coordinated biblical theology. The answer to this question depends on hermeneutical methods and especially on how to treat the preunderstanding of culturally conditioned interpreters.

## A Hermeneutical Perspective

Since contextualization has a deep connection with biblical interpretation, it is necessary to establish a sound hermeneutical foundation before any contextualization attempt. It is of special importance to evaluate the so-called new hermeneutics because it has challenged the traditional hermeneutical approach of the evangelical community and caused serious confusion. An example of this unrest is found in the lack of agreement among representative evangelical scholars at the Lausanne Consultation on Gospel and Culture in 1978 concerning how to view human culture in theology and contextualization. For the purpose of this study, this section first examines the hermeneutical proposal of Rene Padilla, who incorporates cultural contexts of contemporary interpreters into his hermeneutical model.[51] Then it provides an orthodox evangelical response to his model by identifying points of digression on the foundational hermeneutical issues.

Padilla begins with several contentions in building up his hermeneutical model. He argues that traditional evangelical hermeneutics has not considered the different cultural contexts of the world seriously enough. Consequently, it is confined to a western-oriented hermeneutical method. He also contends that the nature of cultural conditioning of the Bible inevitably prevents interpreters from uncovering the objective meanings of the text. Padilla asserts that the objectivity of biblical interpretation is "neither possible nor desirable."[52] He is critical about the historical-grammatical hermeneutics because its effectiveness is limited to the western cultures.[53]

50 Nicholls, *Contextualization*, 44.

51 Padilla, "Hermeneutics and Culture," 63–94.

52 Padilla, "Hermeneutics and Culture," 67. Padilla stands on a neo-orthodox epistemological foundation when he says that the meaning of biblical text cannot be objective since it should be experienced within the life context of interpreters. His view is closer to Barthian epistemology than orthodox theological epistemology.

53 Padilla, "Hermeneutics and Culture," 71. Padilla affirms the usefulness of the historical-grammatical hermeneutics, but he does not accept it as a universally

Based upon these assertions, Padilla alternatively proposes "the hermeneutical circle," where he considers the dynamic interaction among four factors: "historical context, world-and-life view, Scripture, and theology."[54] This circle consists of the dialogue between the historical situation and Scripture. The hermeneutical procedure begins with analyzing the contemporary context to identify questions residing within it, and then moves to Scripture to answer those questions. In this process, interpreters bring the contemporary issues into the biblical text so that the meaning of the text cogently produces transformations in the concrete human situation, which is the ultimate goal of the interpretive process.

The digressions of Padilla's hermeneutical circle from the traditional evangelical approach can be understood by comparing the two. The first is found in his view of the Bible. When Padilla takes the Bible as God's revelation within a cultural conditioning, he seems to consider biblical revelation relative. Similar to the neo-orthodox theological notion, he refuses the objective absolute truth value of biblical revelation for all cultural contexts. Instead, he only approves its subjective value as long as it is experienced in human life.[55]

An orthodox evangelical view of the Bible in regards to its relationship with human culture is well-described by J. I. Packer: "God's revelation of himself is culture-bound, in the sense of being culturally particularized (being historical, it had to be), but not at all in the sense of culturally being distorted."[56] Padilla's use of "cultural conditioning" moves closer to the latter sense in Packer's distinction, cultural distortion, because Padilla uses the cultural conditioning of the Bible as the basis of relativizing biblical truth. The presupposition of an orthodox evangelical position is succinctly summarized by Nicholls:

> Evangelicals recognize the inseparable connection between biblical event and interpretation. In conceptual terms there is an inseparable relationship between the content and form of the Word of God. Both are overshadowed by the Holy Spirit so that the inscripturated Word is the authoritative Word that God intended. This biblical content-form carries its own objectivity.

---

applicable principle.

54 Padilla, "Hermeneutics and Culture," 75–77.

55 As was discussed in the preceding sections, on philosophical and theological perspectives, Padilla stands close to the Barthian neo-orthodox understanding of God's revelation and the Bible.

56 Packer, "Gospel," 101.

It is not dependent on the relativity of the interpreters' own culture or the culture into which he contextualizes it.[57]

The orthodox evangelicals, therefore, argue that the goal of hermeneutics should be to find the original meaning or authorial intent within the original context independent of its interpreters' contexts. They contend that this goal is not only possible but also necessary. After this original meaning is found, then it can be applied or appropriated to contemporary contexts in multiple ways. Grant R. Osborne uses E. D. Hirsch's distinction between "the author's intended meaning of a text, a core that is unvarying, and the multiform significance or implications of a text for individual readers, an application of the original meaning that varies depending upon the diverse circumstances."[58] According to this view, the objective meaning of biblical revelation relies on authorial intent irrespective of human cultural contexts of interpreters.

Another digression of Padilla's hermeneutical circle from the traditional evangelical position is found in his acceptance of the interpreter's cultural conditioning as part of the hermeneutical and theologizing process. Padilla is so preoccupied by the subjective nature of an interpreter's perception or preunderstanding that he thinks it impossible to find any objective meaning. In the historical-grammatical hermeneutics, however, the preunderstanding of interpreters is taken into consideration in such a way that it does not affect the original meaning of the text. In the rigorous historical-grammatical hermeneutics, the role of preunderstanding is clearly defined. Osborne, for example, provides an elaborated explanation of its significance and role.[59] He admits that preunderstanding inevitably brings differences of opinions, but he contends that it is not impossible to reach the text's intended meaning so long as interpreters remain open to critical dialogue in the hermeneutical process.[60] Furthermore, Osborne distinguishes its positive role from its negative use: "Preunderstanding is primarily a positive (and only potentially a negative) component of interpretation. Preunderstanding only becomes negative if it degenerates into an a prior grid that determines the meaning of a text before the act of reading even begins."[61] Padilla is rightly critical about the prejudice of interpreters

---

57 Nicholls, *Contextualization*, 45.

58 Osborne, *Hermeneutical Spiral*, 7. Osborne refers to contextualization as "application of original meaning" and "the cross-cultural communication of a text's significance for today."

59 Osborne, *Hermeneutical Spiral*, 412–15.

60 Osborne, *Hermeneutical Spiral*, 412.

61 Osborne, *Hermeneutical Spiral*, 412.

being an obstacle in the hermeneutical process, but he fails to observe the positive roles of preunderstanding.

D. A. Carson also carefully distinguishes two separate ways of defining preunderstanding: "a 'functional non-negotiable,' which can be amended into a stance with increased proximity to the text," and "something like 'immutable non-negotiables,' a function of an entire world view at odds with Scripture."[62] He astutely warns against the danger of confusing the two different uses of this term:

> To confuse these two uses of "pre-understanding" is to devastate both theology and epistemology. The one use helps us to be more careful, encourages us to follow the "hermeneutical spiral" to bring our horizon of understanding into line with the horizon of understanding of the original author, and ultimately brings our mind into increasing proximity with what the text actually says; but the second becomes a reason for transmuting the text into something else. The arguments in favor of a sympathetic treatment of "pre-understanding" are *formally* the same in the two cases; but in the first case they lead to improved hermeneutical self-criticism, whereas in the latter they lead to epistemological solipsism and a complete inability to hear any word from God with which we cannot agree.[63]

Larkin basically shares the same view when he demonstrates how preunderstanding can help biblical interpretation by categorizing it into three kinds: biblical preunderstanding, preliminary study of the text in context, and cultural preunderstanding.[64] Even if the preunderstanding of interpreters falls into prejudice, the safeguard of historical-grammatical hermeneutics secures an honest encounter between the text and interpreters' preunderstanding so that the text occupies the priority and "challenges, reshapes and directs presuppositions."[65] This is why the authority and primacy of Scripture is paramount in the evangelical hermeneutical approach.

## An Anthropological Perspective

Anthropology has played a significant role in developing modern missiology. It has contributed to an improved understanding of human culture and cultural dynamics in cross-cultural communication. When missionaries

---

62 Carson, "Sketch of the Factors," 12–13.
63 Carson, "Sketch of the Factors," 13 (emphasis in the original).
64 Larkin, *Culture and Biblical Hermeneutics*, 326–34.
65 Osborne, *Hermeneutical Spiral*, 412–13.

incorporated cultural anthropology into missiology, a new academic discipline called "missionary anthropology" was birthed and has a profound impact on many aspects of contemporary missiological thinking.[66] In the meantime, when anthropological insights and assertions were uncritically introduced into missiological thinking together with unbiblical presuppositions, some biblical foundations were challenged or neglected. It is, therefore, imperative to investigate the theoretical assertions and presuppositions of popular Christian anthropology and to lay sound biblical and theological foundations for the anthropological dimension of any contextualization model.[67]

The first step to laying such a foundation is to establish a biblical view of culture. Tennent laments the lack of a theology of culture on the part of Christian church because the contemporary study of culture is dominated by cultural anthropology.[68] A dominant view of culture within Christian anthropology is a functionalist view in which culture is understood mainly by anthropological observations of human life.[69] Since culture is taken to be a closed system, there is no clearly defined space for supracultural interaction between God, man, and other spiritual beings. No biblical value judgment can be made upon human culture according to this view. Culture

---

66 Historically, the birth of anthropology as an academic discipline had much to do with missionaries. Anthropologists, however, soon became very critical of missionaries for their western ethnocentrism during the imperial period. Later missionaries have developed their own brand of "missionary anthropology" as a separate field from the secular one in order to incorporate a Christian perspective. For a detailed history, see Taber, *World Is Too Much*. Concerning the impact of missionary anthropology on contemporary missiology, Taber identifies six specific areas: "understanding and respecting cultures; communication and translation; the indigenous church; the homogeneous unit principle; functional (formerly dynamic) equivalence; and 'redemptive analogies.'" Taber, *World Is Too Much*, 135.

67 Taber identifies a popular form of missionary anthropology as "functionalism" and provides a critical analysis of both its positive and negative influences in the field of missiology. Taber, *World Is Too Much*. Several other scholars also point out the dangers and problems of this functionalist anthropology, including Conn, *Eternal Word*; and Wan, "Critique of Functional Missionary," 18–22.

68 Tennent, *Invitation to World Missions*, 160.

69 Louis J. Luzbetak provides a summary of the functionalist view: "Culture is a system and more like a living organism or a complicated machine in full operation. Culture has a content as well as an organization of that content. Culture is structurally organized or integrated by means of function; it is psychologically integrated by means of configuration. 'Function' refers to the role each part plays in relation to the other parts and the whole. The integration we call 'structure.' 'Integration' is the 'oneness' of culture." See Luzbetak, *Church and Cultures*, 141.

simply becomes a neutral vehicle for human life. It is apparent that the functionalist view cannot be a sound biblical theological model of culture.[70]

Another foundational problem of this functional anthropological view arises from the incompatible presuppositions prevalent between anthropology and biblical truth. The prominent presupposition of functionalist anthropology is the dichotomous relationship between culture and the Gospel, so that both are taken to be completely separable entities. One typical example of this dichotomy is seen in Richard Niebuhr's masterpiece, *Christ and Culture*, which is one of the most influential Christian books among missiologists. Tennent is, however, critical about such dichotomy in Niebuhr's typology:

> The secular foundation of Niebuhr's understanding of culture means that his entire method posits Christ and culture as two wholly separate entities or forces. However, God is the author of human culture and His ongoing sustenance of, and redemptive activity within, human culture is integral to a biblical view of God. This dichotomization creates serious theological difficulties that are never fully resolved by Niebuhr.[71]

It is imperative, therefore, to consider culture and the divine dimension as integral parts of the whole in the process of formulating an evangelical theology of culture. Biblical revelation should occupy the place of superior ascendancy over human culture and play the role of an authoritative criterion to evaluate and judge cultural dimensions.

The functionalist anthropology tends to perceive human culture as a neutral or even positive entity. In observing diverse cultures existing in the world, anthropologists tend to pay greater attention to positive components of human culture. A comparative study of cultural diversity assumes that each has its own uniqueness and that no value judgment can be made against one culture based upon another's norms. The negative historical tag attached to the western imperialistic attitude toward other cultures is "ethnocentrism," and the ideological consequence from it has become "cultural relativism." There is little emphasis on confronting human culture with its supracultural normative value of biblical truth. Tennent criticizes such a positive view of culture and cultural relativism, and even refers to an indiscriminate elevation of human culture as "uncritical *divinization*."[72] Cultural

---

70 Wan explains the reason why functional anthropology cannot adequately serve as a biblical theological model of culture in "Critique of Functional Missionary," 18.

71 Tennent, *Invitation to World Missions*, 163. For an extensive critique of Tennent on Niebuhr's analysis, see pp. 160–67. See also Niebuhr, *Christ and Culture*.

72 Tennent, *Invitation to World Missions*, 181 (emphasis in the original).

## An Analytical Framework for Contextualization among Muslims 79

diversity itself is a descriptive truth, but it does not mean that every culture with all its dimensions is approved as normative as is treated within the functionalist anthropological framework.

Several corollaries from this particular functionalist view of culture have led to various missiological concepts and applications that seem reasonable from a pragmatic point of view. There are, however, serious concerns about these missiological praxes when the presuppositions are evaluated from a biblical theological perspective. This calls for a more carefully delineated and well-balanced biblical theology of culture from an evangelical perspective. Tennent's proposal of a "new creation model of culture" based upon the Trinitarian framework meets this need.[73] He begins with four major Christian affirmations based upon the four realities revealed in the biblical history:

> First, *Christians affirm that God is the source and sustainer of both physical and social culture.*
> Second, *Christians affirm the objective reality of sin, rooted in the doctrine of the Fall, which has both personal and collective implications for human society.*
> Third, *Christians affirm that God has revealed Himself within the context of human culture.*
> Fourth, *Christians affirm that a future, eschatological culture, known as the New Creation, already had broken into the present.*[74]

Several points in his model are distinguishable from a functionalist view of culture. First, biblical revelation holds the highest authority in understanding human culture. The Bible is held as the primary source of evaluating human culture, though social science can provide helpful insights for missiological reflections. Second, divine interaction becomes a crucial part of the dynamics of human culture and its changes. Therefore, culture is no longer a closed system removed from the divine interactions of God, man, and Satan.

Third, the reality of human sin and its consequential results are taken into account in defining the nature of human culture. Fallen humanity, the very universal norm in every culture, produces sinful culture. On the other hand, the image of God in humanity has not completely disappeared; the goodness of creation and man still produces the beauty and positive virtues in human culture. In reflecting upon this contrasting reality, Tennent states, "Human cultures, therefore, are simultaneously a sign of God's creative

---

73 Tennent, *Invitation to World Missions*, 163–90.

74 Tennent, *Invitation to World Missions*, 171–75 (emphasis in the original).

design as well as a manifestation of human sin, which stands in opposition to God's rule."[75] Fourth, God's revelation is understood through both an objective and a subjective dimension. Surely it took on cultural particularity as God revealed himself to men through forms and mediums in cultural contexts. God's revelation itself, however, represents a supracultural message which transcends the human cultural realm.[76]

One important corollary of an evangelical theology of culture is the integration of a theology of religions into the discussion of contextualization; how to view other religions becomes an important criterion to determine the degree and method of contextualization. The traditional way of analyzing various theologies of religions uses three categories: exclusivism, inclusivism, and pluralism.[77] The traditional evangelical view known as exclusivism or particularism stands on three affirmations:

> 1) The unique authority of Jesus Christ is the apex of revelation and the norm by which all other beliefs must be critiqued; 2) The Christian faith is centered on the proclamation of the historical death and resurrection of Jesus Christ as the decisive event in human history (Acts 2:31–32); and 3) No one can be saved without an explicit act of repentance and faith based on the knowledge of Christ (John 3:16–18, 36; Mark 16:15–16).[78]

Based upon these affirmations, those who hold the exclusivist view emphasize a "radical discontinuity" between the Christian faith and other religions, and generally make a critical assessment of other world religions and their scriptures.[79]

In the contextualization discussion, scholars continue to debate what constitutes a correct biblical theological understanding of other religions. Especially, a significant challenge comes from an increasing influence of

---

75  Tennent, *Invitation to World Missions*, 172.

76  Tennent, *Invitation to World Missions*, 173. The "cultural particularity" of God's revelation needs to be distinguished from the concept of "cultural-conditioning"; the latter leads to the notion that God's revelation cannot claim to have absolute value because of the cultural-conditioning of the Bible and its interpreters under the neo-orthodox epistemology.

77  Several representative works to evaluate these three categories from an evangelical perspective include: Netland, *Dissonant Voices*, 1–35; Netland, *Encountering Religious Pluralism*, 47–54; Nash, *Is Jesus the Only Savior*, 11–25. For an extensive scholarly interaction on this subject among representative scholars of different views including John Hick, Clark Pinnock, Alister McGrath, and Douglas Geivett and Gary Phillips, see Okholm and Phillips, *Four Views on Salvation*.

78  Tennent, *Invitation to World Missions*, 197.

79  Kraemer, *Christian Message*, 74.

inclusivism. While some inclusivists make various cases based on certain biblical passages, others argue for a more sympathetic view of world religions by using a comparative religions approach. Inclusivism's influence, when accompanied by the rampantly intensifying claims of religious pluralism, pressurizes the evangelical community to provide a sound biblical theology of religions.[80]

The most important difference between exclusivism and inclusivism is that inclusivists do not agree with the third statement of Tennent's three affirmations of exclusivism. The inclusivist view can be summarized as follows: "Since the majority of people in the world do not have a viable access to the Christian message, the inclusivists believe that this access has been available through general revelation, God's providential workings in history, and even other religions."[81] Inclusivists argue that no explicit knowledge of Jesus Christ and his atoning death and resurrection is required for salvation, but the salvific grace of God is available outside of the realm of special revelation. Inclusivists use biblical examples to show that the faith factor, even outside the covenant community of God, has proved to be sufficient for salvation. The biblical examples include: Melchizedek (Gen 14), Rahab (Josh 2), the Ninevites (Jonah 3), Naaman (2 Kgs 8), and Cornelius (Acts 10), among others. They contend that the believers in the Old Testament were saved although they did not have the explicit knowledge of Jesus Christ.

There are several reasons for evangelicals to dismiss inclusivism. First and foremost, biblical theological truth does not support inclusivism even though several passages are taken to do so by inclusivists. After exegetically examining biblical passages that inclusivists use, Walter C. Kaiser concludes that all these passages actually support exclusivism.[82] Moreover, when the overarching theme of biblical theology in the Bible is taken into consideration, there is no way to deny the biblical stance of exclusivism.

Second, there is little emphasis on the object or content of faith for salvation in inclusivism. Rather a greater emphasis is placed on implicit faith and personal experience. The biblical content of faith is disregarded for the sake of personal faith experience, and various channels of God's revelation remain open in addition to the written Scriptures. The central issue lies in the role of general revelation with respect to salvation. Even though inclusivists contend for the maximal role of general revelation and affirm the possibility of salvation through other religions, biblical evidence clearly

---

80 Two representative Protestant scholars who hold inclusivism include: Pinnock, *Wideness in God's Mercy*; and Sanders, *No Other Name*.

81 Tennent, *Invitation to World Missions*, 201.

82 Kaiser, "Holy Pagans," 124–42.

suggests that general revelation holds no salvific role, but only holds people accountable to God's judgment (Rom 1:18–23).[83]

The problem of general revelation has significant implications for the contextualization discussion. Beyond a soteriological concern, it involves issues of other religions. When the Islamic context is considered, the questions become even more complicated: "Is it biblically permissible to recognize or approve any factors in other religions in light of general revelation? What is the view of other religious scriptures? Can one use them for the Gospel witness? If so, how can they be used?" All these rest on how much weight one gives to the role of general revelation in other religions.

## A Communication Perspective

Modern communication theories have contributed to missiology as they relate to the following questions on a most fundamental level: "How valid is the language? What is meaning and where is it to be found? What happens when we communicate?"[84] Depending on the responses to these questions, Christian contextualizers have utilized the fruits of modern communication theories for a more effective communication, but sometimes they uncritically incorporated ideas and assumptions of communication theories that are not biblically acceptable. This section examines the foundational aspects of communication theories and their influence on missiological thinking.

Hesselgrave and Rommen provide a concise snapshot of the main claims of modern communication theories in regards to contextualization.[85] They point out that communication theories and semantics have helped missionaries to communicate more effectively.[86] Four issues of modern communication theories deserve an examination through an evangelical lens to better grasp their missiological implications for contextualization. First, some modern communication theories stand on postmodern epistemology that promotes the subjective nature of human perception of reality. They deny the possibility of asserting objective truth claims for re-

---

83 See Demarest and Harpel, "Don Richardson's 'Redemptive Analogies,'" 330–40.

84 Hesselgrave and Rommen, *Contextualization*, 181.

85 Hesselgrave and Rommen, *Contextualization*, 180–96. They provide seven axiomatic ideas on which most semanticists and communicologists would agree and an evaluation of their pros and cons from an evangelical point of view.

86 Hesselgrave and Rommen list five positive ways in which modern theories enhance the effectiveness of missionary communication. Hesselgrave and Rommen, *Contextualization*, 188–90. For example, two helpful concepts for the articulation of the Gospel are the felt-need and receptor-oriented approaches, although they should be used within certain boundaries.

ligious affirmations. Consequently, absolutes are seen with skepticism, and any human message, including biblical revelation, is seen as relative in essence. More importantly, it is argued that all religious statements can only carry "subjective and emotive meanings" and thus the claim of the objective, absolute truth of biblical revelation is simply denied.[87]

A traditional evangelical response to this challenge is that God reveals himself in particular historical human contexts through the limits of human language. This cultural conditioning, however, does not destroy the divine nature of God's revelation and its normative value. Conservative evangelical scholars do not deny that human perceptions or formulations of the divine revelation are fallible, but they instead contend for the infallibility and the inerrancy of Scripture. Hesselgrave succinctly summarizes a representative traditional evangelical view on this matter:

> What they [scholars such as Carl F. H. Henry, Francis Schaeffer, Harold Lindsell] claim is that *divine* disclosures and formulations are undistorted, authoritative, and true. Even though mediated through fallible, human, and limited linguistic instruments and even though we "see through a glass darkly," what we are looking at is *divine*. The Lord Jesus insisted on precisely that when he said that the Scriptures cannot be broken (John 10:35) and that even the smallest markings in the text of the law would not pass away until all has been fulfilled (Matt 5:18).[88]

The subjective nature of human perception of divine truth should not be confused with the objective, absolute nature of God's revelation in Scripture. The Bible's own witness must be taken seriously because it evidences that the supracultural absolute truth of God is communicated through human instruments, and that the communicated message maintains its absolute truth value. When the subjective nature of human perception is extended too far, as in modern communication theories, religious statements lose the value of objective propositional truths and become a matter of relative personal truths.

Second, modern theories of communication commonly stand upon the contention that meaning is found in persons (sources and receptors), not in the messages, things, or events. When a communicator delivers a message, meaning is determined in the minds of its receptors.[89] This notion provides a ground for the so-called receptor-oriented communication principle. As long as the correct meaning is delivered to receptors, it is asserted

---

87 Hesselgrave, *Communicating Christ*, 69.
88 Hesselgrave and Rommen, *Contextualization*, 195 (emphasis in the original).
89 Kraft, *Communication Theory*, 89–108.

that communication has accomplished its goal. In this process, there is little emphasis on the content of a message, and the impact on receptors becomes the most important element of communication.

Hesselgrave and Rommen refer to this view as "the instrumentalistic, functional view of language" and describe the danger of taking it to extremity as follows:

> When . . . taken to its extreme, the emphasis shifts from propositional truths to dispositional attitudes. The focus tends to move from the fidelity of the message to the autonomy of source and receptor, from content to impact, from form to function, from adherence to the conventions of language usage to the convolutions of the receptor's brain. The results of this can be little short of disastrous, especially from a Christian point of view.[90]

In line with their critique, several points of concern deserve mentioning. First of all, as the instrumentalist epistemology plays a central role in this view, the authority of Scripture is seriously undermined. One cannot claim to apply objective criteria to test truth because meanings are simply a matter of receptors' subjective perception. When applied to a Christian context, the contents of the Gospel message become a secondary matter, while overemphasis is given to the impact upon the hearers. Consequently, one cannot guarantee an objective basis to test whether the intended meaning of the Christian message has been faithfully conveyed to its receptors. Hesselgrave makes a straightforward case against the contention of modern communication theories from a biblical stance:

> Is meaning to be found in the world? So much so that people are under judgment for misinterpreting or disregarding it! Is meaning to be found in the words of Scripture? So much so that the significance of every letter and marking will be taken into consideration in the fulfillment of them! . . . But clearly, the emphasis of Scripture is on the clear and consistent *content* of general revelation in creation and of special revelation in the Bible, not on the prerogative of humanity to interpret it as we think best.[91]

Third, the instrumentalist epistemological presupposition leads to the notion that forms and meanings are separable. During the nineteenth century, positivism was the major epistemological paradigm under which forms and meanings were taken to be identical and inseparable. No

---

90 Hesselgrave and Rommen, *Contextualization*, 191.
91 Hesselgrave, *Communicating Christ*, 65 (emphasis in the original).

indigenous cultural forms were used for communicating the Gospel because they were perceived to contain unbiblical meanings. In the twentieth century, however, instrumentalist epistemology gained power in most of the scientific disciplines, including anthropology and linguistics. Form and meaning were no longer taken to be identical because private meanings attached to forms were considered to be the most important factor in communication.[92] Since the effectiveness of communication was measured only subjectively by receptors, old cultural and religious forms could be used for communicating new meanings. This paradigm opened up a new potential for using indigenous cultural and religious forms for the communication of the Gospel.

The dynamic equivalence principle is an output of this instrumentalist view and has become popularized among communicologists and cross-cultural missionaries. In the beginning, the idea of dynamic equivalence was restricted to the area of translation between languages. It was claimed that effective communication requires the transmission of equivalent meaning through dynamically equivalent forms instead of sticking to equivalent forms, which is known as formal correspondence. Use of the dynamic equivalence principle, however, has been extended from linguistics to general areas of communication, including the use of local cultural and religious forms. Although this principle holds certain validity in translation, it is not without limit even when it comes to Bible translation.[93] Moreover, there is a serious doubt about extending its scope into cultural and religious forms. It is important to evaluate the right use of this principle within the question of whether forms and meanings are separable.

Paul Hiebert provides a warning against the dangers this instrumentalist view introduces.[94] First, the total separation of form and meaning stands on too simple a view or too positive a view of culture. The assumption behind this view ignores the sinful nature of the fallen humanity and sees the cultural products as value free. It is a false assumption that all cultural practices can be used for the Gospel communication. Second, this view ignores both the social and historical dimensions of culture when it separates form and meaning. Since the meaning of every form is established by social acceptance in historical context, one cannot ignore the social and historical effect on the link between form and meaning. Third, this view is a product of the individualistic view of human experience. Lastly, Hiebert contends that "the greatest danger in separating meaning from form is the relativism

---

92 Hiebert, "Form and Meaning," 102–5.
93 Carson, "Limits of Dynamic Equivalence," 200–213.
94 Hiebert, "Form and Meaning," 105–8.

and pragmatism this introduces."[95] In short, separating form from meaning can produce dangerous results in cross-cultural communication.

A biblical response to this issue is to take into account different types of relationship between the two according to the nature of symbols. Hiebert provides four categories of relating form and meaning: "arbitrarily linked, loosely linked, tightly linked, and equated."[96] The question of whether form and meaning can be separated should be answered by considering the types of relationship along this spectrum. Hiebert concisely summarizes various relationships between forms and meanings:

> In some the relationship is arbitrary, so forms can readily be changed in order to preserve meanings. In other symbols the relationship is more complex, ranging from loose to tight linkages. To change the forms in these inevitably changes the meanings in some way. In still other symbols, meaning and form are essentially one. To change the form is to change the meaning.[97]

The nature of symbols demands an examination to determine whether local cultural and religious forms can be used in the attempt of contextualization. This examination involves not only the symbols of the Bible and the church, but also the symbols of recipient cultures.[98]

The last important issue in contextualization from a communicational perspective involves the choice between two contrasting approaches: "the common ground approach" and "the point of contact approach."[99] A careful understanding of these two approaches, with their respective potential dangers considered, is crucial in determining to what extent one can use cultural and religious forms of other religions in contextualization. The common ground approach focuses on similarities and common factors between two cultures or religions whether it is thoughts, rituals, cultural forms, or behaviors. Some Christian missionaries in the past favored this approach based upon the notion that Christianity was the fulfillment of other religions.[100] Several underlying assumptions are involved in this contention. First, it is easier to communicate cross-culturally by starting with common factors and similarities between two different cultures. The Christian Gospel may look less foreign and less intimidating because it is portrayed as sharing commonness with the recipient religion. Second, the

---

95 Hiebert, "Form and Meaning," 108.
96 Hiebert, "Form and Meaning," 109–16.
97 Hiebert, "Form and Meaning," 109.
98 Hiebert, "Form and Meaning," 109–10.
99 Nida, *Message and Mission*, 211.
100 Nida, *Message and Mission*, 213.

common ground approach assumes that the referents of common factors are the same thing so that they can produce a better understanding on the part of the receptor. Third, therefore, it is assumed that focusing on common ground leads to a more effective cross-cultural communication.

These assumptions, however, are not valid. The first assumption is refuted by the biblical and historical fact of the early church because the Bible clearly reveals that the apostolic proclamation of the Gospel challenges the status quo of the era through confrontation. The second assumption is flawed simply because the referents of common factors between two religions cannot be exactly the same. Nida explains the reason, "It is impossible to take any element of belief out of its context and still have the same belief. Religions are systems, and the individual beliefs have meaning only in terms of the system to which they belong. . . . Thus no two beliefs in any two systems, despite their superficial similarities, present a basis for 'common ground.'"[101] For example, the concept of God's revelation in Christianity and in Islam is not the same. Since the first and the second assumptions prove faulty, the third is consequently flawed.[102]

A biblical position seems closer to the point of contact approach. It differs from the common ground approach in several ways. It emphasizes "parallelism in order to provide one with an intelligible basis for communication, without involving any initial field of agreement."[103] The point of contact approach takes note of the parallel features but soon moves from the point of contact to the Gospel proclamation. For this reason, Nida rightly refers to a point of contact as "'a point of departure' for intelligent communication."[104] This approach is more in line with the biblical examples than the common ground approach, which will be further discussed in the next two chapters.

## A CRITICAL EVALUATION OF CHARLES H. KRAFT'S MISSIOLOGICAL MODEL

Kraft has been an influential missiologist among evangelicals for the last several decades. His influential writings containing thought provoking

---

101 Nida, *Message and Mission*, 214. Hendrick Kraemer shares the same view in his monumental work, *Christian Message*, 130–41.

102 In contrast to the third assumption, Hesselgrave argues that emphasizing differences between two religious systems can promote a more effective communication than emphasizing similarities. See Hesselgrave, "Christian Communication," 131–38.

103 Nida, *Message and Mission*, 214.

104 Nida, *Message and Mission*, 214.

concepts and assertions have affected the missiological approaches of the evangelical community.[105] Most notably, his anthropological background has enabled him to approach missiology from a fresh perspective by incorporating the insights from social sciences, such as anthropology, linguistics, and communication theory. His extensive use of the insights from social sciences has challenged the traditional evangelical missiological approach, and as a result, innovative contributions have produced a variety of radical missionary practices and ministry models of the evangelical missionaries.

While Kraft's contributions to contemporary missiology and his passion for missions are commendable, several evangelical scholars express concerns on his missiological approach. Carl Henry criticizes Kraft's arbitrary redefinition of biblical revelation.[106] Edward N. Gross provides a more comprehensive critique by analyzing Kraft's missiological thinking in six areas and demonstrates how Kraft deviates from an orthodox evangelical theological position.[107] Enoch Wan provides another critique of Kraft's use/misuse of social sciences in biblical interpretation and missiological formulation.[108] Wan reveals how Kraft violates the biblical inerrancy statement of evangelical community in his innovative attempt to use social science for his missiological thinking.

The apex of Kraft's missiological model is contextualization as he formulates a transcultural model of communicating the Christian faith or of appropriating Christianity into other cultural contexts.[109] Some evangelical missionaries and missiologists have incorporated Kraft's innovative concepts and proposals into their contextualization models without recognizing the potential dangers involved when they use his model uncritically. It is expedient to critically evaluate Kraft's missiological model before one adopts the innovative notions of his missiological model. This section applies the analytical framework developed in the previous section to Kraft's missiological model to see if his model remains within evangelical bound-

105 All the published works of Kraft are compiled in the recent edited work. See Kraft et al., *Paradigm Shifts*, 137–45.

106 Henry, "Cultural Relativizing," 153–64. This article is a critique of Kraft, *Christianity in Culture* in 1979 edition. The second edition under the same title is published in 2005 and the rest of this paper will use the second edition. Kraft, *Christianity in Culture*.

107 Gross, *Is Charles Kraft an Evangelical?*. The six categories are revelation, hermeneutics, theology, soteriology, ethics, and the Christian ministry.

108 Wan, "Critique of Charles Kraft's Use/Misuse," 121–64.

109 In his most recent work, Kraft uses the term "appropriate Christianity" in replacement of "contextualization." See Kraft, *Appropriate Christianity*. Although this is an edited volume by Kraft, the major bulk of the book is his own works. This can be regarded as the most comprehensive collection of his writings on contextualization.

aries of contextualization by investigating its underlying assumptions and theoretical foundations. The examination of Kraft's model reveals that many facets of the IM are in close proximity with Kraft's missiological thinking. This is understandably so because several IM advocates use his missiological model as the foundation for validating the IM.[110]

## A Philosophical Perspective

The fundamental departure of Kraft's missiological model from an orthodox evangelical position occurs when he redefines the biblical notion of revelation and thus changes the nature of the Bible through the lens of anthropology, linguistics, and communication theory. Four major issues will be addressed with clearly articulated evangelical responses to the points of deviation. First, Kraft establishes his missiological model on a new definition of biblical revelation. Although he plainly accepts "the cardinal evangelical doctrines including the Bible as both inspired by God and an accurate record of the Spirit-guided perceptions of human beings who were committed to God," what he means strikingly differs from the orthodox evangelical view of Scripture.[111] Kraft applies anthropological and communicational theories to theological interpretation inspired by Bernard Ramm's suggestion: "When . . . an immense amount of sober research has gone into the nature of language theory and communication, we might have to develop a whole new theory of inspiration and revelation."[112] Kraft develops a whole new theory of inspiration and revelation, which is a significant digression from the traditional orthodox evangelical view.

At least two notable digressions deserve the notice. Kraft defines revelation not as propositional truth in the written Word of God but as "stimulus to action." He states, "'God's disclosure' consists of far more than mere information. God's disclosures of himself stimulate to action."[113] Since the purpose of God's revelation is to stimulate to action, Kraft asserts that revelation is essentially personal and relational as is exemplified in the incarnation.[114] He refers to the propositional truth of God's revelation as

110 Some IM advocates were former students of Kraft. Travis, for example, is a former student of Kraft's from Fuller Theological Seminary and contributes one chapter to Kraft's recent book, *Appropriate Christianity*. Kraft is a strong proponent of the IM as he sees it as the representative application of appropriate Christianity in the Muslim context. Kraft, *Appropriate Christianity*, 12.

111 Kraft, *Christianity in Culture*, 27.

112 Kraft, *Christianity in Culture*, 133.

113 Kraft, *Christianity in Culture*, 143.

114 Kraft, *Christianity in Culture*, 136–40. Kraft takes the incarnation as the prime

"information" and relates it with his own redefinition of revelation, which is "personal impact," "experiential knowledge," or "stimulus to action."[115] Kraft denies the authoritative nature of propositional truth in biblical revelation by using his communication theory as the guideline for theologizing. The other digression occurs in his assertion that God's revelation is "a dynamic, continuing communicational process, rather than something that started and stopped in the past and has now become static."[116] Kraft asserts that revelation continues even today because God discloses something new about himself whenever he reveals himself to his people. He concludes, therefore, that revelation is not objective and complete, but subjective and continuing.[117]

As a consequence of these two digressions, the nature of the Bible turns into something radically different from the biblical witness. First, Kraft's definition of revelation as "personal impact" or "stimulus to action" has no scriptural basis. On the contrary, as Carl Henry states, "the Christian belief in inspiration as well as in revelation rests both on explicit biblical assertions and on the pervading mood of the scriptural record."[118] Kraft's view of revelation is an imaginative, yet arbitrary personal redefinition based on anthropological and communication perspectives with no scriptural validation.[119] Kraft's denial of the propositional truth of Scripture as God's revelation in turn undermines the authority of the Bible. The fundamental reason for this is his problematic epistemology, a so-called "critical realism," which he claims to have borrowed from Paul Hiebert.[120] Hiebert defines

---

case of receptor-oriented revelation.

115 Kraft, *Christianity in Culture*, 133–200.

116 Kraft, *Christianity in Culture*, 308, 140–45.

117 Kraft, *Christianity in Culture*, 145.

118 Henry, "Bible, Inspiration of," 160.

119 Kraft, *Christianity in Culture*, 145. Kraft's radical departure from the orthodox evangelical position is evident in the following statement: "While the Bible is the inspired product of God's revealing, it points beyond itself to the contemporary re-creation within contemporary hearers of the process that it records. Therefore, though the Bible is today a most important means to revelatory ends, it should never be itself regarded as the only product of the revelatory process."

120 For critical realism, see Hiebert, *Missiological Implications*, 68–116. Hiebert provides a summary of critical realism in three subheadings: 1) "Nature of knowledge: The external world is real. Our knowledge of it is partial but can be true. Science is a map or model. It is made up of successive paradigms that bring us to closer approximations of reality and about truth." 2) "Relationship between systems of knowledge: Each field in science presents a different blueprint of reality. These are complementary to one another. Integration is achieved, not by reducing them all to one model, but by seeing their interrelationship. Each gives us partial insights into reality." 3) "The Umpire's response: I call it the way I see it, but there is a real pitch and an objective standard

critical realism as an epistemology which "affirms the presence of objective truth but recognizes that this is subjectively apprehended."[121] An important distinction is made between the ontological reality (R) independent of human perception and the reality (r) within a limited human perception of it.

A cautious distinction is necessary. Even though the same term "critical realism" is used, Kraft's understanding of critical realism fundamentally differs from Hiebert's original proposal. Philip Barnes points out that Kraft's epistemology is closer to instrumentalism than to critical realism within Hiebert's epistemological taxonomy.[122]

One critical difference between Kraft's and Hiebert's views of critical realism concerns the question of objectivity of truth and objective criteria to judge the truth. Hiebert contends that humans can know truth, though only partially, and that this knowledge of truth can be objectively judged. On the other hand, Kraft denies the possibility of knowing truth objectively and objective measurements to test truths. Kraft states one assumption of his own definition of critical realism:

> Critical Realism *sees the observer as both very important and very limited in the observational process*. . . . And those differing perspectives may result in quite a variety of understandings of what is written here. And you (not I) will have the final say as to what I mean. Your part, then, becomes at least as important as mine in determining the reality of what I intend.[123]

According to this statement, Kraft does not accept any objective criteria for judging between the truth and falsity of different perspectives. He says that human perceptions of reality (R) are merely "interpretations of REALITY (or parts of it) seen imperfectly and partially by human beings through lenses affected by culture, personality, experience, sin, and probably a myriad of other limiting and distorting factors."[124] He also contends that the subjectivity of human perception does not allow for an objective measurement.

---

against which I must judge it. It can be shown to be right or wrong." See Hiebert, *Missiological Implications*, 37. In an earlier article, Hiebert uses this statement to describe his critical realism: "If knowledge is a map, it is not an absolute statement of reality, but an approximation of it." Hiebert, "Missions and Anthropology," 177. Norman L. Geisler provides a critique of Hiebert's critical realism in his essay, "Response to Paul G. Hiebert," 129–43.

121 Hiebert, *Missiological Implications*, 69.

122 Barnes, "Missiology," 196–98. For Hiebert's taxonomy of various epistemological positions, see Hiebert, *Missiological Implications*, 37–38.

123 Kraft, *Worldview for Christian Witness*, 63 (emphasis in the original).

124 Kraft, *Worldview for Christian Witness*, 67.

Hiebert, however, refers to this notion as "instrumentalism" and criticizes it: "Because no one claims to know the truth and because there are no objective criteria on which decisions can be made, disagreements do not drive the participants to reexamine their positions seriously."[125] Kraft clearly misunderstands Hiebert's critical realism and misuses that ill-perceived concept for his own missiological model. Due to his flawed epistemology, Kraft denies the absolute truth value of Scripture even though he acknowledges Scripture as God's inspired Word. He believes that the limitedness and subjectivity of human interpretation make Scripture fail to be the absolute truth of God. Kraft distinguishes "the inspired data of the Bible from the fallible interpretations of theologizing human beings."[126] By making the subjective nature of human perception of revelation a part of God's revelatory activities, Kraft makes God's written Word an incomplete revelation. His epistemological stance essentially departs from the orthodox biblical position.

Second, concerning the inspiration and inerrancy of the Bible, Kraft makes another dangerous departure:

> I believe strongly that the Scriptures are inspired and that this inspiration may properly be labeled "verbal" (that is, inspiration attaches to the wording employed) and "plenary" (that is, the *whole* Bible is inspired). These terms label what is inspired (i.e., all the words). But the words are inspired almost incidentally. For the primary focus of inspiration (as of all ethnolinguistic communication) is on the meanings. *Only in societies like ours that, under the influence of simplistic views of language, have chosen to focus almost exclusively on words, would one get theories of inspiration that concentrate almost exclusively on words.* . . . I contend that a word-focused doctrine of inspiration is also inadequate.[127]

According to this paragraph, Kraft neither accepts the verbal plenary inspiration nor the inerrancy of the Bible in the same manner which they are understood by the majority of evangelical scholarship. He twists the definition of inspiration so that the inspired word is limited only to meanings. He finds the traditional evangelical view of inspiration "too static," believing that God's inspiration should be understood as dynamic in terms of "the

---

125 Hiebert, *Missiological Implications*, 46.
126 Kraft, *Christianity in Culture*, 21–22 and 33.
127 Kraft, *Christianity in Culture*, 161 (emphasis in the original).

continual leading activity of God."[128] Furthermore, he criticizes conservative evangelical scholars for their narrow definition of biblical inerrancy:

> In defending the Bible's inspiration, such closed conservatives feel compelled to sink or swim on the basis of an equation between inspiration and inerrancy. This is a "chancy" kind of decision at best, given the fact that such an equation is based on philosophical presuppositions, not on scriptural statements. For the Bible, though claiming inspiration (2 Tim 3:16), never claims inerrancy.[129]

Kraft's own formulation concerning inspiration does not coincide with the Bible's own witness in 2 Tim 3:16. His view of biblical inerrancy deviates from the evangelical position as it is explicitly described in the Chicago Statement of Biblical Inerrancy. In fact, his notion of revelation is closer to that of a neo-orthodox theological view.

Third, based upon the preceding assertions on biblical revelation, inspiration, and inerrancy, Kraft makes several striking statements about the Bible. He defines the Bible as an "inspired classic casebook" in the sense that the Bible contains "an inspired collection of classic cases from history, exemplifying certain of God's past interactions with human beings for the instruction and guidance of those who now seek to follow in their footsteps."[130] He asserts that the Bible carries the normative values for all cultures only through the powerful use of "appropriate analogy" to understand its meanings.[131] Consequently analogy becomes the major interpretive method in his missiological model.

> The Bible assumes that, in spite of significant differences in culture, there are impressive basic human similarities between peoples. It assumes, further, that these are sufficient to provide the necessary experiential commonality to make the cases of divine-human interaction described appropriate analogies. It also assumes that the hearers/readers are good enough at the job of learning by analogy to be able to deduce the principles being illustrated and to 'transculturate' them into their life within their culture.[132]

128 Kraft, *Christianity in Culture*, 161.
129 Kraft, *Christianity in Culture*, 162.
130 Kraft, *Christianity in Culture*, 155.
131 Kraft's principal hermeneutical method in biblical interpretation is highly dependent on analogy. This analogical interpretive method can lead to a liberal understanding of the meaning of the biblical text and thus can be dangerous.
132 Kraft, *Christianity in Culture*, 156. According to this description, analogy

For Kraft, the Bible is simply "a most important means to revelatory ends," but "not the only product of the revelatory process."[133] The Bible itself cannot fully be the revelation of God without a subjective human application or appropriation of biblical revelation, as he claims, "The information contained in what we call the Word of God if used improperly (as by Satan) is neither revelation nor God's Word."[134] This is, in fact, a questionable assertion because it makes man's response to "God's information [revelation]" in the Bible play a determining role for whether the Bible becomes God's revelation or not.[135]

Kraft's doctrine of the Bible, regarding its authority, revelation, inspiration, and inerrancy, deviates from the orthodox evangelical position. Consequently, his missiological model creates serious problems in the area of contextualization. The doctrine of the Bible occupies an important place in Christian theology and praxis. If evangelicals forsake this fundamental doctrine of Scripture, they will inevitably lose the foundation for all other Christian doctrines as well as for all appropriate Christian praxis, including contextualization.

Kraft defines general and special revelation in an unconventional way by using communication theories in his missiological model. Kraft rejects the traditional evangelical distinction between general and special revelations.[136] He denies the qualitative difference between the revelations and claims that general revelation is "not deficient, even as a basis for salvation."[137] This contradicts biblical teaching on general revelation. This kind of arbitrary expression blurs theological precision, which frequently occurs in Kraft's missiological model due to his extensive use of anthropology and communication theory.

---

becomes the primary hermeneutical method in Kraft's missiological model, and this hermeneutical method is used throughout his book. Gross points out that Kraft's faulty interpretation of 1 Cor 13:12, which he quotes more than any other biblical reference in *Christianity in Culture*, leads him to make such a firm foundational statement as "absolute truth cannot be known." Gross, *Is Charles Kraft an Evangelical?*, 45.

133 Kraft, *Christianity in Culture*, 145.
134 Kraft, *Christianity in Culture*, 148.
135 Gross, *Is Charles Kraft an Evangelical?*, 14.
136 Kraft, *Christianity in Culture*, 171. He criticizes the protestant scholars because they consider general revelation "a flawed type of information" and special revelation "an unflawed type of information that somehow has greater (even magical) power in itself." This is a false accusation against Protestant scholars because they do not contend that general revelation is "flawed." General revelation is still God's revelation although its purpose is different from that of special revelation.
137 Kraft, *Christianity in Culture*, 171.

Kraft also undermines the biblical teaching of general revelation when he claims that it is not a deficient basis for salvation.[138] According to Kraft, general revelation itself is sufficiently salvific so that God can save people through general revelation without the explicit knowledge of Jesus. Kraft even makes a striking claim about "those who have never heard":

> Can people who are chronologically A.D., but in terms of knowledge, B.C. (i.e., they have not heard of Christ), or those who are indoctrinated with a wrong understanding of Christ, be saved by committing themselves to faith in God as Abraham and the rest of those who were chronologically B.C. did (Heb 11)? Could such persons be saved by "giving as much of themselves as they can give to as much of God as they can understand"? I personally believe they can and many have.[139]

Kraft alters the biblical teaching of general and special revelation and of salvation by regarding general revelation as being salvific. By redefining revelation as impact or stimulus, with the sole purpose of creating a more effective cross-cultural communication, Kraft deviates from the clear biblical teaching of salvation. The biblical position clearly stresses that general revelation alone, apart from special revelation, cannot lead people to the saving grace of God.

## A Theological Perspective

The goal of Kraft's missiological model is to develop a cross-cultural ethnotheology which arises from a need for "a more broadly based, multiculturally applicable theological perspective" by utilizing anthropology, linguistics, translation theory, and communication science.[140] The ethnotheology starts from his assertions that western theology is too narrow to be applied to other cultural contexts, and that theology in general is a culturally conditioned product, as human perceptions of reality (R) differ depending on the worldviews of individuals. For Kraft, a cultural context is a neutral channel for the occurrence of dynamic revelation. Therefore, each cultural context should be received with respect. This high respect for the ethno-cultural conditioning of God's revelation stands upon his epistemological assumption that God's revelation continues even in the contemporary era in every human cultural context as long as the Scriptures produce impacts or stimuli.

---

138 Kraft, *Christianity in Culture*, 171.
139 Kraft, *Christianity in Culture*, 198.
140 Kraft, *Christianity in Culture*, 10.

Theologically speaking, Kraft comes closer to the neo-orthodox theological position in his view of Scripture and revelation, especially to Barthian theology. Both Karl Barth and Kraft agree that revelation should be viewed more as relational and personal truth than as propositional. Both would agree on the statement that "Scripture contains the Word but is not the Word." Both reject biblical inerrancy. They come to this conclusion, however, for slightly different reasons. Kraft reaches this conclusion based on the culture-bound nature of Scripture and the different human perceptions of reality in biblical revelation, while Barth makes his theological claim based upon the distinction between the written Word of God and Jesus the incarnate Word.[141] Barth emphasizes the Christ event in history as God's revelation whereas Kraft gives an emphasis on contemporary human experience of God's revelation.

Kraft's ethnotheology departs from the orthodox evangelical theological foundation in several ways. First of all, his questionable epistemology, as explained above, inevitably leads him to the rejection of the orthodox evangelical doctrine of the Bible: the propositional truth of biblical revelation, verbal plenary inspiration, and biblical inerrancy. Second, his assertion that Scripture contains both supracultural truths and cultural factors needs a careful evaluation. Carson rightly criticizes Kraft's ambiguous use of "supracultural" to refer to the sub-content revealed by God in Scripture, and argues for the impossibility of isolating it from Scripture:

> If it [the term, supracultural truth] simply refers to the fact that God has revealed certain truth that is objectively true in every culture, it is not offensive; but if there is an attempt to distinguish among parts of the Bible, for instance, according to whether this snippet or that is supracultural or culture-bound, then the attempt is fundamentally misguided and the pursuit of the supracultural an impossible undertaking. The point I am making is that every truth from God comes to us in cultural guise: even the language used and the symbols adopted are cultural expression.[142]

Third, his overemphasis on cultural conditioning of biblical revelation undermines the absolute nature of God's truth and makes every theology relative. Kraft assumes that "theologizing is a human, fallible process" and that "no theology is perfect or absolute."[143] Kraft implies that imposing any theological system upon another cultural context is simply "theologi-

---

141 Schnucker, "Neo-orthodoxy, History," 820.
142 Carson, "Sketch of Factors," 19.
143 Kraft, "Contextualization of Theology," 34.

cal imperialism." Kraft emphasizes that this warning is necessary for the incarnational nature of Christianity because it can prevent Christians from committing the error of making human institutions absolute.[144] Kraft's view is ambiguous because he acknowledges the absolute truth of God as supracultural on the one hand, but rejects the normative value of Scripture on the other, due to the fact that the theological expressions of biblical writers are culturally conditioned and thus relative.

Kraft's assertion that God's revelation continues in the present cultural contexts is important for contextualization because one must carefully discern God's revelation by observing what God is doing in the contemporary contexts. This is referred to as prophetic contextualization by Hesselgrave and Rommen.[145] Kraft takes the notion of "discovering what God is doing today" as the main rubric in his contextualization model.[146] In Kraft's method, therefore, theologians should pay attention to what God is doing in cultural contexts to discover God's truth in light of Scripture. There is a dialectic interaction between human contexts and Scripture. His neo-orthodox theological position leads him to promote the contextualization method of discovering truth in cultural contexts. This notion of discovering truth, however, does not coincide with the biblical principle of contextualization, which is didactic in essence.

While he relativizes theology and elevates human cultural contexts as a valid source of theologizing, Kraft denies the normative value of historic Christianity. For instance, he contends that historic creeds have relatively little value in themselves because they are historically and culturally conditioned products with no normative value.[147] He asserts, "We are to re-create the scripturally endorsed theologizing process, not simply transmit the theological products of yesterday."[148] If he is referring to specific forms of historic creeds, Kraft's point is acceptable. If it involves changing the contents of the creeds due to contextual consideration, his assertion cannot be accepted. His view is closer to the latter case because his view of historic heresies in church history indicates so: "It is likely that most of the 'heresies' can validly be classified as cultural adaptations rather than as theological aberrations."[149] Kraft unfortunately does not provide any example of these

144 Kraft, "Contextualization of Theology," 98.

145 Hesselgrave and Rommen, *Contextualization*, 150.

146 This same expression frequently appears in the writings of IM advocates as it will be revealed later in chapter 5.

147 Kraft, *Christianity in Culture*, 228.

148 Kraft, *Christianity in Culture*, 228.

149 Kraft, *Christianity in Culture*, 233.

historic heresies to substantiate his claim. Gross argues that "Kraft cannot expect to be accepted as an Evangelical while defending doctrines labeled heretical by Evangelicalism, unless, of course, he removes all right to label anything as heresy."[150] Kraft's comments on historic creeds and heresies make one suspicious about the possibility of changing not only the forms but also the contents of creeds.

## A Hermeneutical Perspective

Kraft develops his own hermeneutical method based upon his epistemological and theological ground. It is called "ethnolinguistic hermeneutics" or "ethnohermeneutics," whose major concern is to decode the meanings from the biblical texts by looking into "language and culture both at the biblical end and with respect to their influence on the interpreter."[151] His approach stands on the epistemic assumptions that human perception is culturally bound and that language is culturally restricted in communicating the same meaning cross-culturally. The skeptical view of human perception and language leads him to criticize traditional evangelical hermeneutics, historical-grammatical hermeneutics, for having the tendency to "overestimate the possibility of objectivity on the part of the contemporary scholarly interpreter."[152] Searching for authorial intent is not the main objective in his hermeneutical process.

Kraft's hermeneutics shares many common features with the new hermeneutics of neo-orthodox theologians, such as Padilla.[153] Kraft agrees with Padilla on "the hermeneutical circle" and refers to it as a "two-culture dialogic interpretation" in his formulation of ethnohermeneutics. While adopting this new hermeneutics, Kraft deviates from the traditional evangelical hermeneutics. One notable deviation occurs when he assumes that the original meaning of biblical text cannot be objectively found. He states two reasons for this claim: the human cultural conditioning of biblical texts, and the cultural conditioning of contemporary interpreters. Kraft's use of cultural conditioning in the former is closer to the notion that God's revelation is imperfectly reflected in Scripture. Kraft sees the cultural conditioning of the Bible as an obstacle to biblical writers' communicating the true biblical revelation in a perfectly objective manner. Thus, the scriptural

---

150 Gross, *Is Kraft an Evangelical?*, 51.
151 Kraft, *Christianity in Culture*, 104.
152 Kraft, *Christianity in Culture*, 112.
153 Padilla, "Hermeneutics and Culture," 63–94.

witness to God's revelation in human cultural contexts is undermined as being an imperfect revelation.

Kraft is skeptical about the ability of interpreters in the hermeneutical process. He describes five factors which limit human perception of God's truth.[154] The critical issue is how to deal with the cultural conditioning of contemporary interpreters in the hermeneutical and theologizing process. In the traditional evangelical hermeneutics, this is referred to as preunderstanding. Kraft is critical about the cultural bias or prejudice of interpreters, but he fails to appreciate how historical-grammatical hermeneutics prevents the preunderstanding of interpreters from affecting the objective meaning of biblical text. As explained earlier, this is the reason scriptural authority must be maintained in biblical interpretation. Ultimately, it is scriptural authority which prevents interpreters from distorting the meaning of biblical texts, as Scripture corrects their biases or prejudices in their approach to biblical texts.

## An Anthropological Perspective

Kraft's missiological model uses anthropology so extensively that many facets of his anthropological thinking demand a careful evaluation from a biblical perspective. The first problem lies in the incompatibility of the presuppositions of humanistic anthropology with those of biblical revelation. For instance, Kraft's view of culture stands against the biblical view of culture. Kraft takes culture as a neutral vehicle God uses for communication of his revelation. He finds biblical support for this claim from Paul's attitude toward culture in 1 Cor 9:19–22. He further notes, "Culture is not in and of itself either an enemy or a friend to God or humans. It is, rather, something that is there to be used by personal beings such as humans, God, and Satan."[155] Furthermore, by utilizing the typological analysis of Niebuhr, Kraft identifies his view as "the general 'God-above-culture' perspective in viewing God as transcendent and absolute, completely beyond and outside of culture."[156] He separates himself from secular anthropologists by proposing "biblical cultural relativism" in contrast to "absolute cultural relativism" of secular anthropologists.[157]

---

154 Kraft, *Christianity in Culture*, 101. The five factors are the limitations of the revelations, human finiteness, human sinfulness, human cultural conditioning, and human individual psychological and experiential conditioning.

155 Kraft, *Christianity in Culture*, 89.

156 Kraft, *Christianity in Culture*, 88.

157 Kraft, *Christianity in Culture*, 99. Describing biblical cultural relativism, he

Nevertheless, Kraft's effort to establish missionary anthropology upon a biblical foundation is not completely successful. First, his view of culture stands on the dichotomous distinction between Christ and culture as in Niebuhr's framework. This model has a critical weakness in that human culture is separated from God's sovereign rule in the totality of human life, as mentioned above in Tennent's critique. Second, Kraft holds a positive view or at least a neutral view of culture, which plays a determining role in every aspect of his missiological model. This view comes from the fundamental presupposition of anthropology, which defines culture as "a closed integrated system with components playing different functions" under the paradigm of functionalism.[158] Wan points out the danger of this anthropological presupposition:

> Unfortunately the Christian functionalist anthropologists are preoccupied with the abstraction of "the integrated system" and its component parts with "manifest function" and "latent function" meeting the needs of members within the cultural system. Instead of delineating the dynamic interaction between God, man, Satan and the world, they have consigned their Christian faith to "functionalism's box 'religion'—a part of culture."[159]

As a consequence of the high view of culture, it is easy for Kraft to be critical about "ethnocentrism" and to be in favor of "cultural relativism." No normative rule is recognized to evaluate or judge human cultures because every culture is validated within its own cultural context. Even biblical values have a limited role in making normative value judgments on human cultures within this ideological framework. Tennant is critical about the one-sided positive view of culture by denoting cultural relativism as "uncritical *divinization of culture*."[160] While Kraft rejects "absolute cultural relativism" of anthropologists, he partly admits the notion of cultural relativism in his "biblical cultural relativism" in which his high view of culture is maintained. Kraft one-sidedly emphasizes the positive aspect of culture and minimizes the sinfulness of human culture with the intention of making culture a neutral vehicle for God's communication in his missiological model.

---

says that "we see in the Bible a relativism with respect to the extent of the revelational information available to given culture-bound human beings." The fact that God uses human culture, and communicates his revelation through culture, seems to give Kraft a firm conviction that culture either must be neutral or should be considered as a positive factor.

158 Luzbetak, *Church and Cultures*, 141.
159 Wan, "Critique of Functional Missionary," 18.
160 Tennant, *Invitation to World Missions*, 181 (emphasis in the original).

Kraft's unhealthy theology of culture is reflected in his theology of religions so that he holds a high view of other religions. At the very least Kraft makes two mistakes in his theology of religions. First, his view of general revelation leads to unbiblical conclusions about other religions. He contends that general revelation has sufficiently salvific impact and that there might be a possibility of salvation in other religious traditions as long as the faith factor is seen in the hearts of people. While his view is quite similar to inclusivism in accepting potential salvation opportunities in other religions, Kraft does not completely agree with inclusivists because he believes that no one can be saved other than through Christ.[161] On the other hand, he departs from the traditional evangelical position because he asserts that no explicit knowledge of Jesus Christ and his atoning death and resurrection is required for salvation because the salvific grace of God is available outside of the realm of special revelation.

As a strong evidence for his assertion, Kraft contends that believers in the Old Testament are saved by the same faith factor as believers in the New Testament, even though the former did not have explicit knowledge of Jesus Christ. Based upon several biblical passages, Kraft argues that those who are living under other religious faiths are not completely excluded from the saving work of God, because the faith factor is at work within their religious traditions.[162] This view deviates from exclusivism of a biblical evangelical stance.

Second, Kraft redefines salvation. He criticizes the western cultural theological notion for defining "salvation by positional basis" because, he believes, it is almost impossible to distinguish Christians from non-Christians based upon their outward behavior. Instead Kraft claims that God has a directional basis for accepting humans and that salvation should be viewed directionally through the lens of faith or faithfulness:

> His [God's] basis, however, would seem to place the emphasis on the direction in which people are going. Some may (like the young wheat) behave very much like a non-Christian. But, since they are growing in the direction of greater Christlikeness, they are among the saved. Others may (like the tares) look very much

---

161 Kraft, *Christianity in Culture*, 198. Kraft's assertions on this issue are both ambiguous and inconsistent. On the one hand, he asserts that no explicit knowledge of Jesus is required for salvation, as is the case with the Old Testament believers. On the other hand, he asserts that Jesus is the only way of salvation. He contends, therefore, that the ontological and historical fact of Christ's redemptive work is sufficient for salvation, whether or not one is aware of this fact.

162 Kraft, *Christianity in Culture*, 198–99.

like Christians on the outside. But they are growing away from Christlikeness and are therefore among the lost.[163]

When Kraft redefines salvation, he endangers the traditional biblical doctrine of salvation. He seems to believe that either faithfulness to God or God-ward movement is sufficient for salvation because salvation is understood in terms of a "relational interaction between human faith-response (allegiance) and the divine invitation."[164] In regards to other religious faiths, he defines salvation in terms of allegiance:

> The Scriptures . . . do not often focus on either the fact or the nature of the initiation of this allegiance. In dealing with Gentiles there is reference to the newness and consequent *discontinuity* of such an allegiance with their previous commitment (e.g., Acts 17:30). For Jews, though, the focus is more often on the *continuity* between the Jewish commitment to God and that advocated by Christianity (e.g., Luke 24:25–27; Acts 2; etc.). The necessity for a conscious pledge of allegiance on the part of the members of each of these groups is emphasized, but whether such a pledge involved radical discontinuity with the past or simply a renewed affirmation of one's commitment to the same God on the basis of new information (concerning Christ) does not seem important to the authors of Scripture.[165]

Kraft makes a radical assertion that deep-seated discontinuity does not have to be part of conversion as long as "new information" (revelation) concerning Christ renews one's commitment to the same God in their previous religious context. One can remain within the previous religious system as long as he reveals allegiance to God through Christ based upon new information. The most explicit application of this idea is the IM.

Kraft departs from the fundamental biblical principle of conversion in order to make his anthropology-driven missiological model work toward a more effective communication of the Gospel. This is accomplished by his innovative redefinition of key theological terms at the cost of the most important soteriological doctrine of biblical Christianity. In this process, Kraft does injustice to biblical and historic Christianity.

---

163 Kraft, *Christianity in Culture*, 187–88.
164 Kraft, *Christianity in Culture*, 261.
165 Kraft, *Christianity in Culture*, 262 (emphasis in the original).

## A Communication Perspective

Kraft builds up his missiological model by extensively employing modern communication theories because contextualization primarily involves an effective cross-cultural communication of the Gospel. In assessing Kraft's communication theory, three issues are of special importance. First, following the presupposition of modern communication theories, Kraft emphasizes the subjective nature of a human perception of external reality and rejects the possibility of asserting objective truth claims into the realm of religious statement. By doing this, Kraft falls into the danger of changing all religious statements into completely relativistic personal truths and denying the nature of the objective propositional truth.

Second, Kraft accepts the common assertion of modern communication theories or semantics that meaning is found in persons (sources and receptors). When the message is delivered, meaning is found in the minds of the source and the receptor. Kraft postulates that communication accomplishes only the transmission of a message, not of the meanings.[166] According to Hesselgrave, Kraft holds "the instrumentalistic functional view of language" and takes it to an extreme to produce dangerous assertions.[167] Kraft's missiological model leads essentially to the denial of objective propositional truth and the arbitrary redefinition of many theological terms in an unbiblical way.[168] In his missiological model, many of biblical and theological terms are either reinterpreted or redefined by using concepts or assumptions in communication theories and anthropology. The most fundamental flaw of his model is the diminished authority of Scripture through the subjective interpretation of biblical notions and the arbitrary redefinitions by uncritically borrowing anthropocentric academic disciplines.

Third, Kraft asserts that form and meaning can be separable and thus promotes the dynamic equivalence principle. Since forms and meanings are taken to be separable, and since the goal of Christian communication is the transmission of meanings, Kraft argues that it is not formal correspondence but dynamic- or meaning-equivalence principle that should be the fundamental principle in Christian communication.[169] Kraft extends this principle into other areas of missiology, such as transculturation of the message, theologizing, church and leadership. The problems of this approach are discussed in the earlier section of this chapter.

---

166 Kraft, *Communication Theory*, 83–85.
167 Hesselgrave and Rommen, *Contextualization*, 191.
168 Conversion is one example. See Kraft, *Christianity in Culture*, 257–69.
169 Kraft, *Christianity in Culture*, 203–56.

In a recent article, Kraft contends that faith response to God can be expressed in a "multiplicity of cultural forms."[170] He makes a radical assertion:

> Could, for example, Christian faith be expressed in cultural forms ordinarily associated with Islam, Hinduism, or Buddhism? I believe it can, and movements such as that in Bangladesh among Muslim converts that work at a C4 or C5 level and that among Hindus spoken about by Herbert Hoefer in Churchless Christianity testify to this possibility. Using the name of the cultural package to refer to the culture and Christianity to refer to the faith thus gives us combinations such as "Hindu Christianity," "Buddhist Christianity," or "Muslim Christianity."[171]

Kraft commits at least two critical errors in this assertion. First, he arbitrarily refers to religious terms (Hindu, Buddhist, and Muslim) as cultural, so that an irreconcilable combination between Muslim and Christian is actually made viable. No devout person, either Muslim or Christian, would admit such terminology. Second, what he refers to as "cultural forms ordinarily associated with Islam" is in fact religious forms. The fact that he does not provide examples weakens his argument. Kraft's distinction between culture and religion seems to be intentionally blurred in order to make it possible to borrow Islamic cultural forms for the Christian faith which he identifies as an essential.

## CONCLUSION

This chapter has established a comprehensive analytical framework for evaluating contextualization models by utilizing the five perspectives of Hesselgrave and Rommen's framework. It is emphasized that the contextualization discussion not only focuses on practical features but also examines various underlying presuppositions and theoretical underpinnings behind individual models. This framework provides an evaluative tool for examining whether central features of each model remain within biblically acceptable parameters, such as scriptural authority based on the biblical notion of revelation and inspiration, biblical inerrancy, historical-grammatical hermeneutics that seeks for authorial intent, biblical theology of culture and religions, and biblical epistemology. This analytical framework needs some modification in order to have greater relevance to various cultural and religious contexts by incorporating context-specific issues of contextualization.

---

170 Kraft, "Contextualization of Essential Christianity," 82.
171 Kraft, "Contextualization of Essential Christianity," 84.

## An Analytical Framework for Contextualization among Muslims 105

When the analytical framework was applied to the missiological model of Kraft, it is demonstrated that his model deviates from a biblically permissible traditional evangelical foundation. The first and foremost digression occurs when he undermines the authority of Scripture by holding a flawed epistemology which is not compatible with a biblical worldview. Kraft finds the validity of many aspects of his missiological model in sources other than Scripture, primarily anthropology, communication theory, and linguistics. He admits the questionable presuppositions of social sciences into his missiological model even though they seriously violate central biblical teachings. It is highly likely that the unhealthy roots of his missiological model will jeopardize the fruits of any contextualization attempt which stands on the notions or methods of his model. The IM is such a representative case as will be demonstrated in the following chapters of this study.

# 4

# An Evaluation of the Biblical Interpretations of Insider Movement Advocates

ANY MISSIOLOGICAL MODEL THAT claims to be in line with historic evangelicalism must pass the test of biblical validation. IM advocates have taken a commendable step toward validating the IM on biblical and theological grounds. In the early days the IM discussion revolved around describing what was happening in the Islamic world among Muslims, especially MBBs who turned to follow Jesus. However, more heated and sharpened discussion of the IM has forced both advocates and critics of the movement to refine their arguments as well as to supply corresponding responses. The most fruitful development in this process has been the refinement of the biblical and theological validation of the IM by its proponents. Kevin Higgins has made the most notable contribution to this biblical discussion through his semi-exegetical studies of key biblical passages.[1]

This chapter evaluates the biblical interpretations of IM advocates on the biblical passages they use to validate the IM. Special attention will be given to both the exegetical process and the conclusion of key passages. Since both C4 advocates and C5 (the IM) advocates have used the same biblical passages, and yet, come to different conclusions, this examination

[1] Higgins (writing under the pseudonym of Stuart Caldwell) provides exegetical studies on the following passages: John 4 in Caldwell, "Jesus in Samaria"; Acts 2–3, 2 Kgs 5, John 4, Acts 17 in "Key to Insider Movements," 155–65; Acts 15, 1 Cor 8 in "Acts 15," 29–40; Acts 17 in "Inside What," 74–91. Many IM advocates, however, do not rely on their exegetical studies for their arguments, but make assertions based upon simple parallelism in these passages or borrowing observations of other writers.

*An Evaluation of the Biblical Interpretations of Insider Movement Advocates* 107

of the exegetical process will clarify many areas of confusion in the IM debates.² When the IM was introduced, IM advocates defined the approach as a descriptive phenomenon occurring in Muslim nations. While IM advocates have made biblical validation over the years, the nature of the IM became both descriptive and prescriptive as it is reflected in the writings of IM advocates.³ It is the prescriptive nature of IM advocates' claim that demands a careful exegetical study of their biblical validation. That is, IM advocates contend that the IM is a biblically acceptable ministry approach among Muslims and that the IM should be allowed for Muslim Insiders. This chapter evaluates the biblical interpretations of IM advocates on key biblical passages. This will also reveal various features of the IM so that the analytical framework from the five perspectives of contextualization can be applied to the evaluation the IM in chapter 5.

## THE MAIN ASSERTIONS OF IM ADVOCATES

Although the main characteristics of the IM were reviewed in chapter 1, it seems helpful at this point to summarize the main assertions of IM advocates related to their key biblical passages. The argument of IM advocates includes two basic components. First, they want to prove biblically that Muslim Insiders can remain within the Islamic community alongside maintaining Muslim identity. Second, they also want to demonstrate how it is biblical for Muslim Insiders to observe the Islamic cultural and religious practices with proper modifications or reinterpretations.⁴ Woodberry summarizes the two components in the following:

> The [Jewish] leaders of the Temple and synagogues had corrupted Judaic worship and rejected Jesus, but he and his first

2 Parshall takes note of the fact that both C4 and C5 advocates use the same biblical passages and yet come to totally different conclusions in Travis et al., "Four Responses," 124.

3 Travis, for example, emphasizes the descriptive nature of the IM in his earlier articles: Travis, "C1 to C6 Spectrum," 408; Travis, "Messianic Muslim," 55. There is an indication, however, that some missionaries and missiologists intentionally experimented with the IM approach by using the earlier proposals that might have been in an embryonic form. Travis mentions a number of key missiologists, who suggested "the idea of Muslim followers of Jesus or messianic mosques," such as Winter, Kraft, Conn, and Woodberry. See Travis, "Must All Muslims," 414. Even this original idea of these missiologists might have been derived either from the field observation (descriptive) or from a missiological proposal (prescriptive). The IM approach seems to have taken place by some intentional experiments probably in addition to an ongoing field situation with Muslim believers.

4 Corwin and Winter, "Reviewing September–October," 19–20.

followers continued to identify with Judaism and to participate in temple and synagogue worship. Therefore a case may be made for Muslims who follow Jesus to continue to identify with their Muslim community and participate, to the extent their consciences allow, in its religious observance.[5]

The most common approach to the biblical validation of IM advocates is simply to provide biblical *examples* that appear to support their two propositional statements. The most prominent example they utilize is the early Jewish Christians in the book of Acts, especially in chapters 2, 3, and 15, because these early believers certainly maintained their Jewish religious identity and remained within the Jewish religious community by observing Jewish religious practices at least for a certain time period. Noting several parallel features between Islam and Judaism, IM advocates establish a case for the IM from the historical experience of the early church. Moreover, taking notice of parallelism between the contemporary Messianic Jewish movement and the IM, they refer to Muslim Insiders as "Messianic Muslims" in comparison to "Messianic Jews," the Jews who believe in Jesus as their Messiah.[6]

The imperative question becomes, "Is it valid to make this parallelism between the early Jewish Christians and Muslim Insiders in an attempt to validate the IM?" This presupposition that undergirds the IM advocates' argument depends on the assumed parallelism between Judaism and Islam. Woodberry emphasizes similarities between the Jewish worldview and that of most Muslims and between Mosaic Law and much of Islamic Law to support the validity of this parallelism.[7] Generally, other IM advocates do not further prove the validity of using parallelism between Judaism and Islam, but simply assume that it is valid. Any reasoning by parallelism can be easily refuted by showing major differences between items of comparison. In this case, if one can simply show major differences between Judaism and Islam, the presupposition of IM advocates can be rejected and all the other subsequent reasoning will collapse.

Other biblical examples of validation include Jesus' ministry to the Samaritans in John 4, Naaman in 2 Kgs 5, and the so-called holy pagans, such as Melchizedek, sailors in the Book of Jonah, and Cornelius. Some IM advocates have tried to validate Muslim Insiders' practice of Islamic religious rituals by establishing a theology of religions from Acts 17.[8] After

---

5 Woodberry, "To the Muslim," 24.
6 Travis, "Messianic Muslim," 53.
7 Woodberry, "To the Muslim," 24.
8 Higgins and Lewis are the two representative advocates who deal with Acts 17

his exegesis of Acts 17, Higgins asserts that "God is at work in the world, including the religions of the world."[9] This notion has enormous implications for understanding Islam as a religion and for a missionary approach to Muslims. Other IM advocates have used various aspects of Paul's teachings to the Corinthian church (mainly from 1 Cor 8–11), which encountered complicated problems with idol worship and the practice of religious rituals.

In the process of evaluating IM advocates' biblical validation, two methods will be employed with these examples. First, each biblical case will be tested through an exegetical study. Second, the usage of biblical precedents as grounds for biblical validation will be tested. Finding a similar case in the Bible does not necessarily mean that one can make that case a normative principle for Christian life and ministry.[10] By providing their biblical validation for the IM, IM advocates have exposed their missiological thinking and presuppositions. These presuppositions and assertions have been hoisted onto the biblical text, and so make one wonder whether their biblical interpretations are exegetically sound. The following presentation evaluates their biblical interpretations on five key passages that they rely on to validate the IM.[11]

## AN EVALUATION OF BIBLICAL INTERPRETATIONS

### The Early Church (Acts 2–3)

IM advocates pay special attention to the early church context to find biblical precedents concerning the two key questions presented earlier. One, is it biblically permissible to maintain dual identity: "followers of Jesus" on the one hand and "Muslim" on the other?[12] Two, is it biblically permissible

---

to discuss theology of religions. Higgins, "Key to Insider Movements," 160–63; Higgins, "Inside What," 81–88; Lewis, "Insider Movements," 17.

9 Higgins, "Inside What," 86.

10 This involves a hermeneutical principle that will be discussed in the next chapter.

11 Five passages are merely a selective, not exhaustive, list due to the space limit. These passages, nevertheless, sufficiently reveal the essence of the biblical reasoning of IM advocates.

12 Most IM advocates intentionally avoid using the term "Christian," not only because it has a bad connotation in the minds of Muslims, but also because "Christian" in a traditional sense is not compatible with the term "Muslim." A new term, "Messianic Muslim follower of Jesus," however, is compatible because Muslim is taken to be a cultural term. Kraft, for example, contends, "Using the name of the cultural package [Muslim] to refer to the culture and Christianity to refer to the faith thus gives us combinations, such as 'Hindu Christianity,' 'Buddhist Christianity,' or 'Muslim Christianity.'" See Kraft, "Contextualization of Essential Christianity," 84.

to continue to practice former religious practices even after coming to the faith in Jesus? By focusing only on parallel features between the early Jewish Christians and Muslim Insiders, IM advocates contend that Muslim Insiders can likewise remain within their Islamic cultural and religious community by maintaining dual identity, Muslim followers of Jesus, and by participating in Islamic religious practices. An important biblical precedent for them is the early Jewish Christians who remained within the Jewish religious community by maintaining dual identity, Jewish religious and Christian identity, and who continued to observe the Jewish religious practices by participating in the temple worship, the temple prayer, and the Passover supper.[13]

IM advocates take Acts 2–3 as a primary biblical basis for examining the context of the early church. Not so many advocates, however, exegete the passage through their critical interactions with commentaries written by evangelical scholars. The only exception is Higgins who provides an exegetical study of Acts 2–3, and it is for this reason that his exegetical work is taken up here for critical evaluation.[14]

With the desire to discover "the models and dynamics of a healthy, vital movement to Jesus," Higgins identifies six "keys" to describe the dynamics of such a movement and contends that "every movement to Jesus is inside of a culture or some aspects of culture."[15] Most of these six "devoted's" correctly describe the main features of a healthy, dynamic movement to Jesus, and some of them still holds their contemporary relevance as well. Several exegetical problems, however, appear in his analysis of the biblical text.

Higgins takes "the breaking of bread" to refer to "early celebrations of the Lord's Supper" and "the prayers" to refer to "prayers in the Temple" respectively.[16] By taking note of the combined use of these two terms, he contends that the early church was "devoted to expressions of worship that included the Lord's Supper and Temple prayers."[17] He takes this combina-

---

13 Jameson and Scalevich, "First-Century Jews," 33–39.

14 Higgins, "Key to Insider Movements," 156–60.

15 Higgins connects "keys" to the Greek term *proskartereo* which means "devoted." Six contents of the devotedness include "prayer, the apostles' teaching and fellowship, the breaking of bread and the prayers, meeting in the Temple and house to house, the Word and prayer by leaders, and relational discipleship." Higgins, "Key to Insider Movements," 156–57.

16 Probably Higgins takes the Greek term *tais proseuchais*, which is plural with the definite article, to imply formal religious set prayers in Judaism although he does not explicitly mention it.

17 Higgins, "Key to Insider Movements," 158–59. Travis shares a similar conclusion: "The first-century Jews gathered regularly in the temple with non-Messianic Jews, and in homes with fellow Messianic Jews." See Travis, "Messianic Muslim," 59.

tion as an indication that "even as new community continued to embrace the temple prayers, it also added major new emphases and interpretations."[18] According to Higgins, the Lord's Supper is "the radically reinterpreted Passover supper that had been inaugurated by Jesus Himself."[19]

Consequently, he concludes, "Insider Movements, even as they continue to embrace old forms and expressions, also bring in radically new meanings and truths."[20] While emphasizing possible parallels between early Jewish believers in Acts 2–3 and Muslim Insiders, Higgins believes that it is biblically acceptable for Muslim Insiders to remain in the Islamic community and to continue to observe the Islamic religious practices either by reinterpreting or attaching new meanings to old forms.[21] The exegetical conclusions of Higgins on Acts 2:42 deserve a careful evaluation.

First, there is no definite evidence for the "breaking of bread" as a reference to "the Lord's Supper" in Acts 2:42. Rather, the reference is to a regular communal meal where the Lord's Table might have been a part of it.[22] Darrell Bock, for example, makes his case in favor of a communal meal based on the contextual consideration because Acts 2:42–47 emphasizes the newness and radicalness of new community of believers who are distinguishing themselves from the old Jewish religious tradition.[23] Bock concludes that Acts 2:42 primarily describes the practice of a regular communal church life rather than the formal temple rite. Higgins's specific claim that former religious rituals in Judaism are in view from Acts 2:42 seems fragile in view of this contextual evidence.

Moreover, by noting that the Greek term *tais proseuchais*, "the prayers," has the definite article in the plural form, Bock does not deny a possibility that it might have referred to set prayers used in Judaism, possibly tied to

---

18  Higgins, "Key to Insider Movements," 159.

19  Higgins, "Key to Insider Movements," 159.

20  Higgins, "Key to Insider Movements," 159. Concerning the religious forms of the early Christians, Travis says, "Just as early Jewish followers of Jesus changed few of their outward Jewish religious forms, so too C5 believers change little in their outward Muslim religious forms." Travis, "Messianic Muslim," 54–55.

21  Higgins summarizes the exegetical conclusion of Acts 2:42: "Proponents of Insider Movements, especially among Muslims, have pointed to possible parallel here. They have argued from this passage and others that a biblical precedent exists for new believers from Islam to remain in the mosque and continue to practice other religious expressions of Islamic life." See Higgins, "Key to Insider Movements," 158.

22  Bock, *Acts*, 150–51.

23  Bock concludes, "The setting here of the community functioning by itself apart from a temple rite suggests, however, that the reference to prayer is broad, although it may well have included such set features." Bock, *Acts*, 151.

temple worship.²⁴ However, the usage of the definite article provides a clue for understanding this verse. Daniel Wallace identifies the syntactical usage of this definite article as "well-known or celebrity article."²⁵ He explains the definite article in 2:42 as follows: "The article points out an object that is well known. . . . Either the pattern of worship was well known in the early church because it was the *common* manner in which it was done, or Luke was attempting to convey that each element of the worship was the only one deserving of the name (par excellence)."²⁶ Therefore, prayer has to be viewed as an integral part of the early church life in connection with the Apostles' teachings, the fellowship, and the breaking of bread. There is no indication of a particular type of set prayers in Judaism.

Therefore, it is far more likely that *tais proseuchais* (the prayers) is a general term for community prayer life in the early church.²⁷ Based upon these exegetical points, it is inaccurate to assert that early Jewish believers intentionally continued to observe former religious practices in order to remain within the socioreligious community of Judaism. On the contrary, the main emphasis of Acts 2–3 lies in the radical break, or discontinuity, rather than continuity between the old Judaism and the new faith in Christ with its radical lifestyle.

In his interpretation of Acts 2:46, Higgins interprets the fact that "every day they [early Jewish believers] continued to meet together in the temple courts" to mean "their participation in the worship in the Temple led by priests who did not follow Jesus."²⁸ He also takes "Peter's habit of going to the temple at set times for prayer" (Acts 3:1) to be an indication that the early church continued to participate in temple and synagogue worship with much devotion.²⁹ His claims, however, do not find exegetical support in Acts 2:46. There is no concrete indication that the disciples participated in temple worship and practiced Jewish rituals strictly within the traditions of Judaism as Higgins contends. Although it is true that the apostles went to

---

24 Bock explains the reasons why one may take it as set prayers although he does not hold this view. He states, "The use of set prayer on occasion is likely in light of the facts that (1) set prayers existed in Judaism, (2) a tie to the temple where set prayers were made is expressed in 2:46 and 3:1, and (3) the Lord taught the disciples such a fixed prayer (Luke 11:2–4)." Bock, *Acts*, 151.

25 Wallace, *Greek Grammar*, 225.

26 Wallace, *Greek Grammar*, 225 (emphasis in the original).

27 Bruce agrees with Bock on this point. See Bruce, *Acts of the Apostles*, 132.

28 Higgins, "Key to Insider Movements," 159.

29 Higgins, "Key to Insider Movements," 158. He brings the same reasoning to the IM context to imply that Muslim Insiders can participate in mosque worship with other Muslims even though Muslim leaders in mosque would teach something different from what Muslim Insiders believe.

the temple, their visit to the temple was not for their continued practice of the old rituals and religious practices of Judaism.

While Higgins's interpretation is rejected, one must ask why early Jewish believers continued to meet together in the temple courts. Peterson contends that the disciples went to the temple courts for various reasons: "to teach and encourage one another (Acts 2:46; 5:12) and to give public testimony to the gospel about Jesus."[30] He notes the significance of the temple gathering to be both practical and evangelistic. Practically the temple was a place for a large crowd gathering, and evangelistically the disciples wanted to take the Gospel to the center of Judaism.[31] Blomberg in the same line agrees that the disciples gathered in the temple courts because it was the only place for a large public gathering and an optimal site for witnessing and proclamation.[32] Therefore, it is far more reasonable to conclude that the disciples used the temple meetings for a practical reason as well as for an evangelistic purpose. There is no contextual evidence that supports the view that their primary motive was to remain within Judaism and to practice former religious rituals.

Concerning the association of early Jewish believers within Judaism, the relationship was indeed a historical reality, but not as IM advocates have perceived. First of all, it was only a temporary phenomenon in the unique historical setting of the birth of the early church. The transition from the old covenant to the new occurred in this unique historical period. Second, it took some time to make this transition and to make a complete break with Judaism because the early church had to work out their theological differences on practical matters under the new covenant by figuring out how these differences were to be expressed in relation to the old Jewish religious life. More importantly, the disciples believed that their task was to be a witness of Jesus before their fellow Jews. The temporary association of the early disciples with Judaism needs to be understood from this historical light.

The disciples preached Christ's death and resurrection in the temple courts and experienced oppositions and persecutions (Acts 4:3; 5:25–26), even while going to the temple. This was not compliance to Judaism, but a proclamation of Christ in spite of oppositions. Peterson notes, "Preaching about the centrality of the exalted Christ in God's plans for Israel suggested

---

30 Peterson, "Worship," 375. Peterson states that "meeting together in the temple courts (2:46) appears to have been for the express purpose of hearing the apostolic preaching (cf. 3:11–26; 5:21), although there were also opportunities in the home context." Peterson, "Worship," 390.

31 Peterson, "Worship," 375.

32 Blomberg, "Christian and the Law of Moses," 402. John B. Polhill expresses the same view in Polhill, *Acts*, 121.

that he was a replacement for the temple, the law and the whole structure of worship associated with it. Such a message inevitably led to the exclusion of Christians from the temple and in due course also from the synagogues."[33] The theological distinctiveness of the Gospel and the incompatible teachings of Jesus necessitated early Jewish believers to move away from the old religious life of Judaism. It is, therefore, the theologically incompatible nature of new faith in Christ that forced the early disciples to separate themselves from old Judaism. This aspect clearly contradicts the speculative assertion of Higgins.

Concerning the break of the disciples from Judaism, Higgins makes two points. First, it took possibly more than fifty years before early Jewish believers finally stopped participating in temple worship. Second, it occurred mainly because of persecution from outside, not because of theological incompatibility.[34] In response to Higgins's first point, it is a historical fact that the break occurred over time, but it is difficult to tell a precise date for this separation as he suggests.[35] In regards to his second point, the biblical evidence reveals that the major driving force behind the separation was essentially theological, although persecution played a role as a consequence of theological incompatibility. Stephen's speech to the Sanhedrin in Acts 7 indicates that there exists an insurmountable gulf between the old covenant and the new covenant. The Jewish religious leaders became agitated and began to persecute Christians after hearing his sermon. Although oppressions and persecutions by Jews played a role in the separation of Christians from Judaism, the essential driving force which induced persecution was the theological incompatibility of their new faith in Christ with Judaism.

There is a fundamental problem in the reasoning of IM advocates: the simplistic use of parallelism between early Jewish believers and Muslim Insiders behind their biblical validation. Higgins is aware of this danger and correctly points out the complicated issue of applying the model within Judaism to other religious contexts such as Islam or Hinduism.[36] While he takes into account the criticism that "Islam does not occupy the same posi-

---

33 Peterson, "Worship," 377.

34 Higgins, "Inside What," 77–79. Higgins implies that although Muslim Insiders may eventually break away from the Islamic community, it might take a long time as it was the case with the early Christians. A related implication is that Christian outsiders need to wait patiently until they make the decision while acknowledging them as believers in Christ.

35 Higgins' contention for more than fifty years seems to be rather exaggeration because Stephen's martyrdom in Acts 7 occurred early enough to initiate or even accelerate the separation of Christians from Judaism.

36 Higgins, "Key to Insider Movements," 158; Higgins, "Inside What," 79.

tion in salvation history as Judaism," he bypasses this problem by providing two more biblical examples—Naaman and the Samaritan woman.[37] In the end, he contends for the validity of using parallelism without providing any further exegetical or theological analysis: "So, while I would grant that Judaism is in fact a different case than, say, Islam, the parallel still holds."[38] In another article, he admits that the parallel is "at a practical level," which demises his case for the validity of the IM. Since this problem directly involves hermeneutics of the IM advocates, it will be taken into account in the hermeneutical perspective section in the next chapter.

The real problem in the use of parallelism between early disciples and Muslim Insiders is the unspoken presupposition by IM advocates. First, when they compare Judaism and Islam at a practical level, IM advocates subtly assume that Islam has valid expressions of God's revelation, though imperfect, like Judaism. Second, when they argue for the validity of remaining in the Islamic religious community by maintaining Muslim identity, they suddenly make an important assumption that Islam is a valid religion containing God's revelation as much as Judaism was part of God's revelation in biblical history.

The presupposition is that there exists a valid theological continuity between Christianity and Islam as much as the theological continuity between Judaism and Christianity. Redemptive history progressively develops throughout the Old Testament and the New Testament that Judaism has certain theological connections with Christianity. On the other hand, the continuity between Judaism and Islam cannot be said in the same manner. In order to make such parallelism, it is necessary to assume that Islam, at least partially, contains valid revelation of God which is consistent with the previous revelation in the Old and New Testament. This unspoken presupposition of IM advocates on how to view Islam has to be explicitly discussed within the framework of a theology of religions, which will be discussed in detail in chapter 5.

## The Jerusalem Council (Acts 15)

The Jerusalem Council in Acts 15 is one of the most quoted passages in the contextualization discussion because this incident occurred in a pivotal moment in the cross-cultural expansion of the Gospel into Gentile nations.

---

37  Higgins, "Key to Insider Movements," 158–59.

38  Higgins, "Key to Insider Movements," 59. By purposefully emphasizing the parallel features between early Jewish believers and Muslim Insiders, IM advocates portray the IM as a valid biblical model following its biblical precedent.

As the Gospel moved beyond the Jewish cultural milieu into the Gentiles, the early church encountered such an important contextualization question. Considering the significance of this incident in the book of Acts, Luke records the account in detail, including the major questions, the decision-making process, and the crucial decisions.[39]

Before considering how the Jerusalem Council is related to the contextualization debates, it is important to clarify what the biblical text says in the original historical context. The Jerusalem Council addresses a specific question on whether or not the Gentiles should observe the Law of Moses and be circumcised in order to be saved (Acts 15:1, 5). In view of contextualization, the question can be rephrased: Should the Gentiles become proselytes to be saved by leaving their cultural identity or can they maintain their cultural identity even after receiving the Gospel? Hesselgrave and Rommen identify the issue as "What part of the Jewish religious tradition was an integral, and therefore a supraculturally valid, part of the gospel?"[40] The Jerusalem Council determined the necessary essence of the Gospel which needed to remain intact as it spread to the Gentile nations.

The Jerusalem Council provides a two-fold conclusion in regards to contextualization. One, salvation only by faith in Jesus Christ, not by particular works of the law, is the biblical truth, which cannot be compromised in any circumstance. Two, when it comes to the matter of non-essentials in regards to salvation, believers can show grace to one another by allowing differences for the sake of unity.[41] It is, therefore, necessary to distinguish what is essential for salvation from what are non-essentials in contextualization. Since the Gospel does not demand cultural conversion of believers, missionaries are to proclaim it in culturally relevant ways without compromising the essence of the Gospel.

Higgins provides a detailed exegetical analysis of Acts 15 under three headings: question, process, and conclusion.[42] He translates the "foun-

---

39 Flemming divides the whole chapter into four parts: dissension (15:1–5), discussion (15:6–18), decision (15:19–29), and dissemination (15:30–35). See Flemming, *Contextualization in the New Testament*, 44–48. Higgins also provides three-component analysis of Acts 15—questions, process, and conclusions—in his article, Higgins, "Acts 15," 29–40.

40 Hesselgrave and Rommen, *Contextualization*, 10.

41 Bock, *Acts*, 508.

42 Higgins provides the most extensive and in-depth study of Acts 15 in his article, "Acts 15," 29–40. Most IM advocates simply note the parallel features between the Jerusalem Council and the IM, and conclude that the IM has a biblical precedent for its validation. That is not, however, a strong argument for the biblical validation of the IM. Woodberry, for example, provides seven criteria from the Jerusalem Council to apply to the IM, but he hardly deals with the text exegetically in his article, Woodberry, "To

dational, biblical, and theological issues" of the Jerusalem Council into a single question: "How are the Gentiles saved and what is the place of Torah (including but not limited to circumcision) in the new movement?"[43] He rightly recognizes that the main question in Acts 15 is soteriological. A problem appears, however, when he applies this original question of the Jerusalem Council directly into the IM context and changes the nature of the question:

> For now, let me state what questions I believe the Acts 15 Jerusalem Council would have asked had it been held to discuss insider movements among Muslims: What is necessary for a Muslim to be saved? What is necessary for unity between believers in a movement to Jesus among Muslims and believers from other backgrounds (for example, western Christian)?[44]

Later in the article, he rephrases the question: "*1) What is required of Muslims to be saved; and 2) Are Muslims in fact being saved in insider movements?*"[45] He answers the second question by saying, "Actually, I know of no critic of insider movements who questions whether Muslims are being saved—or can be saved—as 'insiders.'"[46] He asserts that both IM advocates and IM critics admit that Muslim Insiders are saved and are being saved.[47] For the first question, he draws a conclusion that since the cognitive beliefs of Gentile believers in the early church were minimal, "the 'measurement' of salvation is not the cognition-centered measurement so typical of modern western Christianity (articulated primarily in specific belief statements) but one of

---

the Muslim," 25–27.

43 Higgins, "Acts 15," 30.

44 Higgins, "Acts 15," 30.

45 Higgins, "Acts 15," 34 (emphasis in the original).

46 Higgins, "Acts 15," 34.

47 One crucial distinction is necessary on this matter. If what Higgins means by "Muslims" is the Muslim-background believers (MBBs), then it is probably a true statement that no critic questions the salvation of MBBs because they follow Jesus by leaving Islam. If, however, what Higgins refers to is Muslim Insiders maintaining Muslim identity by practicing Islamic religious practices, than many IM critics, if not all, will surely have deep concern about the spiritual status of Muslim Insiders and will not endorse Higgins' statement. Basically, this is the primary reason why IM critics are so critical about the IM and the assertions of IM advocates. Whether Muslim Insiders are saved or not is a quite complicated question, but one can certainly state that their faith stance surely does not stand upon the biblical teaching according to IM critics. It may be true that no critic has explicitly mentioned that Muslim Insiders are not or will not be saved. This, however, cannot be taken as evidence that no critic questions the salvation of Muslim Insiders. IM critics do express their serious concern when they argue against the IM because it betrays the biblical teachings in many ways.

lives transformed by the grace of God through Christ and the outpouring of the Holy Spirit."[48] He contends that life transformation of Muslim Insiders should be emphasized in determining their salvation more than cognitive knowledge of biblical truth.

Higgins asks a wrong set of questions when he applies an exegetical point of Acts 15 to the IM context. While the real question of Acts 15 was soteriological, one cannot simply change the wording by noting parallelism. For example, the simple question, "How can the Gentiles be saved?" is correct as long as the supplementary content is provided, such as "Should they observe the Jewish customs and be circumcised to be saved?" or "Should the Gentiles become proselytes before they are saved by faith in Christ?" The answers to the two supplemental questions are negative. Gentile believers need not observe the Jewish customs or the Jewish religious laws for salvation. If this is the main exegetical finding, the equivalent question when applied to the IM discussion should be such as "Should the MBBs leave their cultural identity in order to be saved?" "Should the MBBs convert to western or eastern cultural Christianity?" The reformulation of Higgins, "What is necessary for a Muslim to be saved?" is certainly not equivalent to the exegetical focus of Acts 15. Higgins casts a wrong set of questions by focusing on the seemingly parallel features between the Jerusalem Council and the IM in order to draw his predetermined conclusion.

Higgins contends that the process of the Jerusalem Council is applicable to contemporary missiological discussions. To a certain degree, the Jerusalem Council provides a pattern for the Christian church to emulate for contextualization discussions, such as a wider ecclesiological scope, a sufficient amount of time and energy for discussion and debate, a careful search for scriptural and theological foundation, and some field reports and experiences among nationals and missionaries. When the Christian church encounters a new missiological issue on contextualization, a wider body of the Christian church can follow such a pattern revealed in the Jerusalem Council.

This pattern, however, should be limited to an *application* of biblical principle that comes from the biblical text, and cannot be extended to determine or develop new biblical-theological principles due to new experiences or encounters in various human contexts. The Jerusalem Council was a unique biblical-theological problem encountered by the early church in the historical expansion of the Gospel among the Gentiles.[49] The conclusion,

---

48 Higgins, "Acts 15," 34.

49 Corwin, "Humble Appeal," 11. Corwin states, "The Jerusalem Council of Acts 15, and the story of Cornelius in Acts 10 for that matter, rather than providing a theological and practical template for us to follow by analogy when introducing the gospel into new

in terms of biblical theological principle, came from the careful exegesis of Scripture based upon scriptural authority, together with the apostolic authority in the unique historical context. The apostolic leadership was able to determine what God's will was in that specific circumstance along with scriptural guidelines about this question in light of the life and work of Jesus Christ. Since the apostolic authority in the interpretation of the Old Testament and of the experiences in the missionary journeys of the apostles is involved in the process, it is not possible for the contemporary church to claim the same authority to repeat the pattern in determining biblical-theological principles for new contextual problems.

A hermeneutical principle of biblical narratives in Scripture strengthens this conclusion. Gordon Fee and Douglas Stuart provide a well-reasoned guideline to interpret and apply biblical narratives and historical precedents in the book of Acts.[50] Several points of their work shed light on the present question whether the pattern of the Jerusalem Council can be repeated by a contemporary church.

> 1. It is probably never valid to use an *analogy* based on biblical precedent as giving biblical authority for present-day actions....
> 2. Although it may not have been the author's primary purpose, biblical narratives do have illustrative and, sometimes, "pattern" value.... But none of us has God's authority to reproduce the sort of exegesis and analogical analyses that the New Testament authors occasionally applied to the Old Testament. It should be noted especially in cases where the precedent justifies a present action, that *the precedent does not establish a norm for specific action*.... A warning is in order here. If one wishes to use a biblical precedent to justify some present action, one is on safer ground if the principle of the action is taught elsewhere, where it is the primary intent so to teach.[51]

---

contexts, should perhaps be understood only as a one-time seminal event marking the final stage in the early church coming to fully understand that the old covenant and its requirements were fulfilled in Christ and that the new covenant was for all people and peoples, Jews and Gentiles." IM advocates do not seem to understand Corwin's point about a hermeneutical principle. Brother Yusuf, for example, says, "Are you saying that we remove these two chapters from the Scripture, or just ignore them? I do not believe that these verses have been abrogated." Lewis also argues that the same decision-making process in the Jerusalem Council can be modeled for the contemporary church. She does not feel it necessary to explain what hermeneutical method is involved in the process. See Yusuf's and Lewis' responses in Corwin, "Humble Appeal," 11.

50 Fee and Stuart, *How to Read the Bible*, 78–112.
51 Fee and Stuart, *How to Read the Bible*, 110–11 (emphasis in the original).

The hermeneutical principles of Fee and Stuart lessen the possibility of admitting Higgins's claim for using the Jerusalem Council as a historical precedent of the IM. His interpretive method, analogy or parallelism, then is tenuous. The primary intent of Acts 15, however, cannot be used to define how Muslims or people of other religions can be saved, as Higgins wishes to assert, but to clarify the biblical teaching on the salvation of Gentiles in view of the relationship between the essence of the Gospel and human cultures. The Jerusalem Council does not provide a repeatable biblical principle by which the contemporary church can discuss new contextual issues and determine biblical-theological answers through new interpretation of the biblical text in Acts 15.

From the beginning of the IM debate, IM critics have expressed their concerns about the biblical and theological understandings of Muslim Insiders. Higgins addresses this concern by asking the following soteriological question: "What is required of Muslims to be saved?" Although Higgins points out that this question should be answered from a wider scope of biblical witness, he draws major points exclusively from Acts 15.[52] Recognizing that IM critics question the spiritual status of Muslim Insiders, Higgins contends that the cognitive aspects of faith and biblical teaching should not be the sole measurement of determining the salvation of Muslim Insiders, and that one should consider "the behavioral and affective dimensions of faith and conversion."[53] He also argues that "the actual amount of such cognitive understanding necessary for salvation is actually relatively small."[54] Brown agrees with Higgins when he formulates a soteriological question as follows: "What must one believe about Jesus for salvation?" He answers, "What is required is simply to put one's faith personally in Jesus as the Christ, the Messiah, meaning one's Lord and Savior. Saving faith, in both its propositional and relational aspects, is simply saying 'Yes' to Jesus."[55] They commonly contend that one places less emphasis on cognitive factor of biblical and theological contents, and more emphasis on the behavioral factor of transformed lives in the soteriological question.

One may accept Higgins's assertion that the cognitive dimension of Muslim Insiders needs not to be extensive in the initial stage because they can grow over time. The real problem lies in the fact that IM advocates hold

---

52 He says, "I am sure we would all agree, God is the one who saves by his own action (see Ephesians 2:1–10)." Higgins, "Acts 15," 34–35.

53 Higgins, "Acts 15," 34. Higgins seems to admit the fact that Muslim Insiders lack the cognitive understanding of the orthodox theological and doctrinal foundation of Christian faith.

54 Higgins, "Acts 15," 35.

55 Brown, "What Must One Believe," 20.

onto a "minimalist viewpoint" of salvation when they talk about the salvation of Muslim Insiders. Both Higgins and Brown emphasize a faith factor and undermine the contents of the saving faith in terms of the propositional truth of Christianity.[56] One must remember that this faith factor certainly includes biblical truth about the person and work of Jesus Christ within the larger framework of biblical theology. It is simple faith that leads one to salvation, but the contents of that faith should be emphasized as much as the faith factor itself.

Tennent makes a valid critique when he changes the focus of the question from the faith of an individual to the collective faith of a community of believers. He reformulates Brown's question into "What is the minimal core confession of the church regarding salvation?"[57] This question weaves the personal faith factor with faith content and soteriological perspective with ecclesiological perspective. In this way, one can have a more solid foundation to prevent individuals from falling into a subjective, arbitrary understanding of the Gospel and salvation.

A fundamental missionary approach to preaching the Gospel of salvation should be to teach the biblical truth of salvation in its entirety from the whole counsel of God's Word (Matt 28:19–20). It is neither IM advocates nor IM critics who can judge whether Muslim Insiders are saved or not based on the present condition of their faith in Christ and their life as Muslims. Only God knows everyone's heart and faith in Jesus. The responsibility of Christians, however, is to preach the apostolic teaching that has been transmitted throughout history (Jude 3) and the whole counsel of God's truth without any compromise, not reducing the truth of God into minimal requirements for salvation. If the approach of IM advocates to Muslim Insiders is to intentionally avoid some biblical truths that might cause conflicts, confusions, and confrontations, there is a danger of distorting the Gospel.[58]

Tennent is right in his critique of IM advocates' question on the minimal requirements for the Muslims Insiders to be saved.[59] He criticizes IM advocates for committing an error of theological reductionism when they

---

56 This is portrayed in Brown's statement: One's salvation is dependent on his "personal faith in Jesus as the Christ, the Messiah." Brown, "What Must One Believe," 20.

57 Tennent, "Followers of Jesus," 109–12.

58 This writer is contending that IM advocates employ this approach of using selective biblical truths that are theologically compatible with Muslim Insiders' theological understanding. Nevertheless, the minimalist arguments of IM advocates suggest that they avoid some biblical materials that might become stumbling blocks for Muslims even though they are foundational to the Christian faith. Examples include biblical materials related to the deity of Christ, the Son of God, and the Trinity.

59 Tennent, "Followers of Jesus," 109–12.

mistakenly identify the notion of salvation only with justification. Since Scripture teaches three dimensions of salvation (justification, sanctification, and glorification), equating salvation only with justification is simply an error of theological reductionism. After pointing out the most serious implication of this error is that "it gives rise [to] a general minimalist emphasis in this discussion,"[60] Tennent suggests that "the issue be reframed, by a broader, and more biblically informed understanding of the word 'salvation.'"[61] In view of the forgone discussion, the soteriological question of IM advocates is irrelevant to what Acts 15 addresses. Their conclusion in answering their own question is both theologically reductionistic and misleading. Acts 15 does not provide a biblical basis for the IM.

The second part of Higgins's exegetical conclusion involves the "four prohibitions" in Acts 15:19–21 and 15:29. Higgins rightly observes that these four items concern table fellowship between Gentile and Jewish believers, meaning "the unity of the church."[62] In his interpretation of these four items, Higgins makes detailed distinctions: "Blood and strangled meat relate to food (and table fellowship). Fornication, on the other hand, relates to the fundamental ethical issue of sexuality, and idolatry to a fundamental shift in allegiance and worldview."[63] While he takes the first two as cultural elements so that they become a matter of concession for the unity of the church, he takes the last two items to be non-cultural matters: "abstaining from fornication" as a moral requirement and "abstaining from idolatry" as a theological requirement.[64]

The implications of making these two items as ethical and theological issues is significant for the validation process of the IM because Higgins asserts, "We should emphasize here that nowhere in the Acts 15 passage was there any hint that keeping this requirement was an issue of salvation for the Gentiles."[65] Higgins reformulates the question once again by incorporating a newfound implication: "What are the essentials for unity, including ethi-

---

60 Tennent, "Followers of Jesus," 110. When the question is formulated in such a manner as "what is the absolute bottom-line minimum an individual needs to know in order to be justified?" Tennent acknowledges that the answer is "very, very little, indeed." This way of formulating a question, however, is completely misleading in his view.

61 Tennent, "Followers of Jesus," 110.

62 Higgins, "Acts 15," 30.

63 Higgins, "Acts 15," 30.

64 Higgins contends that "two of the four 'necessary things' can appropriately be called 'concessions' while the remaining two are issues of ethics and theology." Higgins, "Acts 15," 32.

65 Higgins, "Acts 15," 32.

cal/theological 'minimums' and cultural concession?"⁶⁶ The main question becomes the theological minimum that is required of Muslim Insiders for the unity of the church. He concludes that the essential minimum theological requirement is not an issue of salvation, but an issue of unity of the church.

He further contends that even this theological requirement should be minimal, which he refers to as "salvation starting points," because "the Holy Spirit takes believers through a long-term process where they develop a biblical theology in their own specific cultural context."⁶⁷ While making the theological differences of Muslim Insiders from the historic, orthodox theology a matter of the unity of the church rather than an issue of salvation, Higgins contends that Muslim Insiders should be admitted into the body of Christ by other Christians because they believe in Jesus as the Christ and the Lord. He also contends that the theological compliance of Muslim Insiders to the orthodox theological stance must be kept minimal as long as they are under the guidance of the Holy Spirit.

In response to Higgins's exegetical argument, the first objection involves the validity of his distinction on the four items in Acts 15:20. One questions whether Higgins is right in categorizing the four items into three: cultural, ethical, and theological. Scholars have approached the four prohibitions by asking three related questions: the sources, the nature, and the purpose of the prohibitions.⁶⁸ The most directly related questions in regards to Higgins's conclusions are the nature and the purpose of the prohibitions. Concerning the nature of the prohibition, Charles H. Savelle concludes that "the societal or cultic views seem to present the most likely options" among three major views (the ethical, the societal, and the cultic view).⁶⁹ The societal view sees the prohibitions as necessary conditions from the perspective of Jew-Gentile relations. The prohibitions deal with ritual practices of Gentiles. Richard Longenecker, who holds a societal view, contends:

> They [the prohibitions] should be viewed not as dealing with the principal issue of the council but as meeting certain practical concerns; *not as being primarily theological but more sociological in nature*; not as divine ordinances for acceptance before God but as concessions to the scruples of others for the sake of

---

66 Higgins, "Acts 15," 35.

67 Higgins, "Acts 15," 36. Higgins also contends that Muslim Insiders are ultimately the decision-makers under the guidance of the Holy Spirit concerning the theological requirement. Higgins, "Acts 15," 37.

68 Savelle, "Reexamination," 449–68.

69 Savelle, "Reexamination," 463–64.

> harmony within the church and the continuance of the Jewish Christian mission.[70]

The cultic view, on the other hand, takes the prohibitions to be associated with pagan religious practices, as Ben Witherington finds its evidence from, "the choking of the sacrifice, strangling it, and drinking or tasting of blood transpired in pagan temples."[71] In this view, even sexual immorality is taken to refer to temple prostitution, not a simple ethical code.[72] Gentile believers were required to avoid ritual participation so that they do not put a hindrance for the Jews to enjoy fellowship with them.

Considering these two views that are not mutually exclusive, the essential nature of these prohibitions has to do with ritual or religious practices among Gentiles that can hinder fellowship between Gentile and Jewish believers. Higgins's categorization of four prohibitions into cultural, ethical, and theological requirements is unlikely after reviewing different views of representative biblical scholars. The way Higgins brings about a notion of "minimum theological requirement" starts with a misreading of the biblical text in Acts 15:20 because the Greek text says, "abstain from things contaminated by idols," and does not say, "abstain from idolatry."[73] Higgins translates the Greek term as "food sacrificed to idols" and extends this "beyond table fellowship to concerns about actual idolatry."[74] This misreading of the text and the imposition of his predetermined conclusion lead him to a misguided result. The attempt to make theological requirements as an issue of unity of the church, not as part of an issue of salvation, is simply unconvincing. Savelle's exegetical conclusions on the four prohibitions are helpful:

> All four were associated to some degree with pagan religious practices. Since this association was highly offensive to Jews, Gentile believers were asked to avoid even the appearance of evil by avoiding such practices altogether. Thus the purpose of the decree and its prohibitions were to promote unity among believing Jews and believing Gentiles.[75]

---

70 Longenecker, "Acts," 448 (emphasis added).

71 Witherington, *Acts of the Apostles*, 464.

72 Savelle, "Reexamination," 464.

73 Higgins, "Acts 15," 32. Out of the major English translations, only NIV mentions "food polluted by idols" while all the other translations take the Greek word, *alisgēmatōn tōn eidōlōn*, as "things contaminated by idols" (NASB) or "things polluted by idols" (NRSV).

74 Higgins, "Acts 15," 30.

75 Savelle, "Reexamination," 468.

Larkin also draws a biblical lesson for contextualization from this passage in the following words:

> James' proposal, then, teaches us three things about life together in a culturally diverse church. We must say no to any form of cultural imperialism that demands others' conformity to our cultural standards before we will accept them and their spiritual experience. We must say yes to mutual respect for our differences. And we must live out that respect even to the extent of using our freedom to forgo what is permissible in other circumstances.[76]

In summary, IM advocates have not succeeded in proving that Acts 15 provides biblical evidence for the IM. In fact, the Jerusalem Council in Acts 15 provides a biblical basis for C4 contextualization, not C5 or the IM. In using Acts 15 as a biblical basis for the IM, IM advocates must prove two main points that distinguish the IM (C5) from C4: the validity of maintaining Muslim religious identity on the part of Muslim Insiders, and the validity of practicing Islamic religious rituals even after becoming believers in Christ. Higgins has not succeeded in proving the two main points while other IM advocates have not even attempted to do so exegetically.[77]

---

76 Larkin, *Acts*, 225.

77 Some notable hermeneutical features of IM advocates in Acts 15 include heavy reliance on simple parallelism or analogy, placing wrong questions and drawing wrong conclusions, or too hasty conclusions in favor of the IM. IM advocates need to pay more attention to exegetical works utilizing a consistent biblical hermeneutical method. Rebecca Lewis asks a question, "Does one have to go through Christianity to enter God's family? Do all believers in Jesus Christ have to go through Judaism in order to enter God's family?" Asking these questions is misleading because Acts 15 is not intended to talk about "going through Judaism or Christianity," but to answer the question about the prerequisite of salvation for Gentile believers and the essentials for fellowship between Jewish and Gentile believers. Although her questions sound related to the text, they are misrepresenting the authorial intent of the text. See Lewis, "Insider Movements," 17. One surprisingly faulty statement on the four prohibitions comes from Brian Petersen: "These four prohibitions all have to do with their sanctification. Although they were free in Christ to continue living as salt and light within the context of their birth communities and did not therefore have to transfer into the Jewish socioreligious community, yet these Roman and Greek believers needed to make sure that their influence was backed by authentic godly living." See Petersen, "Possibility of a Hindu Christ-Follower," 90. Petersen's conclusion is doubtful because the prohibitions are to be viewed within the unity theme, not sanctification. Although Petersen quotes Witherington and other biblical scholars, he simply misrepresents the respective views.

## Paul at Athens (Acts 17)

Paul's evangelistic approach at Athens in Acts 17 has been an arena for contextualization debates, and IM advocates utilize it for the IM within the framework of a biblical theology of religions and culture. Higgins provides an extensive exegetical treatment of this passage and reveals his view.[78] Higgins's exegetical argument of Acts 17 with respect to the IM can be summarized by two assertions. First, he asserts that Paul not only affirms the religiosity of Athenians, but also "sees the altar to an unknown god as preparation for what he will say about the gospel."[79] He goes on to state:

> A Jewish monotheist (Paul) is using a pagan altar as a sign that the people he addresses are religious and that they have in fact been worshipping the true God without knowing it. This is not the same thing as saying that this "anonymous worship" is salvific. I am not arguing that, nor do I believe it. But Paul *is* assuming they have been worshipping the true God without knowing Him.[80]

Higgins is mistaken at several points. One, it is not so definite that Paul was positively affirming the religious tendency of the Athenians when he says "you are religious in all aspects" (Acts 17:22). The Greek word, *deisidaimonesterous*, which is a "comparative adjective being used as a superlative," is difficult to translate because it can be rendered in two ways: positive or negative.[81] While this term may refer to a "sincere pursuit of a divine transcendent being (whether a true pursuit or not)" in a positive sense, it may refer to "an embracing of superstition" in a negative sense.[82] It may be reasonable to assume that Paul uses the term in a positive sense to recognize their religious devotion to an unknown god since this is the beginning of his speech.[83] As he starts his speech, Paul simply wants to draw attention from his audience by recognizing their religious zeal for their gods. Paul's recognition of the religious pursuit undertaken by the Athenians, however, cannot be taken to mean that "Paul is assuming the Athenians were worshiping the true God" as Higgins asserts. Paul's dissatisfaction due to the idol-worshiping condition of the city (Acts 17:16) indicates that he is

---

78 Higgins, "Key to Insider Movements," 160–64.
79 Higgins, "Key to Insider Movements," 161.
80 Higgins, "Key to Insider Movements," (emphasis in the original).
81 Wallace, *Greek Grammar*, 133.
82 BDAG 216.
83 Bock, *Acts*, 564; BDAG 173.

not commending the Athenians for their true worship of God in their idol worship.[84]

Two, Higgins's assertion that Paul is equating the god worshiped by the Athenians with the God he preaches cannot be supported if the whole passage of Acts 17 is examined. In the latter part of his speech, Paul becomes confrontational by challenging his audience to repent in view of God's future judgment (17:30–31).[85] Paul points out the ignorance and the inability of mankind in spite of devout religious pursuit (17:30–31). Moreover, in other biblical passages on this issue, such as Rom 1–3, Paul rejects such a notion because he critically mentions the inability of fallen humanity in pursuing and knowing God (Rom 3:10–18). Higgins's assertion that Paul equates an unknown god of the Athenians with the God of Paul's Gospel is not supported exegetically.

On the basis of the two preceding points, Higgins's notion of *preparation* in dealing with "an altar to an unknown god" is to be rejected. This is referred to as a fulfillment theory in theology of religions. While the critique of this theory is beyond the scope of this study, it is noteworthy to observe that Higgins uses two pairs of parallelism for supporting his notion of preparation: that between Old Testament types and prophecies and their fulfillment in Christ and that between pagan religious and cultural elements and their complete fulfillments in Christ. This theory stands upon a great amount of assumption, such as the presence of God's revelation in other religions and the continuity between biblical revelation and other religions. Higgins's assertion of this theory cannot stand because all these assumptions are too difficult to prove on the basis of the biblical data in Acts 17.

The other assertion of Higgins from Acts 17 is that Paul's use of the pagan altar and the poets provides valid grounds for missionaries to use both cultural and religious elements of other religions in contemporary evangelism.[86] This conclusion comes from various exegetical points he makes from Acts 17. Higgins takes Paul's mention of the inscription at the altar in Acts 17:23 to be a positive affirmation of their religious worship of God. He contends that Paul only needed to better inform the Athenians with the true knowledge of God through Jesus. Moreover, Higgins takes Paul's quotation of pagan poets in Acts 17:28 to be another evidence for the validity of using other religious sources as long as they support biblical truths. He further elaborates his view on theology of religions based upon Acts 15:26–27:

---

84  Carson, *Gagging of God*, 498.
85  Bock, *Acts*, 565.
86  Higgins, "Key to Insider Movements," 161–62.

In these verses Paul argues that God has created every nation, every culture, "*pan ethnos*." And not only did He create them, He also determined the *era* of history in which they would live and the geographical *area* they would inhabit. This is very careful, sovereign planning on God's part, and encompasses, again, every nation and people. But there is a purpose for this careful planning and design; verse 27 makes this very clear. The purpose is so that they (the nations) should "seek God," "feel after Him," and indeed "find Him," although in fact "He is not far from us." . . . Paul's use of the altar and the poets is very logical outworking of his worldview, which can be summarized in this way: The true God has designed the cultures, seasons, and locations of the nations to further the process by which all peoples might seek after and actually find Him.[87]

According to this description, Higgins makes an error that seriously weakens his assertion. While Acts 17:26 apparently describes God's sovereignty over all nations in terms of the divine care and providence for his creation, the purpose statement in Acts 17:27 does not support Higgins's conclusion of "actually finding God." Paul is simply referring to general revelation through which "people *would* seek God." That means, Paul does not affirm cultures and religions as the product of God's design and does not approve them as a valid process for finding God. This point is clearly revealed in the use of two optative verbs, *psēlaphēseian* (feel, touch, handle, grope) and *heuroien* (find, discover), which express only a possibility of groping or finding God.[88] It neither describes actual seeking for God nor actual finding of God through cultures and religions. In contrast to Higgins's positive view of religions as a valid foundation for seeking God, Hesselgrave contends that "it is wrong to assume that the search for God is common" among men because "that idea is in stark contrast to biblical teachings, which indicate that it is God who searches and God who draws men and women to himself."[89] Therefore, one may say that Higgins's arguments from

---

87 Higgins, "Key to Insider Movements," 161 (emphasis in the original).

88 For the syntactical significance of the optative verb, see Wallace, *Greek Grammar*, 483–84 and 699–701. The optative is used to denote "a possible condition in the future, usually a remote possibility (such as *if he could do something, if perhaps this should occur*)." For the lexical meanings of these two verbs, see BDAG 412 and 1097–98. Both Bock and Witherington agree on this point. Bock, *Acts*, 566; Witherington, *Acts of the Apostles*, 528. BDAG translates verse 27, "If perhaps (in the hope that) they might grope for him and find him."

89 Hesselgrave, *Paradigms in Conflict*, 102. Larkin contends that human religious response is only "blind ignorance and foolish rebellion" because sin's intervention produced this serious condition of men. Larkin, "Contribution of the Gospels," 82.

Acts 17 contradict the overarching biblical principle of the total depravity of mankind in knowing God.

Higgins's understanding of Acts 17 is dangerous both theologically and missiologically. Higgins acknowledges the influence of human depravity in the formation of cultures and religions when he contends that not all of paganism can be acceptable and that some areas of paganism should be transformed by biblical truth. Higgins, however, does not clearly state how to understand God's sovereignty over every culture and religion. He does not provide a guideline for differentiating what is acceptable from what is not while he holds such a high view of cultures and other religions based upon his emphasis on God's sovereignty and Lordship among the nations.[90] Higgins's contention for God's sovereignty is too ambiguous that it can lead to a dangerously positive outlook on and affirmation for other cultures and religions.

The problem becomes even more evident when Higgins applies his conclusion to the IM context. Higgins argues that one should be able to "freely use religious and secular aspects of the culture to communicate biblical truth."[91] Since "God's own hand was involved in making that altar," as was the case with Athenians for the purpose of making them find God, Higgins contends that missionaries among Muslims should endeavor to find the Islamic equivalents of "altars to an unknown god" and "poets," such as the Qur'an, the Hadith, worship in the mosque, and in the Haji itself.[92] Higgins refers to them as "God's design" and "the fingerprints of God."

The other application of his conclusion is the validity of reinterpreting other religious sources by the hermeneutical key of Christ. Higgins takes Paul's use of pagan sources to suggest that such sources can and should be reinterpreted from a Christological perspective by new believers. For example, he contends that it is valid to reinterpret the Qur'an through the hermeneutical key of Christ as the apostles did it in their reinterpretation of the Old Testament.[93] Higgins's claim surely demands further biblical evidence, and it is beyond what can be supported by his conclusion from Acts 17.

Rebecca Lewis is another IM advocate who draws an erroneous exegetical conclusion from Acts 17:26. She argues for the validity of retaining the previous socioreligious identity of Muslim Insiders because she simply takes God's sovereign rule over the nations in Acts 17:26 as a normative

---

90 Higgins, "Key to Insider Movements," 161–62.
91 Higgins, "Key to Insider Movements," 162.
92 Higgins, "Key to Insider Movements," 162.
93 Higgins, "Key to Insider Movements," 162–63. He suggests that one should "read the Qur'an with Christ" to draw "many discoveries of altars and poets."

rule, not as a descriptive fact.[94] Lewis states, "The Scriptures seem to indicate that this identity, and the community a person is born into, were [sic] determined in advance by God."[95] If Lewis refers to the cultural and ethnic identity of believers, one might admit that they do not need to leave their cultural-ethnic identity to follow Christ. Yet, Lewis expands the identity as a socioreligious one for a pragmatic reason: "In many countries, it is almost impossible for a new follower of Christ to remain in vital relationship with their community without also retaining their socioreligious identity."[96] When Lewis refers to retaining the religious identity of converts, she cannot use Acts 17 as a biblical basis because the text does not say anything about maintaining one's religious identity.

IM advocates incorrectly use this passage of Acts 17 in an attempt to validate the IM. Higgins asserts that Muslims can be in a relationship with the true God while retaining their Muslim identity.[97] While the claim of IM advocates on retaining religious identity should be evaluated in a larger biblical and theological context, it must be said that Acts 17 does not provide valid biblical support for the claim that retaining religious identity, even after believing in Christ, is acceptable.

## The Assyrian Naaman (2 Kgs 5)

Several IM advocates use the narrative of Naaman and Elisha in 2 Kgs 5 for the validation of the IM. Higgins, for example, considers it as a "possible biblical precedent of Insider Movement" and uses Naaman as an example

---

94 It is unfortunate for her to use the NIV translation for this verse because it might have caused her to reach this faulty conclusion. It reads, "He [God] determined the times set for them and the exact places where they should live." There seems to be a normative sense by the verb "should." One cannot draw a normative rule from this verse simply because the Greek text only uses a phrase without a verb. This can be clearly seen in NASB or other translation: "determined their appointed times and the boundaries of their habitation (NASB)." God's sovereign rule over the nations should be understood as a descriptive fact rather than a normative rule in the sense that each nation should remain wherever they are allocated. The problem lies in that she draws such a theologically loaded claim only by relying on a single verse with an imprecise English translation.

95 Lewis, "Insider Movements," 17.

96 Lewis, "Insider Movements," 17.

97 Higgins contends, "Acts 17 describes God's sovereign design of the times and places in which humans are born. The intention of God behind this is that men and women would seek after Him and actually find Him (see 17:27). This implies that people in other religions can be in relationship to the true God." Also see Higgins, "Inside What?" 86.

of a true believer in God who remained inside his former religious community.[98] Before examining the interpretations of IM advocates, it might be helpful to point out the central theme of this narrative. After God's healing, Naaman is genuinely converted to a worshiper of Yahweh. This is evident because he clearly expresses an exclusive worship and loyalty to Yahweh in 2 Kgs 5:15–17. Upon his return to Assyria, Naaman asks for two things: "two mules' load of earth" and "Yahweh's forgiveness for his bowing down in the house of Rimmon" during his public duty (2 Kgs 5:17–18). In response to his request, Elisha simply says to him, "Go in peace" (2 Kgs 5:19).

Higgins takes Naaman's first request as an indication that Naaman still has "a territorial understanding of the gods" and interprets it as the evidence that it takes a long process to experience worldview changes even after conversion.[99] Higgins recognizes that the general tone of this narrative portrays Naaman in a positive light on the basis of his declaration of Yahweh being the only true God (5:15) and his determination not to offer burnt offerings nor sacrifice to other gods (5:17). Although scholars have differing views on the nature of the first, "two mules' load of earth," request, most agree that his request was connected to his worship of Yahweh.[100] Concerning the second request, Higgins interprets Naaman's request as asking for permission to remain within his former religious community and to participate in former religious practices while worshiping the true God Yahweh in his heart.[101] A controversial discussion involves Elisha's response, "Go in peace!" Higgins takes this response as Elisha's approval, and contends this as the biblical evidence of "a follower of another religion who becomes a believer in the true God and yet continues to worship the true God within the religious life and practices of his prior religion."[102] He also contends that Elisha's saying means "the clear blessing of the prophet upon this practice" more than a simple permission.[103]

Higgins's conclusion moves beyond what the text actually says. First of all, it is clearly wrong to claim that Elisha announced blessing on this "insider" practice. "Go in peace" should be taken not as a blessing, but as a simple permission at best. Considering Naaman's exclusive worship and loyalty to

---

98  Higgins, "Key to Insider Movements," 158.

99  Higgins, "Key to Insider Movements," 158. There are some scholars who support Higgins' view of "territorial understanding." See Keil and Delitzsch, *Commentary*, 226; Hobbs, *2 Kings*, 66. For a brief overview of various scholarly view on the passage, see Baeq, "Contextualizing Religious Form," 197–207.

100  Provan, *1 and 2 Kings*, 193; Cohn et al., *2 Kings*, 39.

101  Higgins, "Key to Insider Movements," 158.

102  Higgins, "Key to Insider Movements," 158.

103  Higgins, "Key to Insider Movements," 158.

Yahweh as God is an overriding theme in this narrative, it makes little sense that he would desire to remain within his previous religious community and voluntarily participate in Rimmon worship. When Naaman asks this request, he uses the same sentence twice in verse 18: "In this matter may the LORD pardon your servant." This reveals that Naaman feels guilty even when he thinks of the future act of bowing down in the house of Rimmon. Naaman does not consider remaining in the Rimmon worshiping community nor participating in the Rimmon worship as a positive matter.[104]

Naaman explains to Elisha the reason why he has to go to the house of Rimmon and bow. It is due to his official service as a public man, who serves under his master. Naaman's motivation was completely different from the way IM advocates, such as Higgins or Travis, contend for the verse to be understood.[105] While many different motivations might be involved in the mosque attendance for Muslim Insiders, Naaman's attendance to the Rimmon temple is completely different in nature.[106] Naaman does not desire to participate in the Rimmon worship, which is understood from his asking for forgiveness twice in verse 18. In contrast, most Muslim Insiders desire to attend mosque worship for their personal reasons, which may include being evangelistic, belonging to the Muslim community, and worshiping the true God in the mosque.

Daniel Baeq identifies "social pressure" as a common factor between the two cases, Naaman's attendance in the Rimmon worship and Muslim Insiders' attendance in the mosque.[107] His argument is not convincing, however, because Naaman was under public duty, not under a social pressure. Naaman could refuse to attend the Rimmon worship by personal choice in encountering social pressure because he was determined not to worship

---

104 According to Mordechai Cogan and Hayim Tadmor, the repetition of "in this matter" and "I bow myself" in Naaman's speech in v. 18 may reveal that he is so hesitant in making these two requests. This indicates the uneasiness of Naaman for his future potential to be under religious obligations in the Rimmon temple as is required from his public duty. Elisha's seemingly embarrassing permission can be read from this nuanced perspective. See Cogan and Tadmor, *II Kings*, 65. Baeq does not consider this important exegetical clue in his evaluation of the text in Baeq, "Contextualizing Religious Form," 201–5.

105 Travis, for example, uses this case as a basis of the mosque attendance by Muslim Insiders in Travis, "Messianic Muslim," 55.

106 Possible reasons for mosque attendance on the part of Muslim Insiders may range from being negative (fear of being isolated, pressure from the Muslim community, etc.) to being positive (evangelistic motivation). The crucial difference is that Muslim Insiders make their decisions in attending mosque themselves while Naaman cannot make this decision for himself. Muslim Insiders cannot say that they attend the mosque worship because of the public duty.

107 Baeq, "Contextualizing Religious Form," 204.

other gods than Yahweh. It was not social pressure, but his public service to his master, which forced him to be present in the Rimmon temple. The mosque attendance of Muslim Insiders, therefore, cannot be an equivalent case of the Naaman narrative. A more equivalent example of Naaman's case may be a convert who is asked to take his elderly parent to the mosque out of his respect for him.[108]

Another way to explain Elisha's permissive reply is to understand his reply to Naaman with respect to his *two* requests, not to the second one alone. When Naaman's two requests are combined together, one can sense his genuine exclusive loyalty to Yahweh. In this light, Elisha gives a positive affirmation to Naaman.[109] In view of Naaman's faithful loyalty to Yahweh, Elisha simply says "go in peace." This is better taken as a simple passive permission than a "religious accomodationism."[110] Higgins's assertion to make Elisha's positive response an active blessing for Naaman's "remaining inside" the Rimmon worship community is unlikely on these exegetical considerations.

One last exegetical point is to understand the author's intent within a larger context. The author of 2 Kings makes a striking contrast between the unbelieving Israelite community and an exceptionally faithful gentile figure, Naaman, who shows enormous loyalty to Yahweh worship in spite of his unwanted personal situation.[111] This positive view on Naaman may reflect the positive reply of Elisha in this narrative. Moreover, if one considers the larger context of the biblical history, Elisha's reply to Naaman is to be taken as an exception rather than as a norm, because an overriding biblical teaching emphasizes an exclusive worship of Yahweh and a prohibition of idol worship.[112] The biblical narrative of Naaman does not provide a biblical basis for a Muslim Insider to remain inside the Islamic community by participating in Islamic religious practices.

---

108 Tennent, "Followers of Jesus," 108; Dixon, "Moving On," 11.

109 Cogan and Tadmor, *II Kings*, 65.

110 Paul House emphasizes that Elisha understands the realities Naaman has as a public man in pagan society and "lays no more guilt on Naaman." House, *1, 2 Kings*, 274.

111 Kaiser, "Holy Pagans," 136–38.

112 Rommen and Netland, *Christianity and the Religions*, 3–140. Several scholars provide a collection of essays on evangelical biblical theology of religions that emphasize the exclusive worship of God throughout the Bible. Hesselgrave provides a convincing argument for exclusivism in *Paradigms in Conflict*, 53–80.

## Paul's Teachings to the Corinthian Church (1 Cor 7–10)

Several passages of 1 Cor 7–10 have become the reason for contextualization debates among missiologists, and several IM advocates attempt to find biblical validation for the IM in these passages. Since Paul's letter to the Corinthian church deals with various contextual issues in the first century, it is right to look for important biblical principles of contextualization for contemporary missiological issues in these passages. This section deals with the three most quoted passages by IM advocates and seeks to evaluate their interpretations.

### Remain in That Condition He Was Called (1 Cor 7:17–24)

The key notion of this passage, which is repeated three times, is that "each believer must remain in the condition in which he was called" (7:17, 20, and 24). In 1976, John Anderson used this passage to assert an unconventional idea by saying that "the converted Muslim should reach his fellow-Muslims by not repudiating the 'state in which he was called.'"[113] He surely wants to see the transformation from within the Islamic community as converts live out their new faith among Muslims. Anderson, however, neither goes further to explain how this biblical text supports his assertion nor prescribes how new converts from Islam can live within the Islamic community.

IM advocates, while sharing the same idea with John Anderson, assert that this passage does provide biblical validation for Muslim Insiders to remain within the Islamic community, which is the condition in which they were called. Joshua Massey provides the most extensive explanation of this passage for the validity of Muslim Insiders' maintaining their Muslim identity.[114] Massey borrows Paul's statement in a literal way and applies it to the IM context. He does this especially when he extends Paul's key statement without considering the original historical context of the passage. Massey makes the "condition" include the issue of religious identity in contending, "Now that the church is predominantly Gentile and not Jewish, the corollary remains true: most Muslim believers should also, by default,

---

113 Anderson, "Approach to Islam," 195–96.

114 Massey, "Misunderstanding C5," 12–13. Among IM advocates, this writer finds Massey most disturbing in his biblical arguments. For example, Massey makes problematic arguments based upon the interpretation of the Messianic Jewish scholar on this passage. He contends that Paul does not forbid the Gentiles from being circumcised and that circumcision can be promoted among Muslims. See Massey, "Living Like Jesus," 60–62.

contentedly *remain in the state they were in when called*, i.e., as Muslims who now follow Jesus as Lord."[115] This faulty application results from a misguided exegesis because he disregards the meaning of the text in the original historical context.

Other IM advocates follow the same line of reasoning. While describing the characteristics of the IM, John Ridgway includes religious identity as part of the conditions by stating, "Understanding our physical identity as being related to our first birth, when we were assigned (1 Cor 7:17) a place and time in history (Acts 17:26) that determines our cultural, social, and religious identity."[116] Without an exegetical explanation, Ridgway simply quotes the reference and contends for the validity of including religious identity in the interpretation of this verse.

Lewis, dealing with the same passage, slightly changes the focus into a matter of religious culture or religious expressions of faith.[117] She contends that "the crux of Paul's argument is actually that no one should consider one religious form of faith in Christ to be superior to another."[118] Lewis, therefore, takes "remain in the condition" to mean that "no religious conversion" is required in following Christ. She plainly states the point: "All of the Apostles later came to a unity of understanding that it was not necessary for Gentiles to convert to the Jewish religion. Further, it was preferable that they do not convert, but remain as they were when God called them (1 Cor 7:17–24)."[119] By implication, Muslim Insiders can follow Christ while remaining within Islam in order to become living witnesses to other Muslims.

The best way to evaluate the interpretations of these IM advocates is to review the exegetical meaning of the text by considering the original contexts, both historical-grammatical and literary. First, Gordon Fee provides a useful clue to understanding the passage in hand by emphasizing the structural flow of the entire chapter. While the passage in view (7:17–24) may seem strange because "neither of the specifics of that section (circumcision and slavery) is related to the subject matter of chap. 7" (i.e., marriage and related matters), Fee contends that this passage (7:17–24) provides Paul's answer to the questions addressed both in the preceding section (7:1–16) and in the following section (7:25–38).[120] The answer to these two categories

---

115  Massey, "Misunderstanding C5," 13 (emphasis in the original).

116. Ridgway, "Insider Movements," 85.

117  Lewis, "Integrity of the Gospel," 45–46.

118  Lewis, "Integrity of the Gospel," 46. She contends that this point was so crucial that Paul made it as a rule for all churches (1 Cor 7:17).

119  Lewis, "Promoting Movements," 76.

120  Fee, *First Epistle*, 268–69. He provides the question of two sections: "vv. 1–16 deal basically with those who are already married, or who have formerly been married

of people, the married (7:1–16) and the unmarried (7:25–38), is the same: "remain in the condition when they were called."

Paul's main concern in this chapter is marriage and the related issues. When he says "remain in that condition in which you were called," he is specifically addressing the status of celibacy, marriage, or mixed marriages. In order to explain this principle with a supportive theological reason, Paul adds two additional illustrations in 7:17–24: circumcision and slavery. The unchanging thread in all three cases is that no matter what conditions they were living in, they could still accomplish God's calling. They did not have to try to change the social and civil condition in order to fulfill God's calling in their lives. David E. Garland's summary of the exegetical conclusion is helpful:

> This reiterated principle provides the theological underpinning guiding his counsel on the practical matters of marriage and celibacy. To alter one's status in life on religious ground gives more importance to that worldly status than it merits and denies God's calling in Christ based on grace alone. The offer of salvation came to them without requiring them to alter their ethnic, social, or, domestic status.[121]

The fundamental problem in the interpretations of IM advocates appears when they include religious identity as part of the conditions. Since Muslim Insiders are called while being Muslims, IM advocates assert that they should remain Muslims and not leave Islam. When one considers the original contextual meaning of the text, however, this claim cannot be accepted, because this condition Paul addresses does not refer to religious identity, but the civil and social statuses.[122] The contention of IM advocates is to be rejected on this exegetical ground.[123]

---

but whose marriage have been dissolved by death; whereas vv. 25–38 speaks to a special group who have yet to be married, to which is added a final word to married women, who are to remain as they are until their husbands' death." David E. Garland reaches the same conclusion based on the structural analysis and identifies the passage 7:17–24 as "guiding principle underlying the discussion: remain as you are." See Garland, *1 Corinthians*, 242–362.

121 Garland, *1 Corinthians*, 299.

122 This exegetical conclusion is shared among most evangelical scholars, including Garland and Fee. See Garland, *1 Corinthians*, 299; Fee, *First Epistle*, 268–69; Johnson, *1 Corinthians*, 119.

123 The principle of "remaining in the condition when called" does not mean "forbidding conversion to different religious forms of faith." Lewis loosely takes this principle and applies it to a very different set of issues. What she says may be acceptable as a general principle: one should not ask for Muslims to convert to cultural religious Christianity. No evangelical missionary would deny that statement. The matter, however, is

The most disturbing problem appears in Massey's discussion on circumcision. He paraphrases 7:19–20: "*For neither Jewish identity counts for anything nor Gentile identity, but keeping the commandments of God is what counts. Everyone should therefore remain as they were when called.*"[124] First, Massey equates circumcision with "changing into Jewish identity" and uncircumcision with "maintaining Gentile identity." Then he argues that what Paul does in this passage is not forbidding Gentiles from circumcision, but simply discouraging them to be circumcised. He argues that some Gentiles were circumcised (full conversion) while most Gentile believers remained uncircumcised (half-converted). In doing so, he claims that circumcision should be allowed to Gentile believers only if they really want to be identified with the Jews.[125] Applying the same reasoning to the IM context, he analogously connects the distinction between full-converted believers and half-converted believers to a dichotomous distinction between "full Muslim converts to Christianity (i.e., C1–3 MBBs who adopt Christian identity) and "God-fearing 'half-converts' to Christianity (i.e., C5 Muslim believers who retain their Muslim identity)."[126] There is an insurmountable leap in his logical reasoning from the biblical text to his conclusion for the IM.

Massey's understanding of circumcision is unbiblical. Paul does not require Gentiles believers to be circumcised, but instead vehemently opposed it (Gal 6:11–16). In the original text of 1 Cor 7:17–18, the distinction of the circumcised and the uncircumcised refers to the distinction between Jews and Gentiles at the time of their conversion. It is not referring to the distinction between "full-converted Gentiles" through circumcision and "half-converted Gentiles" without circumcision. Massey's logical reasoning collapses. Accordingly, his distinction between "full Muslim converts to Christianity" and "half-converts to Christianity" is an arbitrary invention out of his desire to find biblical validation from the passage. While bringing so much predetermined opinions into the text, Massey falls into a trap of eisegesis.

## *I Have Become All Things to All Men (1 Cor 9:19–23)*

IM advocates take note of the literal meaning of Paul's statement and apply it to the IM context to argue for the validity of "becoming a Muslim to

---

that this text she used for her claim does not support it. This is an example of poor exegesis or irrelevant application of the biblical text in the writings of IM advocates.

124 Massey, "Misunderstanding C5," 12 (emphasis in the original).
125 Massey, "Misunderstanding C5," 12–13.
126 Massey, "Misunderstanding C5," 12.

the Muslims." Entitling his article with a rather striking statement, Woodberry asks a hypothetical question: "If Paul were retracing his missionary journeys today, would he add, 'To the Muslim I became a Muslim'?"[127] To begin with, it is important to note that, whether intentional or not, Woodberry misquotes the verse in a seriously misleading manner. The correct translation is not "To the Jews I became a Jew," but "To the Jews I became *like* (or *as*) a Jew."[128] This makes a crucial difference in understanding the principle of Paul's ministry or what the text asserts.

While IM advocates use simple parallelism in this passage for their validation of the IM, they fail to provide a detailed exegetical argument on this passage. Massey, for example, contends that "some C5 believers remain in the Muslim community for as long as they can to 'win Muslims as Muslims' (1 Cor 9:19–23)."[129] While emphasizing the evangelistic motivation of Muslim Insiders, IM advocates contend that it is acceptable for Muslim Insiders to remain Muslims simply because the ultimate goal is decent and desirable. They seem to make a misguided appeal by relying on the idea that "the end justifies the means" without the biblical validation that comes from an exegetical study of the text.[130]

One must read the current passage within its larger literary context, 1 Cor 8:1—11:1. The main theme of this larger unit concerns the issue of "things sacrificed to idols" (8:1). In providing the teaching on this issue, Paul makes a seemingly unrelated statement in 9:17–23. When it is rightly understood, however, there is a clear connection between the current passage and the larger unit. D. A. Carson succinctly summarizes the exegetical point of the current passage by taking note of its connection with the larger literary context:

127 Woodberry, "To the Muslim," 23.

128 Since Woodberry does not provide the source of his translation, there is no way to know how he reaches this statement. All of the major English translations contain either "like" or "as," which is the translation of the Greek conjunction *hōs*. The Greek text reads: *tois Ioudaiois egenomēn hōs Ioudaios*. The conjunction *hōs* is used in a comparative sense. Wallace states that "this use suggests an analogy or comparison between the connected ideas or tells how something is to be done." See Wallace, *Greek Grammar*, 675. According to this syntactical point, Paul's focus is not on maintaining identity, but on explaining the way he would become like a Jew.

129 Massey, "God's Amazing Diversity," 8. Even Woodberry does not deal with the biblical text exegetically even though he entitles his article with the quoted statement from 1 Cor 9. Woodberry, "To the Muslim," 23–28.

130 In this case, the end is "saving some Muslims" and the means is "becoming a Muslim." Although the end of leading Muslims to Christ is important, one should test if the means of becoming a Muslim is biblically acceptable. IM advocates need to prove this point by providing relevant biblical theological validation, but this has not been accomplished by any of these biblical passages so far.

The least that must be said, however, is that within certain absolute boundaries, Paul is clearly prepared to let Christians indulge in such food under some circumstances, and not under others. It is within this framework that Paul himself confesses that he becomes all things to all people, so that by all means he may save some (9:19–23). There is no hint of rigid inflexibility in the great apostle. His motives are stunning: he wants by all means to win some.[131]

The structural development of Paul's argument provides an exegetical clue. Paul begins with two rhetorical questions in 9:1; "Am I not free? Am I not an apostle?" Then he develops his answers in a reverse order. First, he makes a defense of his apostleship and explains why he limits his apostolic rights (9:2–18). Second, he deals with the question of freedom. He emphasizes the principle of limiting his freedom, though he surely is free, for the sake of saving some (9:19–23). This clarifies Paul's intended meaning in his principle statement: "Though I am free from all men, I have made myself a slave to all, so that I may win more (9:17)." This is about limiting one's right voluntarily or giving up of one's freedom for the sake of the Gospel. It has nothing to do with changing religious identity by belonging to the religious people to evangelize.

For further clarification of this principle, one can ask a question about the contents of personal rights and freedom that Paul refers to in the passage. Paul categorizes all men into four categories: "the Jews, those who are under the Law, those who are without the Law, and the weak" (9:20–22). The main question in regards to the current IM debate is whether what Paul refers to by "becoming all things to all men" includes the change of religious identity. In other words, one may ask what Woodberry implies in his article, "Would Paul allow Muslim Insiders to become Muslims in order to save some Muslims according to this principle?"[132] In answering this question, the exegetical investigation must precede to understand what Paul actually meant in the passage.

Most biblical scholars agree that this "becoming all things" relates only to cultural matters, not religious or theological matters.[133] The point to counter the argument of IM advocates lies in clarifying what Paul means by "to the Jews, I became like a Jew" (9:20). Most scholars take "Paul's being like a Jew" to mean that Paul follows the "law-observant patterns of living"

---

131 Carson, *Gagging of God*, 510.

132 Woodberry, "To the Muslim," 23.

133 Fitzmyer, *First Corinthians*, 368–72; Fee, *First Epistle*, 422–35; Soards, *1 Corinthians*, 192–95; Garland, *1 Corinthians*, 1427–37; Larkin, *Culture and Biblical Hermeneutics*, 218–19; Carson, *Cross and Christian Ministry*, 115–37.

of the Jews who were under the law.¹³⁴ Paul's observance of Jewish practices is depicted in Acts in various ways: "having Timothy circumcised (16:1–3); cutting his hair at Cenchreae (because of a Nazirite vow, 18:18); and purifying himself in the Jerusalem Temple (21:23–26)."¹³⁵ It is very important to recognize that though the behavioral actions of Paul were the same with those of the Jews, Paul certainly did not practice them for the same theological reasons that the Jews had. Fee describes this important difference as follows:

> The difference, therefore, between his own behavior and that of his social companions [the Jews] is not in the behavior itself, which will be identical to the observer, but in the reasons for it. The latter abstain because they are "under the law"; it is a matter of religious obligation. Paul abstains because he loves those under the law and wants to win them to Christ. Despite appearances, the differences are as night and day.¹³⁶

Garland, while not rejecting the previous viewpoint, argues from a slightly different perspective that the clearest example is "his description of the thirty-nine lashes he suffered at the hands of the Jews (2 Cor 11:24)."¹³⁷ According to Garland, Paul had the right to avoid this severe Jewish discipline if he had wanted, but did not run away from the penalties. If he had refused to take this Jewish discipline, Paul would have been rejected by the Jewish community and could no longer have maintained membership within the Jewish community. Paul had such a strong sense of obligation for his own people (Rom 9:2–4) that he received this serious penalty in order to maintain the membership and preach the Gospel. Paul suffered hardships because of the message of the cross, which the Jews stood against. Paul surely did not become like a Jew in order to simply maintain membership by compromising his Gospel message. He did not compromise the Gospel of Jesus Christ that he had to suffer greatly from the Jewish companions. Even though he had the right to avoid such hardship and suffering, he remained within the Jewish community so that he could preach the Gospel to the Jews while maintaining the integrity of the Gospel.

---

134  See the same works in the previous footnote. Fee gives a contemporary example of "becoming like a Jew" in the following terms: "Where he was among Jews he was kosher; when he was among Gentiles he was non-kosher—precisely because, as with circumcision, neither mattered to God (cf. 7:19; 8:8)." See Fee, *First Epistle*, 427.

135  Fitzmyer, *First Corinthians*, 369.

136  Fee, *First Epistle*, 429.

137  Garland, *1 Corinthians*, 430.

In either of the two explanations of being a Jew, it is clear that no theological compromise was involved. Paul became like a Jew in a purely cultural sense while he did not alter the message of the Gospel and his theological position. There is no indication for a change of religious identity in Paul's ministry. The general principle, "I have become all things to all men," cannot be understood as an "infinitely flexible" permission for wild applications in any situation.[138] It does not approve the notion that "Paul observes no theological or moral limits to this principle (cf. Gal 2:1–14)"[139] because Paul does not say that he becomes an idolater to idolaters or an adulterer to adulterers, or even a Judaizer to Judaizers.[140] In conclusion, Paul's ministry principle in 1 Cor 9:19–23 does not relate to compromising theological messages or changing religious identities for the sake of the Gospel preaching. The two main claims of IM advocates cannot be supported by this passage.

## *Eating the Meat Sacrificed to Idols (1 Cor 8:16 & 10:23–33)*

Many controversial assertions and applications have been proposed in the missiological circles because of the different interpretations of Paul's stance on food sacrificed idols. IM advocates add some more complications to the debate. As mentioned above, Paul's argument on this issue should be seen in the larger literary unit of 1 Cor 8:1–11:1. Three major interpretative matters deserve an evaluation with respect to the IM.

Most IM advocates make bold statements from the present passage, 1 Cor 10:23–33, without an exegetical analysis. Their assertion goes farther than what the text asserts. Woodberry, for example, uses this passage as a biblical reference to contend that "Paul teaches adaptability even to a pagan culture like Corinth as long as one is guided by conscience and by the desire to glorify God and see people be saved (1 Cor 10:23–33)."[141] He implies that Paul's teaching in 1 Cor 10 would support the IM through the notion of cultural adaptation. While his statement in a general sense is acceptable in support of the C4 contextualization, this is far from being a suitable biblical support for the IM. Woodberry, for example, does not provide specific exegetical reasons concerning how this biblical passage can support the

---

138 Carson, *Cross and Christian Ministry*, 119–20. This is clear when one notes the qualifying constraint Paul places in the text, such as "being under the law of Christ."

139 Johnson, *1 Corinthians*, 148.

140 Lenski, *Interpretation*, 381. He stresses that "in accommodating himself to the standpoint of his missionary subjects Paul never descended to a mere pleasing of men or to connivance with their false religious notions and their sinful practices."

141 Woodberry, "To the Muslim," 24–25.

two main claims of the IM: maintaining Muslim identity and continuing to practice Islamic religious rituals.

Next, some IM advocates argue that Paul's teaching on food sacrificed to idols in 1 Cor 10 stands against the prohibitions that the Jerusalem Council required Gentile believers to keep in Acts 15.[142] Higgins contends that Paul's position about food in 1 Cor 8–10 is not the same as in the letter of the Jerusalem Council because "his rational for encouraging the 'strong' not to eat came from his desire that the 'weak' not be tempted to eat, thus defiling their conscience (1 Corinthians 8:7–9)."[143] Lewis makes a slightly different evaluation concerning the relationship between the prohibitions of the Jerusalem Council and Paul's teachings. She considers the four prohibitions in the Jerusalem Council as "the laws given in Leviticus to the Gentiles by the Council: no eating of blood, strangled meat, or food polluted by idols, nor any practice of sexual immorality."[144] She contends that "all of these laws, except the last one, were removed before the end of the New Testament by Paul, who reduced them to a matter of conscience (Romans 14)."[145] She implies that Paul's teaching on food sacrificed to idols contradicts the decision of the Jerusalem Council.

Based upon the earlier discussion on Acts 15, the following question deserves a consideration: "Is there a discrepancy between the decision of the Jerusalem Council and Paul's teaching in 1 Cor 8–10?" The four prohibitions are not the laws that are required for salvation. The Jerusalem Council suggested that Gentile believers would keep these prohibitions for the fellowship with Jewish believers in order to protect the unity of the Christian community. These were a matter of cultural sensitivity, not of laws.[146] By referring to the prohibitions as "laws," Lewis distorts the nature of the prohibitions. Since the prohibitions were not the laws, it is inaccurate to assert that Paul "removed these laws."

---

142 Lewis, "Integrity of the Gospel," 44; Higgins, "Acts 15," 37. Higgins pointedly states the importance of 1 Cor 8–10 in a biblical defense of the IM: "Did the New Testament encourage or describe any sort of 'insider movement' among pagan Gentiles? This would require a thorough study of 1 Cor 8–10, particularly one that keeps this missiological question in view."

143 Higgins, "Acts 15," 37. By noting that Paul does not quote the letter of the Jerusalem Council on this food issue, Higgins takes it to imply that Paul might have changed his view on food issue while he still holds the same view on fornication and idolatry.

144 Lewis, "Integrity of the Gospel," 44.

145 Lewis, "Integrity of the Gospel," 44. She gives three biblical references in her footnote: Rom 14; 1 Cor 8; and 1 Cor 10:23—11:1.

146 Bock, *Acts*, 507.

On the other hand, Higgins asserts that Paul's teaching on food in 1 Cor 8–10 conflicts with the decision of the Jerusalem Council. Higgins implies that Paul changed the Council's requirements in regards to food, because he allowed "strong" believers to eat food sacrificed to idols in the Corinthian church.[147] Moreover, Higgins implies that since Paul was able to change the theological requirement of the Council later in different religious contexts, any theological requirements could be relativized depending on contexts. The best way to counter Higgins's argument is to understand the exegetical conclusion of the text. Larkin summarizes Paul's teaching on the food issue as follows:

> The Christian actually has a remarkable freedom in cultural encounters, even in the midst of a pagan society. Thus the early Christians were free to purchase meat in the market without raising questions about its origin and to eat it, though it had been offered to idols, unless by eating they offended someone of sensitive conscience (1 Cor 8:4–8; 10:25–26). They could not, however, go to a feast honoring a pagan god and there eat idol's meat function (1 Cor 10:14–22, 27–30). Such a cultural form takes its entire meaning and function from the pagan's religious center and its world-view, so that participating becomes an action against God. Still, the action of eating such meat, where separated from the cultural meaning, was harmless.[148]

Several points can be made from this conclusion. First, the essence of the food issue is simply a cultural matter, and believers can enjoy freedom which is the overarching theme throughout 1 Cor 8:1—11:1. Second, Paul emphasizes the principle of limiting one's freedom on behalf of the interests of others as he shows it in his own life examples (9:1–23). Practically speaking, one may eat food sacrificed to idols, but one can do better if he can limit his own freedom by not eating it for the benefit of other weak believers. Third, Higgins may be right in pointing out that Paul brings a different reason in 1 Cor 8–10 than that of the Council. The difference, however, comes from the different contexts. In the context of Acts 15, the issue is addressed in the relationship between Jewish and Gentile believers. On the other hand, in 1 Corinthian 8–10, the issue is expressed mainly in the relationship between the "strong" Gentile believers and the "weak" Gentile believers within the Corinthian church. If Paul were addressing the same issue in regards to the relationship between Jewish and Gentile believers in

---

147 Higgins, "Acts 15," 32 and 37.
148 Larkin, *Culture and Biblical Hermeneutics*, 219.

another sociocultural context, he would have used the same principle from the Jerusalem Council.

In other words, the principle remains the same. The prohibitions of the Jerusalem Council can be understood through the same reasoning of Paul in 1 Cor 8–10: Gentile believers should avoid detestable cultural practices that would hinder Jewish believers from approaching table fellowship with Gentile believers even though they had freedom on these cultural matters. If one applies the same principle to the context of the Jerusalem Council, one may think that the strong ones are actually Gentile believers while the weak are Jewish believers who may be stumbled by the cultural practices of the other party. The matter is not a theological change of the message, but a matter of cultural difference.

One more important erroneous interpretation of Higgins has to be addressed because his conclusion is directly related to his biblical claim for the IM. In interpreting 1 Cor 8:10, Higgins takes Paul's "strange" comment on a brother sitting at a table in the idol's temple in an unusual way: "Paul's concern in the verse is not that the action was wrong in itself; in fact, he does not criticize the brother for the action."[149] He further states that this case refers to "a Gentile believer who, without committing idolatry, is not only buying meat in the market or eating it in a private home, but is sitting at table in the idol's temple."[150] Higgins contends from this reasoning that Paul assumes "the Cor' continued participation in the act of 'dining in an idol's temple'" in 8:10, and his reason for the correction is due to "its potential affect [sic] on another, weaker, believer and not, apparently, because of actually being at table in a pagan temple."[151] In the end, Higgins takes this case to be a "possible example of a Gentile believer who is still 'inside' part of their religious heritage."[152] Higgins's interpretation deserves a careful evaluation.

Higgins misunderstands Paul's meaning in the text. Paul clearly forbids believers from participating in a sacrificial feast because it means participation in idol worship, a worship of demons (10:14–22). While using the serious consequence of the ancestors as a vivid example, Paul warns the Corinthian believers to avoid the participation in any pagan feast, which means "having fellowship with demons" (10:20–22).[153] Fee and Stuart take brother in 1 Cor 8:10 to refer to "Christians who are arguing for the privilege of continuing to join their pagan neighbors at their feasts in

149  Higgins, "Acts 15," 37.
150  Higgins, "Acts 15," 37.
151  Higgins, "Inside What," 79.
152  Higgins, "Acts 15," 37.
153  Robertson and Plummer, *Critical and Exegetical*, 216.

the idol temples," and reach the following exegetical conclusion: "They are absolutely forbidden to attend the idol feasts because of the stumbling-block principle (8:7–13), because such eating is incompatible with life in Christ as it is experienced at his table (10:16–17), and because it means to participate in the demonic (10:19–22)."[154] Higgins misses the overarching principle of Paul's teaching and the clearer principle in 10:20–22.

The entire passage in 1 Cor 8–10 provides useful insights for the missiological issues regarding contextualization. The central problem lies in that many practitioners of missions do not pay careful attention to sound biblical exegesis and to proper applications that are in line with biblical guidelines. IM advocates often commit this mistake; since they seemingly downplay sound exegetical methods in understanding the biblical texts, they tend to apply "assumed, but unproved" biblical reasoning to the IM context.

## Other Biblical Passages

There are other biblical passages that IM advocates use for the biblical precedents of the IM. Taking Jesus' approach to the Samaritans in John 4 as a biblical example, Higgins contends that Jesus did not demand Samaritans to leave their Samaritan religious life because what ultimately mattered was the worship of God in Spirit and in truth.[155] Although space does not permit a reply to his assertion, it is necessary to stress that Higgins's claim in the case of Samaritans depends on several crucial assumptions that demand a more careful study. He himself uses uncertain expressions such as "it is logical to assume" and "will probably continue" in his article.[156] Tim Lewis and Rebecca Lewis, on the other hand, simply take note of the parallel aspect between the Samaritans and Muslim Insiders to argue for the biblical validity of the IM.[157] These assertions do not carry much weight because of their speculative nature as well as the weak reasoning by too simplistic parallelism.

Other biblical examples IM advocates quote include so-called holy pagans, including Melchizedek, Job, Jethro, Balaam, Naaman, the sailors in

---

154 Fee and Stuart, *How to Read the Bible*, 67–68.

155 Caldwell, "Jesus in Samaria," 25–31; Higgins, "Key to Insider Movements," 158–59.

156 Higgins, "Key to Insider Movements," 159.

157 They state, "The Samaritans, like Muslims today, worshiped the God of Abraham. Like the Samaritans, the Muslims 'worship what they do not know.'" Lewis and Lewis, "Planting Churches," 17.

the book of Jonah, the pagan magi, and Cornelius.[158] Some of the arguments are quite similar to those of the inclusivists represented by Pinnock and Sanders.[159] Since the in-depth study of these biblical figures is not provided in the writings of IM advocates, their respective reasoning cannot be evaluated. One thing about these "holy pagans" is certain: God surely has worked in their lives in one way or another. But this simple fact does not necessarily garner divine approval of the two main claims of IM advocates: maintaining the religious identity and remaining within Islam through participating in Islamic religious practices. Instead, the overarching biblical theological principle of exclusive worship of God is too clear to deny.[160]

## CONCLUSION

This chapter began with the contention that any evangelical mission theology or ministry model needs to be grounded on the biblical foundation for its validity. As pragmatic concerns increasingly play an influential role in the missiological circles, missiologists and missionaries tend to pay less attention to the biblical and theological foundations. By examining the biblical interpretations of IM advocates, this chapter reveals several weaknesses of the IM theology of mission. First, since some IM advocates underestimate grammatical-historical hermeneutics, many of their exegetical conclusions do not correlate to overarching biblical teaching. In several cases, they simply rely on parallelism or analogical reasoning based upon observing similarities between biblical examples and the IM. The hermeneutical method of IM advocates is certainly the foundational cause of their problematic assertions. Second, all these biblical passages used by IM advocates do not prove the two main features of the IM, which differentiate it from the C4 contextualization. Lastly, IM advocates do not pay enough attention to the overarching biblical theological teaching of the entire Bible when they focus on the biblical passages for validating the IM. They give less weight to the overall tone of exclusivism in Scripture. For the reasons mentioned above, Carson's advice deserves a renewed hearing on the part of the evangelical missionary community:

> Missionary training must include substantive courses in biblical theology; for, although the study of contextualization may help the missionary free himself from the cultural accretions of his

---

158 Higgins, "Inside What," 85–86; Higgins, "Key to Insider Movements," 162.

159 Pinnock, *Wideness of God's Mercy*; Pinnock, "Toward an Evangelical Theology," 359–68; Sanders, *No Other Name*, 215–80; Sanders, "Inclusivism," 21–55.

160 Kaiser's detailed analysis is helpful: Kaiser, "Holy Pagans," 123–41.

own society, there is a growing danger that contextualization will be used as a new tool to pervert the gospel into something unrecognizable. Nothing will provide a better safeguard than the constant study of the Word of God.[161]

---

161 Carson, "Response," 231–32.

# 5

# An Evaluation of the Insider Movement through an Analytical Framework

THE CURRENT STUDY BEGAN with a review of the historical developments of Muslim evangelism, so as to help the reader understand the IM from a historical perspective. The historical review revealed that the IM looks like a radical extension of C4 contextualization model. Chapter 3 established a comprehensive analytical framework that can serve as an objective and well-balanced evaluative tool for contextualization models. Chapter 4 evaluated the biblical interpretations of IM advocates in order to examine the biblical and theological reasoning for the validity of the IM.

This chapter applies the five perspective analytical framework proposed in chapter 3 to the IM to examine its presuppositions and theoretical underpinnings. While the evaluation of the biblical interpretations of IM advocates in chapter 4 demonstrated the lack of scriptural validity of the IM, the evaluation of this chapter is more comprehensive in scope and brings to light various dimensions of IM contextualization. Using this analytical framework uncovers the implied presuppositions, theological orientations, and key theoretical backbones from anthropology and the communication theory, which shape the IM theology of mission.

This critical evaluation primarily focuses on the missions theology of IM advocates, but it also deals with the biblical and theological understanding of Muslim Insiders. This is necessary because the missions theology of IM advocates has had a significant impact on Muslim Insiders' understanding of the Gospel and biblical teachings. What IM advocates argue and teach concerning certain contextualization issues will inevitably affect how

Muslim Insiders think and act. For this reason, this chapter will not only deal with how IM advocates think about various contextualization issues, but also consider how Muslim Insiders would think concerning important biblical and theological teachings.

## AN EVALUATION FROM A PHILOSOPHICAL PERSPECTIVE

### The Authority of Scripture

It is crucial for every contextualization attempt to begin with Scripture. One's view of scriptural authority and its subsequent application to contextualization determine the validity and authenticity of each contextualization model. It is, therefore, imperative to evaluate the revelational epistemology of IM advocates in terms of how they view and treat the authority of Scripture in the IM. There is no doubt that IM advocates are Bible-believing evangelical Christians, because they affirm the Bible as God's Word.[1] This simple affirmation, however, demands a further investigation because there are some concerns about how IM advocates view and use the Bible. Some evidence indicates they have weakened the authority of Scripture in their missiological thinking.

First, one can discern that the biblical notion of God's revelation is jeopardized by the dangerously liberal use of the term in the writings of IM advocates. Travis, for example, indicates that God's revelation continues today among peoples: "We need to be aware that the 'validity' of a religious movement such as C5 can only rightly be understood through the interaction of biblical/theological reflection *and* first hand [*sic*] experience of what God is doing today in the Muslim world."[2] In his analysis of the Jerusalem Council, Travis argues that the apostles did not first go to Scripture but to "case studies of what God had been doing among the Gentiles."[3] By making this assertion a normative process for contemporary contextualization, such as the IM, Travis elevates the human experiences of God to a high level and

---

1 Higgins, for example, affirmed a fundamental conviction in his plenary address at Tokyo 2010: "The Bible is God's Word and is both supreme in its authority, and sufficient in its application, for every dimension of discipleship, teaching, training and devotion in any movement." See Higgins, "Beyond Christianity," 12–13.

2 Travis et al., "Four Responses," 124. He similarly argues that both IM advocates and IM critics should remain humble and try to discern "what the Spirit of God is saying to the Church and to Muslims at this juncture in world history." See also his response in Corwin, "Humble Appeal," 8.

3 Travis et al., "Four Responses," 124.

seems to suggest an open canon interpretation of Scripture by observing what God is doing. Higgins shares the same viewpoint on this matter when he says, "Empirical evidence of the work of the Holy Spirit was clearly a deciding factor for those gathered" at the Jerusalem Council.[4]

Bradford Greer expresses a more radical view of revelation: "God is personally engaged in each step of the revelation process with each person and with communities across space and time. The personal testimony of many Muslims that they have come to faith in Christ through visions, dreams, or through a healing demonstrates God's personal involvement in this self-revelatory process."[5] He believes that God's revelatory activity is presently at work, and personal experiences such as dreams and visions are part of His revelation.

One may take this simply as a matter of terminology to describe how God works. Certainly, this writer believes that God is at work among the nations, and consequently, that Christians can rejoice as they see and hear of God's workings among peoples, including Muslim nations. If it is really a matter of terminology, IM advocates need to use such terms as revelation or God's revealing activity, with more care, because they can mislead readers in placing too much authority on these so-called "revelatory" activities of God at the level of the authority of Scripture.

There is a deeper problem, however. The two most prominent IM advocates, Travis and Higgins, contend that empirical evidences of contemporary contexts should play a role in determining the meaning of Scripture in the same manner that the apostles in the Jerusalem Council used their empirical evidence of the first-century context to decide their missiological issue. They take the Jerusalem Council as a biblical precedent and apply it to contemporary contexts through appropriate analogy. This approach is similar to that of Kraft when he treats the Bible as a "classic casebook" and argues for "appropriate analogy" as a tool for effective communication of biblical truth.[6] Travis and Higgins use analogical hermeneutics between the biblical precedent of the Jerusalem Council and the contemporary IM context where human experiences are taken to play such an important role in determining the missiological issue at hand. The logical implication is that since God is bringing Muslim Insiders into His kingdom through revealing

---

4 Higgins, "Acts 15," 30–31. In describing the process of decision making in the Jerusalem Council, Higgins places "listening to what God was doing through his Spirit" before "the Scriptures." He emphasizes empirical experience to an extent that it has almost equal influence with the written Word of God in determining the meaning of the biblical text.

5 Greer, "Review," 206.

6 Kraft, *Christianity in Culture*, 154–58.

activities, such as dreams, visions, and healings, one need to appreciate His new work and understand the current phenomenon of the IM in a new light. In the meantime, one may have to interpret relevant passages of Scripture differently from traditional interpretations.

Several problems are noticeable. First, Travis and Higgins undermine the supremacy of Scripture when they elevate human experience as an interpretive key to the interpretation of Scripture. They place new experiences in human contexts as a deciding factor in their understanding of the biblical text and do not acknowledge authorial intent as the objective meaning of the biblical text. Second, even if the Jerusalem Council used the human experiences of God's deeds among the Gentiles in its interpretation of Scripture, the historical situation was rather unique in that there was no written Word of God. The early church had to depend on the authoritative teachings of the Apostles under the guidance of the Holy Spirit. The contemporary church does not have the same excuse because it possesses and has access to the written Word of God. Travis and Higgins regard Scripture as the written Word of God, but not as the final, perfect revelation of God when they elevate new human experiences in the contemporary contexts.

There are insurmountable differences between the Jerusalem Council and contemporary IM contexts so that one cannot simply use the biblical case as a normative model for deciding missiological issues of the contemporary context. Instead, one must uphold the authority of Scripture and draw biblical principles and meanings through a sound hermeneutical method before applying them to a modern context. By taking the Bible as a casebook and using analogical hermeneutics for the IM context, Travis and Higgins largely move beyond the evangelical foundation of scriptural authority, inspiration, and inerrancy.

## General Revelation

In regards to revelation, some IM advocates take an unconventional view of general revelation and make radical statements about the Qur'an and other Islamic sources. Greer, for example, connects his claim for the ongoing revelation of God to his own definition of general revelation: "God actively revealing himself to people through what he has made and through an active involvement in people's conscience."[7] This definition of general revelation is ambiguous at best because the biblical definition of general revelation includes God's revealing of himself through creation and human conscience (Rom 1:19–20, 2:14–16). If one elevates subjective personal ex-

---

7 Greer, "Review," 206.

periences to the level of general revelation, he can soon lose sight of what the Bible teaches. Greer stresses the ongoing nature of God's revelation by using the term "active involvement" in his statement.

Higgins comments about the biblical writers' use of other religious sources in their writings: "This should encourage our respect for the fact that God is at work beyond the 'canon,' even as we uphold the singular and superior role of the canon as the 'measure' of all truth (as the word canon originally meant)."[8] Furthermore, he asserts, "God can [sic] and has used the Qur'an to set people on the path toward repentance and faith in Christ."[9] Greer shares the same view when he implies that God has impacted the way the Qur'an is read by Muslims so that they can come to faith in Christ.[10] Greer argues that it is valid for Muslim Insider communities to "read the Qur'an through a Christ-centered lens" because of the assumption that God's revealing work is present in this process.

IM advocates assert a positive view of Islam by understanding it within the conceptual framework of general revelation. On the one hand, IM advocates do not affirm the Qur'an as the "Word of God' or inspired scripture. On the other hand, they take the Qur'an to be a valid instrument of God's revealing work among Muslims as they approve that God can use and has used the Qur'an to lead many Muslims to faith in Christ. This aspect is further demonstrated in Higgins's hypothetical notion of considering the IM as a reforming movement within Islam.[11] He expresses his belief:

> I do, however, believe that authentic Jesus movements within Islam will bring transformation (and indeed reform) in the light of God's Word and Spirit as applied from the inside. Views concerning Muhammad, the place of the Qur'an, the value of the *salat*, the meaning of the word "Muslim," the nature of Jesus, the character of Allah, and many other elements of Islamic faith and life will change within and through such movements to Jesus.[12]

In the contemporary Muslim world, a significant number of Muslims have come to know Christ personally through reading the Qur'an. Some Muslims search for true peace and salvation in the Qur'an, and yet, fail to

---

8 Higgins's response appears in Corwin, "Humble Appeal," 10.

9 Corwin, "Humble Appeal," 10. See also Talman, "Comprehensive Contextualization" 8.

10 Greer, "Review," 206.

11 Higgins, "Identity," 121. Travis also favors the notion of reformation within Islam through the IM. See his response in Corwin, "Humble Appeal," 8.

12 Higgins, "Acts 15," 38. In his mind, this is possible through a "radical reinterpretation of the Qur'an, Muhammad, the *Hajj*, and the *Shahadah*."

find them. In many different ways they turn to the Bible, especially the Gospels, and eventually find what they are searching for in Jesus Christ through reading the Bible. In the process, the Qur'an plays a role, but it is another matter entirely to assert that the Qur'an can be accepted as a divinely ordained instrument for revealing God's truth to Muslims. This assertion is unacceptable because the ultimate source of Muslim Insiders' faith in Christ should come from the biblical witness, not from a Qur'anic witness to Jesus. The Qur'an may be a stepping stone for turning people to the Bible so that Muslim Insiders eventually have faith in Christ through the biblical truths of Jesus. Moreover, the primary role of general revelation is not to provide salvation, but to make people accountable to God for their sinfulness and realize their desperate need for salvation.[13] The role of the Qur'an in Muslim evangelism cannot be unduly elevated to the biblical notion of general revelation.

Concerning the positive use of the Qur'an, IM advocates attempt to make their argument from the biblical writers' use of non-canonical material in Scripture. They contend that it is reasonable to use the Qur'an for Christian witness as long as it is interpreted through the lens of Christ. While this issue will be discussed later, a brief mention of several points is in order. First, the use of non-canonical sources is limited and unusual in the Scriptures. Their usage is simply to prove a point in the writer's argument, not to prove the biblical truth. Moreover, non-canonical sources were deployed in such a straightforward way that the simple meaning of each source is conveyed, and that there is no need for reinterpreting those sources for the biblical truth claims.[14]

It is striking to read Higgins's assertion that the IM can serve as a reforming movement within Islam by reinterpreting Islamic rituals and the Qur'an. Travis contends that the reforming nature of the IM should be understood as a new wineskin, which can be compared to the Apostle Paul's ministry and Luther's Reformation in their respective historical contexts.[15]

---

13 Daniel Strange succinctly summarizes an evangelical view of general revelation: "While general revelation serves a crucial role in the sovereign purposes of God, in and of itself it is insufficient to bring salvation. God has prescribed the way of salvation which is faith in Jesus Christ in special revelation ordinarily through the hearing of the gospel message through a human messenger in this life." See Strange, "General Revelation," 54.

14 A more elaborate discussion appears in the section on an anthropological perspective.

15 Travis and Travis, "Contextualization," 15. Also see Travis' response in Corwin, "Humble Appeal," 8. Travis argues that "caution and prayerfulness" are equally necessary both for IM advocates and IM critics. He intends to warn "godly, well-meaning Christians [namely, IM critics] not to be working against what God is doing through

This analogical reasoning is questionable, because, if one accepts the notion of reforming Islam from within, it presupposes that the original thought processes and teachings within Islam were in line with God's truth. Both the ministry of Paul and the Reformation of Luther can be proved in line with biblical truth and the essence of the Gospel, but one cannot say that Islam in its original form has the same standing as biblical revelation.

## Epistemology

All the preceding evidences, including an overemphasis on human experience with a correspondingly lowered emphasis on the written Word of God, a liberal use of general revelation, analogical exegesis, and unsound biblical interpretations, indicate that IM advocates have a problematic revelational epistemology. Since IM advocates do not use the term, "epistemology," in an explicit manner, this discussion relies on evidences available in their writings, which provide sufficient data for recognizing their epistemological presuppositions.

The epistemology of IM advocates resembles the instrumentalism of Kraft.[16] One serious problem of this instrumentalist epistemology is that one cannot claim for the objective meaning of a term or biblical text because no objectivity of truth claims or no objective criteria for measuring truth exists within this epistemological framework. The same term can mean different things to different people in various human cultural contexts. "Being a Muslim" for ordinary Muslims means one thing, while the same term can mean something completely different for Muslim Insiders. As a result, a private redefinition of a term, Muslim, is possible. One cannot judge what others mean by "claiming to be a Muslim," because the meaning of the term is found in persons. For example, Travis contends that Muslim Insiders' views of Islam reflect their own views depending on "the Word and the indwelling Holy Spirit."[17] According to him, no outsiders, Christians or MBBs from the same nation, can impose their own views on Muslim Insiders. Higgins asserts that different positions of how to view Islam are acceptable depending on "the conclusions one makes about Islam's origins, early history, and

---

their opposition to the insider paradigm."

16 The instrumentalist epistemology of Kraft is distinguished from Hiebert's critical realism in chapter 3. It is argued that the two epistemologies differ in the fact that the latter acknowledges the existence of objective truths and the objective criteria of knowing truth while the former does not.

17 Travis, "Messianic Muslim," 53.

subsequent development."[18] No objective criteria for determining the objective meaning of terms are recognized in the writings of IM advocates.

This affects the way IM advocates interpret biblical passages. While Higgins gives careful attention to the exegetical study of biblical passages, other IM advocates do not attempt to exegete key biblical texts. Even when they interpret biblical passages, they employ simple analogy or parallelism as interpretive methods of biblical interpretation. They provide little sound reasoning for making such parallelism, but simply demonstrate similarities to validate their interpretation. In dealing with the biblical passages, they neither acknowledge the objective meaning of the text, nor search for the authorial intent of related passages. In the end, their biblical interpretation reflects imprecision in its meaning, and their application is skewed. Some of the examples are shown in the previous chapter in their interpretation of key passages.

From a philosophical perspective in regards to revelational epistemology, it is clear that IM advocates place too much emphasis on human contexts and experiences and too little emphasis on Scripture.[19] When they deal with biblical texts, their interpretive methods differ from a sound hermeneutical method and their interpretations go off target. The most fundamental problem lies in the instrumentalist epistemology where pragmatism governs the validity of any assertion. In the end, the IM has affinities with what Nicholls refers to as an existential model, which emphasizes the new discovery of "what God is already doing in preexisting contexts" and use it as a key to contextualization.[20] When IM advocates validate the IM by overemphasizing Muslim contexts at the cost of sacrificing Scriptural authority, it is clearly seen that the authority of Scripture does not hold a proper place in contextualization.

## AN EVALUATION FROM A THEOLOGICAL PERSPECTIVE

### Theological Orientation

The initial step in evaluating the IM from a theological perspective is to understand the theological orientation of IM advocates by investigating their writings, because it plays a crucial role in determining the IM theology

---

18 Higgins, "Identity," 120.

19 John Piper refers to this tendency of IM advocates as "minimizing the Bible" and "the loss of faith in the power of God's Word." See Piper, "Minimizing the Bible," 17.

20 Nicholls, *Contextualization*, 24–28.

of missions and contextualization.[21] Although IM advocates do not identify their explicit theological orientation, one can still glean a sufficiently congruent view of theology among them by examining their writings.[22] When the spectrum of four theological orientations of Hesselgrave and Rommen is used as a measure, it can be shown that IM advocates do not stand upon an orthodox theological orientation.[23] First, the starting point of their deviation from orthodoxy is their view of Scripture behind the IM contextualization model. Their understanding of revelational epistemology digresses from the orthodox position, because they overemphasize human cultural elements in their definition of biblical revelation. Even though they acknowledge Scripture as God's Word, it does not occupy the supreme place in their theological orientation.

One fundamental reason behind the comparative loss of scriptural authority comes from such an epistemological contention that people only "see through a glass darkly and have much to learn" in the human understanding of God's truth.[24] Due to the limits of human perception and subjective understanding in the matters of God's truth, Higgins contends, everyone needs to approach the study of God's truth in humility.[25] Travis contends that the limitation of human perception comes from the cultural glasses people wear: "They [People] read the Bible differently at points, due to the different cultural glasses their wear."[26] Since cultural context affects the meaning of Scripture in the human perception of God's truth, every theology based upon biblical revelation should be taken to be relative. While they consider Scripture as God's written Word, they deny its normative meaning and undermine its supreme authority within their theological framework based upon their epistemological presupposition.

---

21 Hesselgrave and Rommen, *Contextualization*, 144–45.

22 It might be that some IM advocates unknowingly deviate from an orthodox theological orientation when they extensively use anthropology or communication theory in their formulation of contextualization.

23 Hesselgrave and Rommen define an orthodox theological orientation in terms of believing in both the authority of Scripture and the historical Christian doctrines. They contend that foundational Christian doctrines can and should remain a crucial criterion to judge between orthodoxy and non-orthodoxy. See Hesselgrave and Rommen, *Contextualization*, 145–46.

24 Higgins, "Beyond Christianity," 13. This is the same biblical phrase, 1 Cor 13:12, that Kraft uses to argue for this instrumentalist epistemology. See Kraft, *Christianity in Culture*, 19, 22, 74, 96.

25 Higgins, "Beyond Christianity," 13. He warns IM critics to be open-minded and humble because if the IM is a correct work of God, they will be found opposing God in the final judgment.

26 See Travis' response in Corwin, "Humble Appeal," 7.

This epistemological notion leads IM advocates to the notion of theological relativism, because they take all theologies to be culturally conditioned or culturally biased, and thus, relative. Harley Talman relates a commonly shared view:

> All theologies are contextually conditioned, emerging out of a certain set of experiences or out of a particular historical situation. There can be no one form of systematic or biblical theology, because any theology is an interpretation of data from a particular point of view. . . . Therefore, Western theologies are incomplete and inadequate for the non-Western world.[27]

Talman further develops a theologizing model for Muslim nations by using the work of a neo-orthodox Catholic theologian, Thomas Schreiter.[28] Talman's theologizing model reflects a neo-orthodox approach for the following reasons: no clear supremacy of Scripture in the theologizing process, the presence of too high a view of human culture, and the taking of human context as a starting point of contextualization. Greer, based upon the notion of theological relativism, draws a logical conclusion that imposing one theological position upon another is simply a form of "theological imperialism," which he refers to as *"theolonialism."*[29] The possibility of claiming a normative biblical theology is removed.

Another characteristic of their neo-orthodox theological orientation appears in the fact that the weight of human cultural contexts or experiences increases in the theologizing process while the weight of Scripture correspondingly decreases. IM advocates consider contemporary human experiences highly in their interpretation of Scripture. This leads to the belief that observing what God is doing in the contemporary Muslim world, in the view of many Muslim Insiders' believing in Jesus within the IM, should guide biblical interpreters into new interpretation of biblical texts as in the case of Acts 15.[30] Travis notes that the apostles went first to the "case studies of what God had been doing among the Gentiles" in order to ascertain the answer to their missiological question.[31]

---

27 Talman, "Comprehensive Contextualization," 9.

28 Talman, "Comprehensive Contextualization," 10. For the original source, see Schreiter, *Constructing Local Theologies*, 87–138.

29 Greer, "Review," 206 (emphasis in the original).

30 Higgins, "Acts 15," 33.

31 Travis et al., "Four Responses," 124. In his support of a contextual theology, Travis states the premise: "A contextual theology can only properly be developed through a dynamic interaction of actual ministry experience, the specific leading of the Spirit and the study of the Word of God." See Travis and Travis, "Contextualization," 13. The ordering of three components deserve noting: the Scriptures take the last while

IM advocates are willing to grant broad theological diversity, even to unorthodox theological viewpoints of Muslim Insiders. While claiming that the IM may be understood as a reformation within Islamic religion, John and Anna Travis acknowledge that the nature of this theologizing process can be "theologically messy."[32] They are willing to allow Muslim Insiders to experience theological unorthodoxy in their theologizing process as long as the IM leads the devoutly searching Muslim souls to Christ. This openness to theological diversity stems from the confidence of IM advocates that Muslim Insiders are under the guidance of the Holy Spirit.[33] Higgins refers to this process as "self-theologizing" in addition to the "Three-self" missiological principles (self-propagating, self-governing, and self-supporting): "The movement is actively engaged in the ongoing process of doing thorough biblical theology 'in culture.'"[34] IM advocates are willing to allow Muslim Insiders to work out their own theology at the risk that Muslim Insiders' biblical and theological understandings may deviate from a sound biblical and theological position or that their theological stances may reveal syncretistic tendency. While this is in contrast to the biblical mandate of "teaching them to obey" (Matt 28:20), another problem lies in that there is no sound mechanism to secure Muslim Insiders to remain within an acceptable biblical and theological boundary.

## Orthodoxy and Historic Creeds

As a result of their view of theology and theologizing, IM advocates place less emphasis on historic Christian doctrines as a necessary theological formulation for new believers to agree upon. Travis asserts, "While we must be careful to guard against syncretism, we must also be mindful that ascent to perfect theological propositions is not the apex of the coming Kingdom that Jesus proclaimed."[35] Since historic creeds are simply the products of a culturally conditioned contextual theologizing process, IM advocates argue, they should not be imposed upon Muslim Insiders because to do so would be theological imperialism.

---

experience and the specific leading of the Holy Spirit come first.

32 Travis and Travis, "Contextualization," 15.

33 Massey, "Misunderstanding C5," 14.

34 Higgins, "Key to Insider Movements," 160. Massey considers this theologizing process as a mark of true indigeneity. See Massey, "Misunderstanding C5," 14.

35 Travis, "Messianic Muslim," 59.

Higgins defines historic creeds as "biblically-based articulations of the faith within the context of the culture and questions of their time."[36] He argues that one should not require Muslim Insiders to accept the current form of historic creeds as "theological necessity" for them to have fellowship with a wide body of Christ. He recognizes the value of the creeds as examples but does not approve its normative value for Muslim Insiders to believe and confess:

> As I consider some of the questions being asked about insider movements today, it seems that these movements are being expected to arrive at an articulation of Christian faith that matches the creeds of the 4th and 5th centuries, but within four or five years. . . . It seems, then, that Trinitarian definitions or understanding the Sonship of Jesus in a Nicene philosophical framework have become for some an "essential." The same is true for numerous other important topics and doctrinal formulations. For example, is it sufficient for a follower of Jesus to affirm the unique and final authority of the Old and New Testaments, or must they articulate a particular definition of infallibility that some western Christians might see as "essential"? Are these understandings important? Of course. Are they essential for salvation? That would be difficult to demonstrate biblically.[37]

Higgins further contends that since the Holy Spirit takes Muslim Insiders "through a long-term process where they are developing a biblical theology in a specific cultural context," the outsiders should show patience toward them.[38]

In his recent article, Higgins clarifies the issue in stating that IM advocates or Muslim Insiders acknowledge the value of the creeds, and that IM advocates do promote the creeds in the ministry of the IM. This fact, however, does not solve the problem. IM advocates argue that Muslim Insiders must develop and articulate the creeds differently from the historic creeds by considering their own context. Higgins does not provide an example of

---

36  Higgins, "Acts 15," 36. Steve Strauss provides an excellent discussion on the form and meaning of historic creeds. He seems to agree with Travis at one point: "Creeds and confessions are expressions of biblical truth for specific times and places." There is a crucial difference between Strauss and Travis in that Strauss stresses the universal essence of historic creeds, which can play a uniting role for the global church around them. Strauss fully affirms that the essential content of historic creeds is universal while allowing different forms to be used for communicating the same meaning depending on contexts. See Strauss, "Creeds, Confessions," 140–56.

37  Higgins, "Acts 15," 36.

38  Higgins, "Acts 15," 36. His view is further clarified in his response to IM critics in Higgins, "Speaking the Truth," 67–68.

different creedal expressions of Muslim Insiders, but he contends for the need to develop different theological formulation or articulation within an Islamic context.[39]

In defense of his view of historic creeds, Higgins finds a biblical precedent in Acts 2:42, where the apostolic teaching played an important role in the life of the early church. In his interpretation of this verse, however, Higgins changes the emphasis of this biblical evidence, taking in another direction:

> This "devoted" includes a commitment not only to right apostolic doctrine, but also to right apostolic ministry. It is not only the message of the apostles that we're to learn and embrace but also their method of ministry. How did they communicate the gospel, plant churches, and build leaders? Being devoted to the apostles' teaching and fellowship means seeking to do apostolic work the apostolic way.[40]

It is strange to see Higgins making this subtle change of emphasis from the message of the apostles to the method of ministry, which maneuvers the apostolic doctrines to a secondary matter. The historical context in Acts 2 indicates that the apostolic teaching was the major center of the early church in terms of its contents, not the apostolic method. Higgins largely misrepresents the biblical testimony for the sake of his argument against the orthodox doctrinal teaching of the historic Christian church.

IM advocates emphasize the crucial role of inductive Bible study under the guidance of the Holy Spirit for the spiritual growth, discipleship, and self-theologizing of Muslim Insiders.[41] An important issue is how one can determine the leading of the Holy Spirit among Muslim Insiders. How can one be sure about the fact that Muslim Insiders will come to figure out and believe biblical truth as the historic Christian Church has believed?

It is apparent that their creedal expressions depart from historical orthodox creeds, because the theological assertions and theologizing methods of IM advocates indicates that direction. IM advocates, for example, do not

---

39 Higgins, "Speaking the Truth," 78–79.

40 Higgins, "Key to Insider Movements," 157.

41 Higgins, "Speaking the Truth," 67–68; Higgins, "Acts 15," 36; Travis and Travis, "Maximizing the Bible," 22. Although inductive Bible study is emphasized, one may wonder why Muslim Insiders do not reach the same biblical theological conclusion that the orthodox Christian church has believed. That is, remaining within Islamic religious community by continuing to practice Islamic rituals is not biblically acceptable. One may wonder how Muslim Insiders would interpret the overarching exclusive theological stance of Yahweism in the Old Testament and the explicitly exclusive statements of the New Testaments (John 14:6; Acts 4:12).

favor a Trinitarian expression of the Chalcedonian creed because the notion of the Trinity becomes a stumbling block to Muslims. It is ambiguous as to how Muslim Insiders develop their own forms or expressions of historic creeds that reflect biblical truth within the Islamic context. If they do not remain within the boundary of the universally agreed essential content of historic creeds, it might be dangerous to give Muslim Insiders the freedom to develop their own theological creedal expressions that are contextually driven. Strauss correctly points out a balanced view of historic creeds:

> They [creeds and confessions] unite the universal church around a common history and serve as examples of theology that is both biblical and relevant. This is the sense in which the universal church *can* unite around the Nicean statement about the Triune God and the Chalcedonian formula regarding the person of Christ. They were accurate expressions of biblical truth for their own context, and the consequently provide the church in *every* context with an example of biblical orthodoxy. But in another sense, no creed, no matter how biblical, can ever be the standard against which all other theologies are measured. Only Scripture itself can stand in judgment of any theological expression. The form through which scriptural truth is expressed in creeds and confessions should not be equated with the truth itself.[42]

Even though their theological articulation and formulation in linguistic forms may differ from historic creeds, the proper exegetical conclusion of inductive Bible study can lead any serious Bible student to the universal nature of biblical truths that are explicated succinctly in the historic creeds.

## Plurality of Theology

IM advocates contend for a diversity of biblical theology and deny the existence of a unified single biblical theology. Since all theology is formulated within a cultural and historical context, they contend for a relativity of all theologies. This view seems to lead them to undermine consistent biblical theological themes throughout the Scriptures. Concerning the question of whether or not the IM upholds the integrity of the Gospel, Lewis asserts, "We must turn to the Bible as the authority for our faith and practice, especially to the book of Acts and the epistles of Paul."[43] While it is certainly commendable for Lewis to regard the Bible as an authoritative source, it is also surprising that she tends to neglect the whole biblical theological

---

42 Strauss, "Creeds, Confessions," 155–56 (emphasis in the original).
43 Lewis, "Integrity of the Gospel," 41–42.

framework as the supreme guideline, but considers a selected portion of the Scriptures, such as Acts and the Pauline Epistles, as a more important source of theologizing.[44]

Due to the lack of a biblical theological perspective, IM advocates tend to deploy certain parts of Scripture while neglecting other unfavorable biblical data. Woodberry seems to be an exception when he underscores the importance of dealing with biblical evidence that stands contrary to the theological foundation of the IM and the need for analyzing the entire biblical data to find a consistent biblical theological answer to the IM. Woodberry presents the book of Hebrews as a potential counter example against the IM: "On the other hand, the Epistle to the Hebrews gives some warnings to some believers who have remained under the umbrella of their original faith."[45] IM advocates need to look into the whole canon of Scripture and evaluate parts within the whole. They should equally treat passages that stress an exclusivist tone and biblical repentance in terms of "turning from" and "turning to." Whenever inconsistency is in view, the overarching biblical theology better serves as a grid to resolve seemingly conflicting matters, and aid in formulating a sound biblical theological framework.[46]

According to the preceding observation, it is viable to identify the IM as a contextualization model based upon neo-orthodox or sub-orthodox theological orientation. The meaning of contextualization behind the IM is identified as prophetic contextualization according to the framework of Hesselgrave and Rommen. Prophetic contextualization sounds positive, but it refers to contextualization which "entails entering a cultural context, discerning what God is doing and saying in that context, and speaking and working for needed change."[47] The supremacy of Scripture has primarily been undermined by elevating human cultural contexts which serve a

---

44 The selective use of the Scriptures is a problematic feature found among some IM advocates. For example, Herbert Hoefer contends that since Muslims do not confess the authority of the Pauline Epistles, one may "forgo the Pauline epistles and focus wholly on the Gospels." See Hoefer, "Muslim-friendly," 51. This is simply an unbearable absurdity to Bible-believing Christians because the whole counsel of God's Word should be respected in life and ministry.

45 Woodberry, "To the Muslim," 26.

46 Hebrews is a challenging text for IM advocates because there is a strong warning for the Jewish believers against returning to old Judaism (Heb 6:4–6).

47 Hesselgrave and Rommen, *Contextualization*, 150. Hesselgrave and Rommen argue that this notion of prophetic contextualization dangerously deviates from an orthodox theological foundation primarily because of the weakened scriptural authority. Kraft, on the contrary, uses the term "prophetic contextualization" in a positive sense in his article: "Contextualization of Essential Christianity," 86.

crucial role in determining the meanings of the biblical text, and thus, has impacted the theologizing process of contextualizers.

This is in a sharp contrast to apostolic contextualization of orthodox theological orientation, which approves the supremacy of Scripture and emphasizes the "supracultural nature of the biblical gospel."[48] Even though God's revelation is clothed with human cultural forms, it does not destroy the absolute nature of the biblical message. Hesselgrave and Rommen describe the relationship between God's revelation and human cultural contexts as follows: "The biblical message, therefore, is unique. The impingements of circumscribed cultures, imperfect authors, and human languages are transcended in such a way as to provide a perfect gospel."[49] The human cultural context, therefore, does not affect the meanings of biblical text, but rather it becomes a venue for applying the objectively given meanings of God's message.

Due to the theological orientation of IM advocates, the IM generally stands upon the neo-orthodox dialectical method of contextualization. This is dialectical, because there is an emphasis on the ongoing relationship between Scripture and human cultural contexts. They attempt to discover truth by observing what God is doing in Muslim contexts and interpreting that truth within the light of Scripture. Therefore, truth, to IM advocates, is not dependent upon what Scripture teaches, but it relies primarily upon the dialectical interaction between human contexts and Scripture.

The danger of the dialectical contextualization method lies in that normative truth does not come solely from God's written Word but from human experiences and reflections in different cultural contexts. According to Hesselgrave and Rommen, the biblical method of contextualization, which is the basis of orthodox theological orientation, relies on a didactic method known as "teaching truth."[50] The apostolic teachings of the early church have been transmitted unaltered throughout generations and remains the core of the Gospel in the church today.

Evaluating the IM from this angle, one can understand why IM advocates often undermine the significance of historic creeds and theological orthodoxy in the life of Muslim Insiders. They understand that the theological positions and doctrinal statements of Muslim Insiders are inevitably different from the apostolic teachings and orthodox doctrines. While they seek to give liberty to Muslim Insiders so they can work out their own theological position in light of Scripture under the guidance of the Holy Spirit,

---

48  Hesselgrave and Rommen, *Contextualization*, 149.
49  Hesselgrave and Rommen, *Contextualization*, 149.
50  Hesselgrave and Rommen, *Contextualization*, 155.

they apparently do not realize the significant factor of Christ's Great Commission: teaching the nations what Christ commanded (Matt 28:19–20) and what the apostles preached. One way to understand the serious implications of the IM is to delineate the theological conclusions of IM advocates or what Muslim Insiders actually believe. Some of the sharply debated topics include the Trinity, Christology, soteriology, and ecclesiology.[51]

## AN EVALUATION FROM A HERMENEUTICAL PERSPECTIVE

### Hermeneutical Circle

The revelational epistemology and the theological orientation influence the hermeneutical features of IM advocates to such a degree that it is imperative to evaluate the IM from a hermeneutical perspective. While not every IM advocate shares the same stance on this matter, there are sufficiently congruent hermeneutical assumptions and methods among IM advocates. As revealed in the revelational epistemology of IM advocates, IM advocates believe that human cultural contexts affect the interpretive lens of Bible interpreters. It is assumed that no interpreter can claim an objective meaning of the biblical text because of the cultural conditioning of interpreters. From the evaluation of the biblical interpretation in chapter 4, one can deduce that IM advocates have not given essential priority to determining the authorial intent of a given biblical text. Their primary interest lies in searching for the significance of the text in a contemporary context.[52] As a result, IM advocates show little regard for the grammatical-historical hermeneutical method, which is the predominant interpretive approach among orthodox evangelical scholars. Instead, they take understanding the contemporary significance of the biblical text as important as finding the meaning of biblical text so that their concern for the IM context often overrides that of a sound hermeneutical process.

The hermeneutical approach of IM advocates is similar to the "new hermeneutics" or "hermeneutical circle" of Padilla in which two major poles stand at an equally important place: human cultural contexts (the IM context) on the one hand and Scripture on the other. The hermeneutical

---

51 See Coleman, "Theological Analysis"; and Hwang, "Is the Muslim Insider Movement."

52 This characteristic is indicated by the lack of their interaction with evangelical commentaries available today. Their interpretations on key biblical passages tend to depart from a range of interpretive views expressed in commentaries written by evangelical scholars.

circle begins with observing what God is doing in the IM context. It enables interpreters to take questions and critical issues to relevant biblical texts; some of these questions might not have been addressed before by other traditional interpreters. This explains why some specific questions IM advocates place upon biblical passages are completely new or foreign to other biblical scholars in their exegetical analyses. It is commonly observed that many evangelical commentaries do not specifically address such issues and questions that IM advocates bring to the biblical text.

IM advocates, for example, typically read Acts 2–3 in order to find relevant biblical validation for the IM by contending that early Jewish believers were examples of maintaining a former socioreligious identity and continuing to observe religious practices. These types of questions and statements are usually not addressed by many commentators as they interact with this text. IM advocates also read Acts 15 in an unconventional way by imposing the IM issues on it. A precise exegetical effort to understand the meaning of the Jerusalem Council in the original historical and literary context is lacking while their attention is placed on how this case can provide a guiding principle in a contemporary IM context. IM advocates take questions from the contemporary context of Muslim ministry to the biblical texts to determine their contemporary meanings. In the process, authorial intention of the texts, which is the determinative factor for objective meaning of the text, becomes a secondary matter for the sake of contemporary relevance.

The other side of the hermeneutical circle involves transferring Scripture to human contexts; this process is referred to as self-theologizing by IM advocates. By observing what Scripture says about the questions and issues, IM advocates make theological assertions about the IM.[53] Through this theologizing process, a new theological perspective is introduced to the IM context so that they can make many practical proposals, such as reinterpreting the Qur'an through a Christocentric lens and allowing for *Shahada* by Muslim Insiders.

Nevertheless, some reasonable objections arise concerning this hermeneutical circle of IM advocates. First, the supremacy of Scripture is ignored in the process because the beginning of their hermeneutics is not Scripture but human context, namely the IM context. The authorial intent of the biblical text is not the central concern of IM advocates so that their interpretations move away from a range of acceptable interpretations measured by the

---

53 The result of the self-theologizing process has become an identifiable theology of missions, namely the IM theology of missions. No IM advocate has succeeded in producing a congruent theological study of the IM, but one can be expected to appear in the near future. When such a comprehensive theological work is available, it will help to reveal fundamental issues, problems, and related missiological impacts of the IM.

authorial intent. Chapter 4 revealed that most of the interpretations of IM advocates stand on shaky exegetical grounds. The objective meaning of the biblical text is replaced by a contextually driven interpretation.

Second, the hermeneutical circle of IM advocates produces many subjective interpretations because no normative hermeneutical method is stressed. The underlying assumption is that every interpreter approaches the biblical text with his own life experiences and culturally conditioned theological presuppositions. By using the illustration of an audience in an auditorium, Massey contends that everyone sits at a different spot and has a different perspective.[54] Depending on different viewpoints, every observer sees the same thing differently.

This reasoning, however, cannot be applied to God's revelation in Scripture because every evangelical Christian should stand upon the clarity and sufficiency of Scripture.[55] God's truth can be known to human beings, because He communicates His divine truth through revealing His will and desire in Scripture. The objective meaning of the biblical text must be understood within the framework of the authorial intent through a sound exegetical method. The ultimate goal of biblical interpretation is to know what God has intended and what a human author intended to communicate in the Scriptures. The most reliable method throughout church history is the grammatical-historical hermeneutical method. The evangelical community has employed this method to establish a commonly shared set of evangelical doctrines and preserved the authentic Gospel until today. While some variations in interpretation exist among evangelicals on minor matters, such as forms of baptism, ecclesiological orders, the essential nature of the Gospel and orthodox doctrines have remained intact throughout history. All these results have been possible because of the emphasis on the objective meaning of the biblical text and the emphasis on the grammatical-historical hermeneutical method in biblical interpretation.

## Hermeneutical Method

IM advocates promote a subjective method of biblical interpretation on the assumption that each interpreter brings his own hermeneutical lens to the biblical text. Greer describes this hermeneutical lens and the hermeneutical process:

---

54  Massey, "Misunderstanding C5," 7.
55  Grudem, *Systematic Theology*, 47–138.

One's hermeneutical lens is often shaped by one's theological and church tradition(s) as well as one's personal journey. After this honest and transparent reflection, if the methodology behind the exegesis is acceptable and the analysis consistent, then the conclusions can be considered viable. A fellow academic may not agree with the fundamental assumptions that compromise an analyst's hermeneutical lens, but the analysis and conclusions are generally to be considered viable. This process is important because evangelicalism embraces a wide range of potentially conflicting theological traditions (such as Presbyterianism, Methodism, Pentecostalism, etc.). This transparency in methodology facilitates us academics to stand united in Christ even though we may disagree on particular theological points.[56]

The most serious problem in Greer's description of the IM hermeneutical method is that there cannot be normative, objective criteria to judge which hermeneutical method and fundamental assumptions are admissible among evangelicals. According to his description, one's interpretation is viable as long as his interpretive method is transparent and the analysis is consistent in dealing with biblical text. Scripture does not serve as a judge in deciding which assumptions and methodologies are biblically permissible. While theological differences among evangelicals do exist among various traditions and denominations, the core of the Gospel has to remain intact because the primacy of Scripture necessarily determines proper hermeneutical methods and presuppositions. The hermeneutical method of IM advocates lacks essential screening mechanism to distinguish correct or permissible interpretations from wrong and impermissible ones. The consequence can become confusing and misleading as is the case with the IM.

Some examples of hermeneutical fallacy in the biblical interpretations of IM advocates may prove the point. One of the most utilized hermeneutical methods among IM advocates is the imprecise use of analogical reasoning. IM advocates assert that there is an analogical relationship between early Jewish believers and Muslim Insiders by taking note of several parallel features between Judaism and Islam, such as their emphasis on laws and outward religious observance.[57] Furthermore, by relating the situation of

---

56 Greer, "Review," 204.

57 Woodberry contends, "Although there are some differences, much of Islamic Law is similar to Mosaic Law and can be internalized and interpreted as fulfilled in Christ." See Woodberry, "To the Muslim," 24. He also notes that the five pillars of Islam have their origins in either Judaism or Christianity. See Woodberry, "Contextualization," 171–86. Analogical parallelism is made between the Samaritans within the Samaritan religion and Muslim Insiders and between Messianic followers of Jesus and Messianic Muslims.

Muslim Insiders analogous to the historical situation of the early church, IM advocates contend that Muslim Insiders can maintain a dual identity as both Muslims and followers of Jesus in the same way that early Jewish believers maintained a dual identity as both Jews and followers of Jesus. Another popular example of using analogical reasoning is found in the contention that just as New Testament writers and the apostles interpreted the Old Testament through a Christocentric hermeneutical lens, Muslim Insiders can interpret the Qur'an through the same Christocentric hermeneutical lens.[58]

When analogical reasoning is applied to Scripture as a hermeneutical method, it necessarily warrants the use of analogical reasoning to the cases at hand by demonstrating sufficient similarities between the two items under comparison.[59] In the case of the IM, early Jewish believers are compared to Muslim Insiders. A subtle assumption behind this comparison is that Judaism can be compared to Islam. If IM advocates deploy analogical reasoning to validate the IM, they are obliged to demonstrate sufficient similarities between early Jewish believers and Muslim Insiders and the two religious movements, Judaism and Islam. As far as the IM writings available today are concerned, there is no sufficient proof for this task. Since there is an insurmountable gap between Judaism and Islam and between the Old Testament and the Qur'an, they have not succeeded in accomplishing this goal. Since this issue is closely related to how IM advocates view Islam, one has to evaluate their theology of religions and more specifically, their biblical theology of Islam. This fundamental hermeneutical problem of IM advocates has not been addressed adequately.

When IM advocates use case-based analogical reasoning, they seem to agree on Kraft's contention that analogy is one of the effective ways of communication.[60] When Kraft takes the Bible as "an inspired collection of classic cases from history," he contends that God communicates divine truth through these cases and appropriate analogy. This view of Scripture and the

---

58 Higgins, "Key to Insider Movements," 163; Jameson and Scalevich, "First-Century Jews," 36.

59 Cosgrove, *Appealing to Scripture*, 51–89. Cosgrove argues, "Analogical reasoning is an appropriate and necessary method for applying scripture to contemporary moral issues." His analysis of how analogical reasoning should work clarifies subtle dangers and problems related to this method. He quotes James M. Gustafson about two problems beset analogical reasoning from Scripture: "One is demonstrating sufficient similarity across the epochal gaps between biblical times and our own. A second is that of control: on what basis do we select some biblical stories and not others?" See also Gustafson, "Place of Scripture," 430–55.

60 Kraft, *Christianity in Culture*, 155.

## An Evaluation of the Insider Movement through an Analytical Framework 169

proposed hermeneutical method of analogy tend to destroy the authority of Scripture as well as distort the objective meaning of Scripture.

### Historical Precedent in Hermeneutics

Another hermeneutical error among IM advocates is found in their importation of historical precedents of Scripture into the IM context. Many IM advocates agree that the Jerusalem Council of Acts 15 can be repeated in the present-day context to discuss missiological issues such as the IM.[61] Higgins, Travis, and Lewis all emphasize that the Jerusalem Council provides a model to emulate for missiological debate over the IM.[62]

This conclusion comes from their negligence of a hermeneutical principle: While interpreting the biblical narrative from historical books or from Acts, it is important not to make the historical precedents of the biblical narratives as normative rules. Stuart and Fee provide a helpful guideline on this matter:

> The crucial hermeneutical question here is whether biblical narratives that describe what *happened* in the early church also function as norms intended to delineate what *must happen* in the ongoing church. Are there instances from Acts of which one may appropriately say, "We *must* do this," or should one merely say, "We *may* do this"? Our assumption, shared by many others, is that *unless Scripture explicitly tells us we must do something, what is only narrated or describes does not function in a normative way*—unless it can be demonstrated on other grounds that the author intended it to function in this way.[63]

Concerning the matters of Christian practices, some biblical precedents may be regarded as repeatable patterns. This might be what IM advocates contend for. Fee and Stuart, however, provide a detailed guideline to determine the repeatable patterns that are legitimate:

> The decision as to whether certain practices or patterns are repeatable should be guided by the following considerations. First, the strongest possible case can be made when only one pattern is found (although one must be careful not to make too much of silence), and when that pattern is repeated within the

---

61 See the writings of IM advocates in the discussion on Acts 15 in chapter 4.

62 Higgins, "Acts 15," 29–40; Travis et al., "Four Responses," 126; Lewis expressed her view in her response in Corwin, "Humble Appeal," 11.

63 Fee and Stuart, *How to Read the Bible*, 105–6 (emphasis in the original).

New Testament itself. Second, when there is an ambiguity of patterns or when a pattern occurs but once, it is repeatable for later Christians only if it appears to have divine approbation or in harmony with what is taught elsewhere in Scripture. Third, what is culturally conditioned is either not repeatable at all, or must be translated into the new or differing culture.[64]

The Jerusalem Council occurred once in the New Testament, and there is no other biblical example. It is unlikely that it should be understood as a normative pattern. Moreover, this historical event cannot be repeated because the apostolic authority cannot be claimed in the contemporary context as was the case of the Jerusalem Council.

The fact that IM advocates do not respect a sound hermeneutical method such as grammatical-historical hermeneutics, leads them to misinterpret important biblical passages and draw wrong exegetical conclusions. The tendency of *eisegesis* inevitably appears in some interpretations of IM advocates. Lewis, for example, takes the translated word "families" in Gen 12:3 to mean "families" in an ordinary sense and applies it to the IM context.[65] She argues that the Gospel was spread through the pre-existing community including families, and she claims that to be "the fulfillment of God's promise to Abraham that all the families of the earth would be blessed (Gen 12:3, 28:14)."[66] This claim appears to be faulty because of the Hebrew word, *mishpachah* in Gen 12:3 meaning, "clans or tribes" or "nations" in the modern sense of the term. It is correct to understand God's promise to Abraham to bless all nations of the earth. Lewis makes a mistake of relying on a modern English translation for establishing an important theological assertion.

The hermeneutical approach of IM advocates becomes a reason for a concern about the interpretive ability of Muslim Insiders. IM advocates seem to have confidence in the ability of Muslim Insiders' understanding of Scripture. Moreover, IM advocates emphasize the presence of the Holy Spirit in leading Muslim Insiders to biblical truth through the inductive Bible study method. If the hermeneutical method of Muslim Insiders is ill-equipped, there will be ad hoc interpretations and arbitrary theological conclusions. This concern is proven to be true when one reads one Muslim Insider's interpretation of Acts 15:

---

64 Fee and Stuart, *How to Read the Bible*, 111–12.

65 Lewis, "Insider Movements," 17. See also Lewis's response in Brogden, "Inside Out," 34.

66 Lewis, "Insider Movements," 17.

> In Acts 15 it was decided that the Gentile believers did not need to follow the Jewish forms of life and worship. They were not required to visit the temple or synagogue, attend the feasts, make the various sacrifices, or even be circumcised. So the Gentiles worshiped God in their own fashion. That sounds like some kind of religious contextualization. . . . The Jerusalem Council said the Gentiles should not eat meat sacrificed to idols. I presume that this was because it would be a form of idol worship. Similarly we teach people to serve God and worship him alone. We teach them to be faithful disciples of the Lord Jesus Christ.[67]

His understanding of Acts 15 is distorted to the degree that he uses a term such as "religious contextualization." Since his thought is preoccupied by his favorable view of the IM, he does not recognize the true meaning of the biblical text and thus, injects the predetermined meaning in favor of the IM. IM advocates must determine a more specific solution for helping Muslim Insiders to be armed with a sound hermeneutical method and to discern correct biblical interpretations. Since Muslim Insiders are separated from the wider believers' community, there is no mechanism for them to be corrected by other believers in their biblical interpretations.

## AN EVALUATION FROM AN ANTHROPOLOGICAL PERSPECTIVE

IM advocates utilize many facets of anthropological findings in their contextualization efforts; such utilization needs careful inspection by evangelical missionaries who desire to guard against the allowing of social science concepts taking precedence over biblical teaching. This section is focused primarily on IM advocates' views of culture and religion, more specifically, their views of Islam and the Qur'an. While IM advocates do not provide a comprehensive view of all the topics mentioned, there is sufficient data available in their writings to evaluate their views.[68]

## Theology of Culture

The fundamental orientation of IM advocates' understanding of culture is commonly labeled as "functionalist" anthropology, which was introduced

---

67 This is an excerpt from Brother Yusuf's response in Corwin, "Humble Appeal," 10.

68 It is not possible to generalize the IM advocate's view of certain topics because not everyone agrees on their viewpoints.

in chapter 3. Higgins, who provides a most detailed explanation on this topic, defines culture as an organic integrated "system" as he borrows Daniel Shaw's understanding of culture in which culture is categorized into five cultural sub-systems.[69] Just as some popular missionary anthropologists rely heavily on "functionalist" anthropology, IM advocates are also influenced by the same stream of anthropological thoughts in their writings.[70] Basically, the "functionalist" view of culture regards human culture from a positive light so that there is little space for the intervention of God and His divine revelation as the normative judgment criteria over human culture.[71] Following Kraft and Van Engen, Higgins contends that culture is simply a vehicle that can carry faith as a passenger.[72] Even though they emphasize the need for discerning and rejecting unbiblical cultural and religious components, IM advocates overall reveal a high regard to Muslim culture.[73]

Higgins makes religion a subset of culture when he categorizes religion as ideology, which is one of the five sub-systems of culture.[74] When religion becomes a sub-system or part of culture in this way, it can be viewed in a positive light as much as culture is evaluated in a positive light. Higgins contends that it is meaningless and unnecessary for Muslims to make a distinction between culture and religion, because Muslims hold a "holistic worldview like the Jews of Jesus' day."[75] He suggests that Islamic culture

69 Higgins, "Inside What," 82–83; Shaw, *Transculturation*, 24. Shaw uses five categories to describe human cultural behaviors: economics, ideology, kinship, social structure, and political organization.

70 Higgins uses the definition of culture from the sources written by general anthropologists, Malefijt, *Religion and Culture*, and Spradley, *Participant Observation*. In his discussion on worldviews, Higgins follows Kraft, a representative functionalist anthropologist, to support his contention that religion can be seen as a subsystem of culture. See the footnote in Higgins, "Inside What," 83.

71 One insightful critique on the functionalist anthropology from a conservative evangelical perspective is provided by Wan, "Critique of Functional Missionary" 18–22.

72 Higgins, "Inside What," 83.

73 Higgins, "Key to Insider Movements," 161. It is rare to see critical comments of IM advocates in their writings about Muslim cultural elements.

74 Higgins, "Inside What," 82–83. Higgins uses Malefijt's definition of religion: "systematic patterns of belief, values, and behavior acquired by man as a member of his society." This definition is viable from an anthropological perspective, but inadequate from a biblical theological perspective. This indicates another important aspect that IM advocates rely on anthropological findings more than a biblical and theological basis.

75 Caldwell, "Jesus in Samaria," 29. Caldwell is the pseudonym of Higgins. On another occasion, he seems to agree that one can separate religion from culture by stating, "Although religions and culture may be inseparable in at least some worldviews." Higgins, "Inside What," 82. Greer agrees with Higgins in his critiques of Coleman: "Coleman is able to speak about Islam as if it can be isolated from Islamic culture." See Greer, "Review," 204.

and religion may be inseparable for Muslims, and that, consequently, they should be taken together in contextualization.

This reasoning carries such import for Higgins's contention that Muslim Insiders can and should be allowed to remain in their Muslim religious community by observing Islamic religious practices. While assuming that Muslim cultures are generally accepted as a viable component in contextualization, Higgins wants to move further to include Islam as a viable component in the contextualization model by placing it within the inseparable part of culture. It is concluded, therefore, that Muslim Insiders can remain within the Islamic religion simply because it is a part of their culture as long as the religious components do not contradict biblical principles.

The fundamental problem of Higgins's argument lies in his faulty assumption of a functionalist anthropological understanding of culture and religion. IM advocates tend not to see the danger of their uncritically high view of culture and thus, place their anthropological notions over biblical authority. The crucial flaw appears in identifying religion as a part of culture so that Islam becomes a neutralized cultural component, which can also be used as a valid vehicle in IM contextualization. This arbitrary conclusion is biblically tenuous. The only solution to this problem is that IM advocates reevaluate their view of culture and religion and reexamine the functionalist anthropological assumptions from a biblical and theological perspective.

## Theology of Religions

While it is disappointing to see Higgins rely on an anthropological basis for his description of culture and religion, it is encouraging to see him attempt to establish a systematic foundation for a theology of religions based on a biblical foundation.[76] He rightly observes the inadequacy of the traditional three-fold typology of an evangelical theology of religions: exclusivism, inclusivism, and religious pluralism. By proposing the "Kingdom Paradigm" as an alternative model, Higgins observes two critical points of the biblical data on religion.[77] First, the Bible describes religion as, "the rejection of the truth of God, a rebellion masked within the form of 'religion.'"[78] Second,

---

76 Higgins, "Inside What," 83–88.

77 Higgins, "Inside What," 83–88. Some scholars have noted that this conventional three-fold categorization is inadequate to represent the biblical data and irrelevant for the contemporary pluralistic society. Morgan, "Inclusivism and Exclusivism," 17–39; Tennent, "Christian Encounter," 292–316.

78 Higgins, "Inside What," 84.

the Bible refers to religion as being "involved in the activity of demons and demonic bondage."[79] This reflection rightly reflects biblical data.

The startling problem, however, appears when he contends the third point: "The Bible describes ways in which God is at work in other religions, and suggests in at least some case that members of other religions are in a relationship with God."[80] He mentions Melchizedek, Amos, Balaam, the sailors in Jonah, the Magi, and Paul's evangelistic approach to the Athenians in Acts 17 as biblical evidence. Based on these biblical data, he asserts, "God is at work in the world, including the religions of the world, and God is drawing people to Himself beyond the confines and boundaries we normally refer to as 'His people.'"[81] When he states, "God is at work in the religious life of mankind," his notion of "the Kingdom paradigm" is extended to include religious sphere in the world.[82]

First, in evaluating IM advocates' theology of religions, it might be helpful to see where Higgins or IM advocates stand on the spectrum of the three-fold typology. Their view falls somewhere between exclusivism and inclusivism. IM advocates are not entirely inclusivists because they believe that faith in Jesus as Lord is necessary for salvation, and there is no salvation other than in Jesus Christ. IM advocates, on the other hand, do not completely agree with exclusivists on at least three important points. First, IM advocates contend there are significant amounts of evidence of God's work in other religions which is framed within the Kingdom paradigm.[83] One representative biblical basis for this claim is the so-called "holy pagans" argument whereby they emphasize the prevalent salvific works of God even among non-Israelites outside the covenant people in the Old Testament.[84] Exclusivists, however, emphasize a fundamental discontinuity between biblical revelation and other religions in that they deny revelatory or salvific factors in other religions.

Second, IM advocates do not demand an "explicit act of repentance" in terms of leaving Muslim identity and the Muslim religious community as a condition of salvation because they believe that God is at work even within the Islamic religion. Exclusivists, however, believe that the biblical principle

---

79 Higgins, "Inside What," 84–85.

80 Higgins, "Inside What," 85.

81 Higgins, "Inside What," 86. Higgins provides four propositional statements to describe his theology of religions in this article.

82 Higgins, "Inside What," 87.

83 The Kingdom paradigm is promoted by Higgins and Lewis. Higgins, "Inside What," 87–88; Lewis, "Insider Movements," 18.

84 Kaiser provides an exegetical reply to inclusivists' claims in "Holy Pagans," 121–41.

## An Evaluation of the Insider Movement through an Analytical Framework

of conversion demands repentance and conversion in terms of both "turning from" and "turning to" (1 Thess 1:9; cf. Acts 2:38, 3:19). Remaining within one's prior religion (Islam) and continuing to practice former religious (Islamic) rituals are thought to be incompatible with biblical faith.

Lastly, IM advocates contend that explicit knowledge of Christ should be maintained at a minimum level because the Bible actually does not require much cognitive knowledge other than faith in Jesus. They argue that it is unnecessary and unbiblical to require Muslim Insiders to have cognitive knowledge about the Trinity and the deity of Christ in the Trinitarian formula for their salvation. Exclusivists, however, contend that the biblical understanding of Jesus Christ is necessary in the framework of the historic Christian confession. According to Tennent, soteriology should not be treated independently of eccelsiology because the historic Christian witness and the apostolic doctrines should be carefully taught to new believers though these do not hold an equal authority with Scripture.[85]

IM advocates' view of theology of religions is much closer to a new category that has recently drawn the attention of some evangelical scholars. Since the conventional three-fold typology of theology of religions does not provide a completely satisfactory solution, some evangelicals create a new category between exclusivism and inclusivism. Tennent identifies this new attempt as a "partial replacement model," a term that originates from Paul Knitter, a Catholic theologian.[86] Tennent summarizes this view:

> While acknowledging that there is no salvation in Hinduism, Buddhism, or Islam, and that general revelation is incapable of saving anyone, some exclusivists nevertheless believe that God provides truths about himself and humanity through general revelation that are accessible to all and that some of these truths have been incorporated into the beliefs of other religions, providing points of continuity whenever there is a consistency with biblical revelation.[87]

The partial replacement model, a modified exclusivism, places an emphasis on the possibility of truths that are available through general revelation in other religions in various manners and on their potential usefulness

---

85 Tennent, "Followers of Jesus," 110–12; Tennent, "Challenge of Churchless Christianity," 171–77.

86 Knitter, *Theologies of Religions*, 33–49; Tennent, "Christian Encounter," 293–97.

87 Tennent, "Christian Encounter," 295. Tennent identifies two evangelical scholars who advocate this model: Gerald McDermott and Harold Netland. Tennent seems to favorably look at this view and makes his case in *Theology in the Context*, 53–75. This discussion deserves a further elaboration, first of all, through a biblical and theological evaluation, but it seems too early to make a final conclusion.

as a point of contact in a cross-cultural communication of the Gospel. The partial replacement model also incorporates the fulfillment concept by focusing on "the continuity between human philosophies or religions and the supernatural religion of Christianity."[88] Tennent describes this factor, "While affirming the final revelation of Christ, the fulfillment theologians see God working through the philosophies and non-Christian religions to prepare people to hear and respond to the Gospel."[89] While this emphasis on the potential of general revelation in other religions can be appreciated, many issues are yet to be solved.

It is important to understand precisely the biblical definition of general revelation in regards to the components of other religions. If one uses the notion of general revelation too loosely, one can open the door for many unsubstantiated claims about the relationship between other religions and biblical revelation. In fact, many have been confused when they find seemingly similar religious elements in non-Christian religions and try to compare them using a comparative approach to religions. In the end, these seemingly similar religious components are proved to have more qualitative differences than similarities. Hendrick Kraemer argues against this comparative religions approach because he believes that individual parts of any religion should be understood within a given religious system, and that they should not be evaluated by being removed from its whole.[90] Though the partial replacement model is not widely accepted by the majority of evangelical scholars, it certainly deserves biblical and theological discussions as a new direction for an adequate evangelical theology of religions.

Although the theology of religions of IM advocates seems to agree with this new model of exclusivism, the partial replacement model, there are critical differences as well. The differences include the second and third points that are mentioned above to describe those between exclusivists and IM advocates. The most subtle, yet, critical difference is that IM advocates use general revelation too loosely to make its notion arbitrarily rephrased or repackaged to lose its biblical meaning. Higgins, for example, uses a fuzzy notion of "people of other religions being in relationship with God" to validate his contention that "God is at work in the religions of the world."[91] He

---

88 Tennent, "Christian Encounter," 296. The fulfillment concept of the partial replacement model should be differentiated from the inclusivists' use of fulfillment theory, which is based upon an evolutionary notion of religions.

89 Tennent, "Christian Encounter," 296.

90 Kraemer, *Christian Message*, 130–41. In other words, Kraemer argues for a totalitarian understanding of religion.

91 Higgins, "Inside What," 85–86. Higgins thinks that this relationship does not necessarily refer to a saving relationship. In other words, he does not contend that

seems to stand upon a subtle assumption that God's revelatory works in other religions are to be viewed as general revelation.

The partial replacement model, however, stands on a carefully defined notion of general revelation and maintains its valid limits according to the biblical guideline that biblical primacy and authority are strictly maintained. Instead of allowing revelatory factors in other religions, the partial replacement model critically evaluates components of other religions through a biblical and theological guideline before they are accommodated in crosscultural communication. An example of the articulation process will be introduced when the use of the Qur'an is discussed below.

Higgins's central assertion that God is at work in other religions, even in Islam, has several flaws.[92] First, this assertion contains certain ambiguity. Surely God works among all peoples in the world, peoples of other religions, to lead them to himself (cf. 1 Tim 2:4; 2 Pet 3:9). This generic statement does not seem to be what Higgins asserts. He seems to indicate that God can and may use religious components of other religions to save people. For example, he contends that God has used the Qur'an to lead Muslims to salvation in Christ.[93] In response to this assertion, two points deserve mentioning. The descriptive fact (God has used the Qur'an to lead Muslims to Christ) does not automatically mean the prescriptive norm (Christians or Muslim Insiders can use the Qur'an to witness to Jesus). Also, more importantly, the biblical data that validates this assertion is so rare in the whole of the Scriptures. Even a few biblical examples IM advocates use to validate their assertion are ambiguous at best so that one should not use these examples as a basis for approving components of general revelation in other religions. It is problematic to construct a generalized principle which has important theological and missiological implications based upon only a few debatable examples in Scripture while overlooking the overarching biblical theological evidences that emphasize exclusivism and discontinuity between biblical revelation and other religions.

Second, the biblical argument behind Higgins's assertion that God is at work in other religions essentially collapses when the biblical cases called holy pagans are carefully evaluated within a larger scope of biblical theology. Higgins is right when he acknowledges that not all of the pagans in

---

general revelation is salvific in one sense, so he differs from inclusivists. On the other hand, he seems to hold an open door for potential of salvation in other religions when he asserts, "God is at work in other religions."

92 For a more comprehensive evaluation of Higgins's theology of religions, see Coleman, *Theological Analysis*, 25–77.

93 See Higgins's response in Corwin, "Humble Appeal," 10.

other religions had a salvific relationship with God.[94] Some of them, whom the Scriptures shed positive light on, became a part of God's covenantal community (e.g. Melchizedek, Ruth) and saving faith, not through general revelation but through special revelation.[95] Kaiser emphasizes that the object of saving faith both in the Old Testament and in the New Testament is the same while the method and means of salvation are not the same for everyone.[96] Carson agrees with Kaiser when he points out a crucial difference between the Old Testament believers and contemporary people of other religious faiths:

> Most of the pre-Christ believers are those who enter into a covenantal, faith-based relationship with the God who had disclosed himself to them in the terms and to the extent recorded up to that time. . . . Inclusivists who draw a parallel between modern non-Christians who have never heard of Christ and such Old Testament believers overlook the fact that these believers on the Old Testament side were responding in faith to special revelation, and were not simply exercising some sort of general "faith" in an undefined "God."[97]

In the end, IM advocates stand on a flawed theology of religions, so that their view of Islam and Islamic sources is skewed. They tend to elevate the positive aspects of the components of other religions while overlooking the importance of the contents of faith. As a result, Muslim Insiders remain vulnerable to syncretistic theological constructs in spite of their efforts to study the Bible. As a result of their theology of religions, they promote several problematic methods of contextualization in the ministries to Muslims as the following discussion demonstrates.

## View of Islam and Muhammad

After contending that the IM conversation should be framed within a discussion about "varying paradigms and assumptions of Islam," Higgins stresses that one's view of Islam plays such a significant role in the IM discussion:

> The point is that part of the C-5 [the IM] discussion needs to be a discussion about Islam itself and not just the (very valid) biblical debate about contextualization and how far it can go. . . .

---

94 Higgins, "Key to Insider Movements," 162; Higgins, "Inside What," 86.
95 Kaiser, "Holy Pagans," 130–32.
96 Kaiser, "Holy Pagans," 132.
97 Carson, *Gagging of God*, 298.

### An Evaluation of the Insider Movement through an Analytical Framework 179

> Without a discussion as to what Islam *is* and *was*, we cannot do actual contextualization. . . . I believe the differences [among missiologists and practitioners concerning the validity of the C-5 among Muslims] are primarily due to examined or unexamined differences about how we understand Islam itself.[98]

One's view of Islam is a central key in evaluating the IM. The fundamental problem of IM advocates comes from the fact that they do not take a biblical stance toward Islam but use a comparative religious approach in their understanding of Islam. Their view of Islam is derived through phenomenological observations without holding high biblical normative guidelines. For example, Woodberry, after taking note of the similarities between the Mosaic Law and the Islamic Law, contends that the Islamic Law can "be internalized and interpreted as fulfilled in Christ."[99] He sees a significant potential to refurbish and reuse Islamic pillars for the expression of biblical faith.[100] He expresses another problematic description of Islam: "Islam may be viewed as originally a contextualization for the Arabs of the monotheism inherited directly from Jews and Christians or indirectly through Arab monotheist."[101] Talman also takes Islamic cultural forms of worship as "largely biblical or of early Christian influence" without much evidence.[102] Their approach to Islam lacks a careful biblical and theological consideration.

These claims are based on the comparative observations of Islam and Islamic religious forms, and there is no serious consideration of the theological meanings of various Islamic forms and terms within an Islamic theological framework. This is a naive view of Islam and is completely disconnected from a biblical theological analysis and an evangelical biblical theology of religions. It is dangerous to claim that religious concepts in other religions are biblical simply because they appear to be similar to the biblical concepts. The notion of sacrifice in Islam, for example, cannot and should not be taken to mean the biblical sense of propitiatory sacrifice because the seemingly similar notion in two religions has completely different theological meanings. This is why Kraemer, an outspoken critic against this comparative religion approach, contends that "presenting Christianity

---

98 Higgins, "Identity," 120 (emphasis in the original).

99 Woodberry, "To the Muslim," 24.

100 Woodberry, "Contextualization," 171–86. He sees the danger of syncretism as well as the benefits from reusing the pillars of Islam: "Despite the dangers, we are seeing God blessing the refurbishing and reusing of the five common pillars in our day as they bear the weight of new allegiances to God in Christ in the Muslim world." See page 171.

101 Woodberry, "Contextualization," 174.

102 Talman, "Comprehensive Contextualization," 9.

as the enrichment of the half-truth of Islam" is impossible.[103] From a biblical theological perspective, it is correct to state that Christianity and Islam are wholly different in character and tendency.

Higgins's view of Islam is somewhat confusing. At first, he follows the conventional view: "I am not saying that Islam as we know and experience it—nor even in its supposedly pure or orthodox form—is 'true,' or that it can be embraced as it is by a believer."[104] Then he abruptly brings a conflicting idea in the footnote: "I do, however, think it is quite possible that there is an 'original Islam' in the Qur'an, an Islam that has been lost through the misinterpretation of what became the 'orthodox' versions, and that this may well be in closer (if not complete) harmony with biblical truth."[105] From this description, one can see that his view of Islam is affirmative because he desires to restore Islam to an original version by reinterpreting the Qur'an through the lens of Christ. This assertion demands more evidence and further exploration which Higgins admits, but it does portray how he desires to picture an original Islam so that Muslim Insiders can dwell in a new version of Islam that is in closer harmony with biblical truth.

Concerning the view of Muhammad, varying opinions exist among IM advocates. One needs to distinguish what IM advocates believe about Muhammad from what Muslim Insiders actually believe about him, although both are related. If IM advocates admit the prophethood of Muhammad, they do so in a historical sense that Muhammad was a social and religious reformer who turned his contemporary Arabs from polytheism to monotheism. No IM advocate has publicly admitted him as a prophet from God in the biblical sense.[106] Even when Higgins proposes three alternative options for Muslim Insiders to admit the prophethood of Muhammad, he personally does not advocate Muslim Insiders to confess the *Shahada* with lip service.[107]

A critical issue in this case, however, lies in the question of how Muslim Insiders view Muhammad. Theoretically, IM advocates do not mind Muslim Insiders' admitting and confessing the prophethood of Muhammad in

---

103 Kraemer, *Christian Message*, 355. Kraemer's notion of biblical realism deserves careful attention from contemporary missiologists including IM advocates. For his description of biblical realism, see pages 126–29.

104 Higgins, "Acts 15," 38.

105 Higgins, "Acts 15," 40. See footnote 27 in this article.

106 It is worthwhile to mention a recent attempt to find a way to acknowledge the prophethood of Muhammad by widening the biblical concept of being a prophet. Talman, "Is Muhammad Also Among the Prophets?" 169–90; Accad, "Towards a Theology," 191–93.

107 Higgins, "Identity," 121 and 123. See also footnote 14 of his article.

various meanings which are only privately defined.[108] IM advocates contend that this should be left to Muslim Insiders and not enforced by outsiders regarding their action or response. This issue of Muhammad's identity causes some important theological problems. Muslim Insiders have some syncretistic theological views between Islam and biblical truth. When Muslim Insiders learn the biblical message of Christ from *Injil*, the Gospels, while simultaneously reading the words of Muhammad in the Qur'an, they will inevitably mix the two faiths as long as the words of the latter are considered as authoritative. Next, IM advocates neglect the importance of teaching the biblical notion of prophethood as they remain passive toward teaching and guiding Muslim Insiders. They intentionally avoid teaching what the Scriptures teach about the prophethood claims of Muhammad from the biblical definition of a prophet. Instead of teaching the biblical notion of a prophet, IM advocates accommodate the Islamic notion of prophethood and use it as if it is in agreement with biblical truth. This approach is misleading and unbiblical. While trying to become relevant to Muslims, they accommodate factors of Islam uncritically and, thus, compromise biblical truth in their contextualization attempt.

## View of the Qur'an and Its Use in Muslim Evangelism

One of the most difficult issues in the IM debate involves how one views the Qur'an. Most IM advocates agree upon the reinterpretation of the Qur'an through a Christocentric lens and make it a useful common ground for Muslim evangelism.[109] Several questions deserve further elaborations: Can the Qur'an be considered as God's revelation? Does the Qur'an contain God's revelation? How valid is it to reinterpret the Qur'an through a Christocentric lens? Can Christians employ the Qur'an in Muslim evangelism? If yes, then in what ways? These questions are beyond the scope of this dissertation, because each question deserves an independent study. Nevertheless, a brief discussion on selective questions that are akin to the IM discussion is in order.

Concerning the question whether the Qur'an is God's revelation, no IM advocate has explicitly given an affirmative answer, although their view of the Qur'an is more than simply positive. Massey, for example, provides

---

108 Brother Yusuf and Brown share their opinions on how it is viable for Muslim Insiders to confess the *Shahada* in their response in Corwin, "Humble Appeal," 12.

109 Higgins and Travis are the strongest proponents of this approach. For example, see Higgins, "Key to Insider Movements," 163–64; Higgins, "Acts 15," 38; Travis, "Must All Muslims," 414; Travis, "Messianic Muslim," 59.

his view as follows: "It is because the Qur'an is so full of references to the matchless wonder of Jesus that many C5 Muslims testify."[110] Higgins takes note of all the constructive components of the Qur'an for biblical truth when he contends for the possibility of restoring the original Islam within the Qur'an.[111] Woodberry is more objective in his description of the Qur'an than the other two: "[The Qur'an] contains much that is affirmed by the Bible along with some statements contrary to the Bible."[112] Woodberry is correct in stating that the Qur'an contains both similar content to that in the Bible and other content that is contradictory to biblical accounts. It is, therefore, reasonable to conclude that even IM advocates do not accept the Qur'an in its entirety as God's revelation.

IM advocates, nevertheless, seem to be willing to admit that the Qur'an contains God's revelation or God's revelatory components as long as the content of the Qur'an is consistent with the Bible. Since there is no explicit statement made by IM advocates, it is difficult to know their position in detail. The only inference gleaned from their writings is that they are willing to take the Qur'anic witness about Jesus seriously as if there are reliable sources of God's truth about Christ that exist in the Qur'an.

The real concern, however, involves how Muslim Insiders view the Qur'an because they seem to take it to contain significant components of God's revelation, if not the supreme revelation of God through Muhammad.[113] It is highly likely that Muslim Insiders take the Qur'an as the revelation of God and find valid ground in reading the former books, *Taurat*, *Zabur*, and *Injil*. Nevertheless, several problems are in view. First, Muslim Insiders have a skewed understanding of the Scriptures. The categorization of these former books is in line with Islamic theology and is not consistent with biblical truth. That is, the Islamic understanding of the Old Testament and the New Testament is completely different from a Christian understanding of the Bible. There is a danger that Muslim Insiders are misled in their view of the Bible. Second, Muslim Insiders may give higher authority to the Qur'an than to the Bible. They may read the Bible, or *Injil*, more than the Qur'an because they love Jesus in the *Injil* more than Jesus in the Qur'an. Yet their perception of the Qur'an still continues to play an important role in their lives. Third, one may wonder how Muslim Insiders solve the prob-

---

110 Massey, "Misunderstanding C5," 14.

111 Higgins, "Acts 15," 40.

112 Woodberry, "Contextualizing," 174.

113 Travis states, "Islam is the only other major world religion that officially accepts the Bible—the *Taurat*, *Zabur*, and *Injil*—as God's inspired Scripture." See Travis, "Producing and Using," 73. He accommodates too much of the Islamic view of the Bible and consequently compromises the precise truth concerning the Christian Bible.

lem of reading conflicting testimonies between the Qur'an and the *Injil* by observing conflicting claims. As long as they maintain the notion of God's revealed Word in Scripture, they must encounter serious questions about the authenticity of either the Qur'an or the *Injil*. IM advocates have not addressed this issue in their writings.

There is yet another serious question about the validity of reinterpreting the Qur'an through a Christocentric lens. IM advocates contend that it is a valid method and that Muslim Insiders do this all the time whenever they read the Qur'an.[114] For his effort to provide biblical validation of this approach, Higgins borrows the example of Jesus and the Apostle Paul, who reinterpreted the Old Testament through a Christocentric lens.[115]

Although it may sound reasonable, it is not difficult to see the faulty reasoning when it comes to the too simplistic parallelism. The Old Testament is God's revelation without any internal inconsistency. Christ is the fulfillment of the Old Testament in that he becomes the central interpretive key to the Old Testament. This is based on the profound truth about Jesus, who is the prophesied Messiah that completely fulfilled all the prophecies in the Old Testament. On the other hand, the Qur'an cannot be claimed as God's revelation because there are many inconsistencies not only within the Qur'an but also between the Bible and the Qur'an. Though the Qur'an contains some truthful accounts of Jesus, one cannot claim that Jesus Christ has fulfilled the Qur'an in the same sense that He fulfilled the Old Testament. The logical reasoning of Higgins, therefore, simply fails to convince, and Higgins's claim loses its validity.

In fact, interpreting the Qur'an through the Christian hermeneutical lens, though it is called Christocentric, has the potential to inflict serious injustice upon the Qur'an.[116] In dealing with the Qur'an, one should treat Islam as a whole rather than in pieces. For example, Patrick Cate contends that in Islam, the Qur'an has a different value from that of the Bible in Christianity inasmuch that one cannot make a simplistic direct comparison between the two.[117] In his doctoral dissertation, Cate contends that Christians

---

114 Higgins, "Acts 15," 38; Higgins, "Key to Insider Movements," 162–63.

115 Higgins, "Acts 15," 38. Higgins states, "Jesus launched a new movement within Judaism that reinterpreted everything through the lens of a 'Jesus Key' to the Old Testament. Paul proclaimed the Gospel to the Athenians by applying a 'Jesus Key' to the interpretation of their poets and religious hymns." Also see Higgins, "Key to Insider Movements," 163.

116 Schlorff, "Hermeneutical Crisis," 145–46. Schlorff contends, "This method is at the root of the hermeneutical crisis in Muslim evangelization," and this is actually "indifferent from the Mormon hermeneutic of the Bible."

117 Cate, "Islamic Values," 358–59.

should have the right to interpret the Bible through a biblical hermeneutics while Muslims have the full right to interpret the Qur'an through their own Islamic theological hermeneutics.[118] Christians cannot inject a biblical hermeneutical view into the Qur'an as much as it is not acceptable for Muslims to interpret the Bible from an Islamic theological perspective. This is the method Ahmed Deedat employs in his attempt to renounce the deity and resurrection of Christ.[119] What right do Christians have in reinterpreting Islamic sources from the Christian perspective? Kraemer's warning deserves a careful hearing on the part of IM advocates.

The last set of questions has to do with the use of the Qur'an in Muslim evangelism. IM advocates strongly believe that it is not only a valid but also an effective method to use the Qur'an in Muslim evangelism. Muslim Insiders also use the Qur'an in their witness to Christ with other Muslims. A central question is not whether it is possible or valid to use the Qur'an in Christian witness because, in one way or another, one cannot avoid mentioning the Qur'an in Muslim evangelism. The core question is how to distinguish a valid method of using the Qur'an from an invalid method on a biblical basis. Sam Schlorff provides an excellent study of various uses of the Qur'an in ministry to Muslims.[120] He identifies two categorical uses of Qur'anic phrases, negative and positive, and critically evaluates them. As Schlorff convincingly argues, one should exercise caution about various methodologies of using the Qur'an because there are dangers involved in each method.[121] While further elaboration is beyond the scope of this study, one question requires consideration in regards to the IM.

Can the way IM advocates use the Qur'an be validated biblically? The main method of IM advocates' use of the Qur'an is to verify the biblical truth of Jesus Christ in the reinterpretation of the Qur'an through a Christocentric hermeneutical lens. They validate this method by using several biblical accounts: the Apostle Paul's mention of the pagan poets and altars in Acts 17, the use of non-canonical material in Jude 14, and the Apostle

---

118 Cate, "Each Other's Scripture," 280–90.

119 Deedat, "Christ in Islam."

120 Schlorff, *Missiological Models*, 50–78. There is an interesting introduction concerning a "new hermeneutic" in Qur'anic interpretation proposed by Kenneth Cragg. This approach seems to have many common features with Higgins's claim for the original Islam in the Qur'an.

121 For example, Schlorff is in favor of negative use of the Qur'an in the sense that one can use the historical-critical study of the Qur'an to "call into question Muslim claims for the Qur'an." But he adds a warning, "Christians should be careful not to go beyond the evidence when appealing to such studies in their witness." Schlorff, *Missiological Models*, 60.

Paul's other quotations of other non-canonical sources such as Titus 1:12 and 1 Cor 15:33.[122]

Tennent provides a clearly delineated framework on this topic under the title "the Canon of the New Testament and its relationship to other [religious] texts."[123] The most directly related discussion on the present question is the issue of how one can use the "biblical texts (or allusions to those texts) incorporated into the sacred texts of non-Christian religions," such as "hundreds of references to biblical texts in the Qur'an."[124] IM advocates actively use various Qur'anic accounts that are considered to be consistent with the Bible as a proof text for biblical truth even though they do not approve the authority of the Qur'an as God's revelation. Even when some traditional interpretations of Qur'anic passages do not coincide with biblical truth, they freely reinterpret them so that they eventually come up with conclusions that are consistent with it. The strongest biblical support for this approach comes from the biblical example in which the Apostle Paul quotes the pagan poet in his preaching to the Athenians.

This Pauline quotation raises the following question: "Can Paul's practice become an example for us to follow?"[125] In what ways should the Qur'an be used? Should there be any guiding principles and proper boundaries? Tennent provides three helpful guidelines:

> First, the use of these texts should be limited to *evangelistic outreach*, where the audience consists predominantly of non-Christians who are acquainted with the texts being quoted. . . . The context of Paul's use of Greek texts seems to provide a good rule of thumb to follow today as well. . . . Second, non-Christian texts should be used only to provide a *corroborative witness* to a biblical message, rather than an independent testimony in isolation from the biblical witness. . . . Using a nonbiblical sacred text as a corroborative witness serves to sharpen the biblical message and helps to demonstrate that Jesus does not arrive in India [or any context] as a stranger, but in answer to the prayers of Hindu [or any religious people's] hearts. . . . Third, any nonbiblical sacred text that is

---

122 For example, see Higgins's response in Corwin, "Humble Appeal," 10. A more elaborated analysis on this topic is provided by Tennent, *Theology in the Context*, 56–59.

123 Tennent, *Theology in the Context*, 55–60. Tennent identifies "four main ways in which the New Testament canon interacts with other sacred and/or authoritative texts": "Old Testament in the New Testament, noncanonical 'Jesus material' used in the canonical texts, noncanonical, non-Christian texts in the New Testaments, and biblical texts appearing in the canon of another religion."

124 Tennent, *Theology in the Context*, 59.

125 Tennent, *Theology in the Context*, 70.

quoted should be lifted out of its original setting and clearly reoriented within a new *Christocentric setting*. He imports the text out of its original context and reorients it within a new, distinctly Christian setting.[126]

These guidelines clearly emphasize the fact that the Apostle Paul's use of the nonbiblical texts should not be understood as an unregulated permission to all kinds of wild practices. This writer, however, argues that these guidelines are not precise in preventing flawed practices. According to these guidelines, IM advocates might claim that all three guidelines are satisfied in their practice of the use of the Qur'anic text. IM advocates may assert that they use the Qur'an in their evangelistic outreach to a corroborative witness to biblical truth by reinterpreting the Qur'an through the Christocentric lens.

While the basic position of Tennent is moderately acceptable concerning the limited use of Qur'anic texts for Christian witness, this writer believes that a more carefully articulated description of these guidelines should be supplied after the exegetical consideration of specific biblical texts. First, the appearance of noncanonical texts is limited in the New Testament so that it is unconvincing to make it a general rule to validate the use of other religious sources for a cross-cultural communication among people of other religions. Biblically speaking, this might be better considered as an exception rather than as a general rule. Second, the Apostle Paul's use of the pagan poets was a simple quotation to make a point of contact in order to move immediately into a biblical message. He did not utilize that text as an authoritative source. Therefore, this example cannot be used for validating IM advocates' and Muslim Insiders' use of the Qur'an because both groups use the Qur'an as the common ground. Paul's use of non-canonical religious source is at best a bridge, not a common ground.[127]

Third, the Apostle Paul's use of the poets in Acts 17 laid the groundwork for his claim of God's judgment against his audience, not for affirming the potential truth of the pagan texts. Their texts laid an important foundation for self-condemning on the part of the Apostle Paul's audience (Acts 17:30–31). This self-defeating or self-condemning feature is a commonly observed pattern in several cases where he quotes other noncanonical resources. The

---

126 Tennent, *Theology in the Context*, 71–72 (emphasis in the original). Kraemer would be critical about the third guideline of Tennent because Tennent proposes to isolate the Qur'anic texts from an Islamic theological context and reorient them within a Christian theological context with a Christocentric emphasis.

127 The exegetical analysis of Paul's use of non-canonical sources is provided in Hwang, "Does the NT Quotation." The difference between the two approaches is further elaborated in the following section.

quotation in Jude 14 appears in the context of God's judgment. The quotation in Titus 1:12 appears in the context of criticism against Cretans, and the quotation in 1 Cor 15:33 appears in a negative statement. The primary method of the Apostle Paul's quotation of noncanonical sources, therefore, must be taken not as a positive or affirmative use but as a negative or passive one. Since this is consistent in the few cases of Scripture, one could conclude that the use of non-canonical texts should be kept at a minimum or be taken as an exception rather than a general principle. It is, therefore, concluded that IM advocates' usage of the Qur'an to assert biblical truth to Muslims, and Muslim Insiders' active use of the Qur'an in their spiritual life through the Christocentric reinterpretation are apparently beyond what the biblical guideline can permit.

## AN EVALUATION FROM A COMMUNICATIONAL PERSPECTIVE

Chapter 3 revealed that Kraft's missiological model has deeply influenced the IM through his communication theory in contextualization. It is important to evaluate the IM from a communicational perspective with a special focus on its theoretical connection to Kraft's communication theory. Four main topics deserve careful evaluation: receptor-oriented communication, forms and meaning, dynamic equivalence theory and Bible translation, and a common ground approach versus a point of contact approach.

### Receptor-Oriented Communication

The instrumentalist epistemology of IM advocates plays an important role in deciding the communicational basis of the IM. Due to the subjective and incomplete nature of human perception of reality, Kraft contends that meanings do not lie in the external world, not in symbols that are used to describe the world, but they are "attached or even created" in the minds of persons who receive message.[128] Based upon the assumption that meaning is found in persons, he establishes the notion of receptor-oriented communication.

Receptor-oriented communication is found in many aspects of IM contextualization. First, IM advocates and Muslim Insiders redefine the term "Muslim" as "the one submitted to Allah"; this is fundamentally

---

128 Kraft, *Communication Theory*, 110–15. For a critical evaluation of Kraft's receptor-oriented communication theory from an evangelical perspective, see Hesselgrave, *Communicating Christ*, 55–77.

reductionistic and different from a standard notion of being a Muslim.[129] Higgins contends that Muslim Insiders can confess the *Shahada* simply because their understanding of Muhammad's prophethood is based on a different definition.[130] All Islamic theological meanings are removed in this private redefinition of the prophethood of Muhammad. In their argument for a dynamic equivalence Bible translation, IM advocates hold the view that meaning is determined by receptors:

> We thoroughly agree with Jay [Smith]. Our goal should be to communicate the meaning *as the original author intended it*, as best we can determine on the basis of grammatical-historical exegesis and the findings of modern evangelical scholarship. But the ultimate judges of whether we have communicated the meaning correctly are readers from our intended audience; if they feel that certain traditional terms communicate that God sexually coupled with a woman and procreated Jesus, we need to listen to them and determine with their input how to appropriately communicate the original meaning.[131]

According to this argument, it is Muslim readers who determine the meaning of the written Word of God. A primary focus in the IM's use of communication theory centers on how Muslims or Muslim Insiders understand the meaning of the Gospel message from their reference points of view.

One corollary of receptor-oriented communication is found in their emphasis on a felt-needs approach to Muslim evangelism. IM advocates generally contend for avoiding some of the biblical and theological terms that are used in a Christian circle simply because they can easily induce miscommunication or create unnecessary hindrances in the minds of Muslims. Brown, for instance, argues that the sonship notion should be avoided because Muslims are simply repelled by such a term.[132] The emotional response of Muslims is taken to be a guiding rule in deciding whether certain biblical and theological terms can be used in ministries to Muslims.

---

129 Travis, "Must All Muslims," 413; Higgins, "Identity," 121. While it is true that there is a variety of Muslims in the world, the standard definition of "Muslim" would include at least two confessional elements: the *Shahada*, meaning the prophethood of Muhammad, and the acceptance of the Qur'an as God's revelation. One may add some additional characteristics based upon orthodox Islamic theologies. It may be difficult to define the term based on practices since not all Muslims would agree upon such definitions. This is also an argument of IM advocates for their private redefinition of the term.

130 Higgins, "Identity," 121.

131 The Al Kalima Editorial Committee, "Response to Jay Smith," 17 (emphasis in the original).

132 Brown, "Why Muslims Are Repelled," 422–29; Brown, "Son of God," 41–52.

Certainly receptor-oriented communication can alert messengers to pay closer attention to testing whether their message is correctly communicated. However, the receptor-oriented approach to communication in the IM has some weaknesses and potential dangers. On a fundamental epistemological level, there is a faulty presupposition that meaning is found in persons. In this epistemological notion, IM advocates unavoidably deny the objective value of propositional truth. This is such an intimidation to the message of the Gospel in biblical revelation. Hesselgrave convincingly states his point:

> Orthodox and evangelical Christians hold to a unified universe and epistemology. . . . Biblical revelation is personal (i.e., God reveals *himself*), and it is also propositional (i.e., God reveals truth *about* himself and his world). The meaning of biblical revelation must be apprehended objectively by reason and subjectively by faith. In other words, one must *assent* to truth and *commit* himself to truth.[133]

IM advocates' emphasis on the human perception of Muslim receptors in the process of determining meanings is unbiblical as Hesselgrave succinctly describes the biblical position: "The emphasis of Scripture is on the clear and consistent *content* of general revelation in creation and of special revelation in the Bible, not on the prerogative of humanity to interpret it as we think best."[134] The objective nature of truth is jeopardized in their private redefinition of key terms, such as Muslim, messianic Muslim, and the prophethood of Muhammad.

When IM advocates emphasize the felt-needs of Muslims in their communication approach, they tend to neglect an important aspect of the Great Commission (Matt 28:19–20): "Teaching them to observe." IM advocates seem to take the didactic nature of the Gospel proclamation in Scripture lightly. Although Muslims may be repelled by certain terms, one must teach the biblical message by explaining it to Muslims with deep sensitivity and keen awareness. No theological compromise or syncretistic mixture should find a place in the process. IM advocates violate this rule of thumb when they use the mindset of Muslims as a reference point and adapt the message through their lens by avoiding all Muslim-adversative terms.

---

133 Hesselgrave, *Communicating Christ*, 69–70 (emphasis in the original).
134 Hesselgrave, *Communicating Christ*, 65 (emphasis in the original).

## Form and Meaning

Many assertions of the IM stand upon a theory that form can be separated from meaning. IM advocates think that inserting Christian meanings into Islamic religious forms is not only valid, but also, an effective way of communicating the Gospel with Muslims. Woodberry, by observing similarities or common features that Islamic pillars share with Jewish or Christian practices, contends that it is possible to reuse the five Islamic pillars.[135] IM advocates consider mosque worship as a possible practice for Muslim Insiders because Muslim Insiders can insert a new biblical meaning to their action. Yet, mosque attendance has a completely different meaning in the minds of Muslim Insiders though the external form remains intact. Massey even proposes how to use the Muslim form of prayer as pertaining to a Christian meaning in his attempt to choreograph the Lord's Prayer.[136]

Higgins makes a case for validating the practice of inserting new meanings to old forms by arguing from a biblical precedent. He contends that the Lord's Supper is "radically reinterpreted Passover supper that had been inaugurated by Jesus Himself" by connecting the Jewish Passover supper with the Lord's Supper in his interpretation of Acts 2:42.[137] After contending that the early church drastically transformed the Jewish ritual practices of the Passover meal both in its meaning (the Lord's Supper) and in its format of observance (more frequent observances than an annual Passover celebration), Higgins asserts, "Insider Movements as they [Muslim Insiders] continue to embrace old forms and expressions, also bring in radically new meanings and truths."[138] It is assumed that forms and meanings are separable in his reasoning.

Higgins's contention fails to convince in several ways. First, the exegetical consideration does not support that the "breaking of the bread" in Acts 2:42 refers to the Lord's Supper, which is discussed in chapter 4. Second, even if he makes the connection between the Jewish Passover supper and the Lord's Supper in the early church, this connection cannot be used as ground to validate reinterpreting Islamic religious forms with Christian meanings. Since Jesus is the fulfillment of the Lamb of God who takes away the sin of the world (John 1:29) as predicted in the Old Testament, it is valid to reinterpret the types or prophecies of the Old Testament in light of Jesus. Islam or Islamic forms are not a part of God's revelation or divinely

---

135 Woodberry, "Contextualization," 171–86.
136 Massey, "Living Like Jesus," 65–66.
137 Higgins, "Key to Insider Movements," 158.
138 Higgins, "Key to Insider Movements," 158.

*An Evaluation of the Insider Movement through an Analytical Framework*    191

ordained types that will be fulfilled through Jesus Christ. They are post-Christ religious expressions that resemble the forms in Scripture or Judaism. Neither IM advocates nor Muslim Insiders can use this case as biblical ground for validating their reinterpretation of Islamic religious forms with biblical meanings.

Many evangelicals think that Muslim forms cannot be easily separated from Islamic meanings, because they are so deeply interwoven. Parshall, for example, contends, "The mosque is pregnant with Islamic theology."[139] Warren Chastain of the Zwemer Institute for Muslim Studies also asserts, "Muslim forms cannot be divorced from their meanings."[140] Chastain sees the danger of syncretism in the IM because of not separating the two:

> A "Christian mosque" is neither fish nor fowl. It confuses converts and outrages Islamic leaders, who see it as a deceptive lure for ignorant Muslims. Other Muslims may see it as an admission of defeat, a sign that Christians are adopting their "superior" form of worship. Westernized, urban Muslims may just laugh at the idea, since many of them no longer practice the traditions of their own religion.[141]

The categorization of Hiebert to explain the relationship between form and meaning is helpful to evaluate this issue. He identifies four types of relationship as "arbitrarily linked, loosely linked, tightly linked, and equated."[142] Whether form can be separated from meaning depends on the relationship between the two. Inserting Christian meanings to Islamic religious forms may create confusion or induce syncretism in the minds of receptors when the relationship is not arbitrarily linked. The level of confusion and syncretism will depend on the degree of how tightly the Islamic form is linked to Islamic theological meaning.

One example of the arbitrarily linked relationship is the use of "Allah" when referring to God. Allah, in Arabic, had been used by Arab Christians even before the birth of Islam; therefore, there is a greater acceptance in using the Arabic term, Allah, to refer to God.[143] This use of Allah, however, should not be taken to mean that the God (Yahweh) of the Bible is identical to the Allah of the Qur'an or in Islam because there is an insurmountable

---

139 Parshall, "Danger!" 409.
140. Bridges, "Of Jesus' Mosques," 49.
141 Bridges, "Of Jesus' Mosques," 49.
142 Hiebert, "Form and Meaning," 105–8.
143 Schlorff, "Missionary Use," 46–71. Travis also takes the same view on this issue in Travis, "Producing and Using," 75.

theological gap between the two.¹⁴⁴ Most Islamic religious forms, however, contain their specific meanings within the Islamic theology that they are generally considered "tightly linked" or "equated" in Hiebert's spectrum. Mosque attendance, for example, demonstrates the foundational confession of Muslim loyalty to Allah, Islamic belief, Muhammad's teachings, and a local and/or global Muslim community. One cannot consider this loyalty as a personal and spiritual matter because it inevitably carries social and historical meanings. Attending the mosque, therefore, carries the meaning of "belonging to Islamic religious community," which does not allow Muslim Insiders to become part of the global community of Bible-believing Christians.¹⁴⁵ A dual identity is implausible.

## Dynamic Equivalence and Bible Translation

IM advocates extensively utilize the method of dynamic equivalence not only in Bible translation, but also in transculturation which is communicating biblical truth in cultural and religious forms. Reusing the five pillars of Islam for communicating biblical truth is a representative example of the latter. Some suggest an alternative cultural form of baptism in various contexts as long as the equivalent meaning is kept intact.¹⁴⁶ Though the issue of transculturation is a complicated missiological issue beyond the scope of this study, it must be said that there is a danger of this approach as mentioned in chapter 3.¹⁴⁷ The central problem in extending dynamic equivalence to

---

144 Geisler and Saleeb, *Answering Islam*, 15–33 and 135–50.

145 This is an example that any theological reflection must consider all the related theological dimensions together, not an individual theology separately. In the case of the IM, there is a close connection between soteriology and ecclesiology. The notion of belonging to the global body of Christ is closely related to the notion of being saved. As a result, if one belongs to the Islamic Muslim community and thus does not belong to the global body of Christ, he cannot be considered a child of God.

146 Kraft identifies the primary function of baptism as initiation in terms of "open commitment of the initiate to allegiance both to God through Christ and to that specific group of Christians." Kraft, *Christianity in Culture*, 67–68. In terms of ritual forms, he proposes some possibilities such as using sand in the desert or a coffin. Travis also proposes some alternative term for "baptism" because this term creates such an enigma for Muslims as it carries the meaning of "a final communal rite separating one from his family and people" in the minds of Muslims. He contends for using alternative terms, including "washing for the forgiveness of sins," "washing as a sign of repentance," "immersion as symbol of unity with Isa," or just "immersion." See Travis, "Producing and Using," 76–77.

147 Taber, *World Is Too Much*, 148; Carson, "Limits of Dynamic Equivalence," 200–213. Taber points out important differences between languages and cultural forms because form and meaning is arbitrarily linked in the former, whereas the two are

general areas of cultural and religious forms lies in the fact that forms and meanings cannot be easily separated. If cultural or religious forms and their intrinsic meanings in the source contexts are deeply interwoven together and thus, cannot be separated, then using dynamically equivalent forms does not secure a clear communication of the same original meanings in the receptors' cultural and religious contexts.

In chapter 3, it is asserted that the dynamic equivalence principle needs to be applied with much caution even in the area of language. IM advocates unapologetically argue that dynamic equivalence translation or meaning-based translation is the most effective method of cross-cultural translation.[148] Space does not allow for a complete elaboration on this issue, but one much debated topic deserves mentioning: the dynamic equivalence translation of "the Son of God" for Muslim readers.

IM advocates deduce that the literal expression of the sonship of Jesus becomes a stumbling block for Muslims because it offends them and creates hostility towards the Bible. IM advocates promote using dynamically equivalent terms for the Son of God because they believe it is not only plausible, but also valid and necessary for an effective communication of the true meaning of the biblical notion of sonship.[149] Nida refers to it as "acceptability" in Bible translation, and he defines it as "a measure of the readiness with which people are happy to receive such a text and read it."[150] Muslim-friendly Bible translation promoted by IM advocates is a typical example of emphasizing the notion of acceptability. Michael Marlowe is willing to admit the acceptability principle to styles in Bible translations. Nevertheless, he expresses a deep concern about this approach because acceptability normally involves "ideologically offensive or in some way objectionable on religious grounds" and consequently tends to cause the distortion of the original meaning.[151]

The real issue is whether the dynamic equivalence translation of the Son of God distorts the biblical and theological meaning. One needs to

---

intrinsically closely linked and thus inseparable in the latter.

148 Higgins, "Speaking the Truth," 84. Also see the view of the representative IM advocate concerning translation issues in Al Kalima Editorial Committee, "Response to Jay Smith," 15–20.

149 Brown, "Why Muslims Are Repelled," 422–29; Higgins, "Speaking the Truth," 84–85; Travis, "Producing and Using," 75. This idea is not completely new among Bible translators as one can find the earlier proponents of this idea. See De Kuiper and Newman, "Jesus, Son of God," 432–38.

150 Nida, "Intelligibility and Acceptability," 301–2.

151 Marlowe, "Against the Theology." Marlowe makes a critical evaluation of the dynamic equivalence theory in a comprehensive manner. See chapter 6 entitled "The Criterion of Acceptability."

question whether IM advocates' proposal for the dynamic equivalent terms for the Son of God can be biblically and theologically validated. Brown, a consultant to Bible translators and an IM advocate, provides four different approaches which he claims are theoretically possible and theologically valid in order to circumvent the taboo term of sonship for Muslim readers.[152] The common feature of all these approaches is that they employ somewhat dynamically equivalent terms for the sonship notion although there are some slightly different nuances. Some of the representative expressions that identify Jesus as the Son of God include: "God's Beloved Christ," "God's Beloved," "God's Eternal Word," "the Christ whom God loves as a Father loves his Son," "the Spiritual Son of God," "the Prince of God," and "the Beloved Son who comes from God."[153] He introduces actual practices in a number of Muslim communities: (1) to translate the divine sonship terminology in non-literal ways that avoid the taboo phrase and (2) to explain their original forms and meanings in the footnotes, glossary or introduction.[154]

Selective Muslim-friendly translations provide a clear picture as to how familial terms, such as the Son of God, the Father, and the Son, are translated in dynamic equivalence translations.[155] All familial language of Scripture which refers to God as the Father and Jesus as the Son is removed and dynamically translated.[156] The Father is replaced by "God," "Guardian," or "Lord" depending on various contexts. "His one and only Son" in John 3:16 is translated as "His unique Son (i.e., His only beloved)" and "His son" in John 3:17 as "His only beloved" while the son of Man is translated as "the master of the humanity" (John 3:14–15).[157]

There is an important underlying theological premise that demands a careful biblical and theological evaluation. Brown contends that the term, "Son of God," in the Bible is dynamically equivalent to "the Messiah or

---

152 Brown, "Why Muslims Are Repelled," 426–28.

153 Brown, "Why Muslims Are Repelled," 426–27.

154 Brown, "Why Muslims Are Repelled," 427.

155 See selective samples in two chapters of a recent publication written by IM critics. Simnowitz, "How Insider Movements Affect Ministry," 163–72; Lingel, "Islamizing the Bible," 215–18.

156 One common characteristic in these samples is that it is so loosely translated without strict verse distinctions, and thus it becomes possible to incorporate non-familial languages.

157 In one Bengali translation, the Son of God is consistently translated as "the Messiah of God," and "Father," referring to God, is translated as "Guardian." In one Malaysian translation, Shellabear Revision, "Son of God" is consistently translated as "Prince of God," while "Son of Man" is translated as "Prince of Flesh." See Lingel, "Islamizing the Gospel," 164–72.

### An Evaluation of the Insider Movement through an Analytical Framework 195

Christ."[158] Brown explores the biblical meaning of the Son of God in several articles and concludes that it is a viable option to translate the familial terms of Scripture into dynamically equivalent expressions.[159] One question arises from his assertion: "Is it true that the Son of God is a biblically and theologically equivalent term to 'the Messiah'?" In other words, the question is whether any significant loss of biblical truth occurs by deploying this dynamic equivalence translation.

While a full scale elaboration of this issue is not possible, it is worth noting the main claim of biblical scholars and IM critics on this issue. They argue that the Messiah cannot be an equivalent term to contain all the rich meaning that the Son of God or other familial expressions communicate in Scripture.[160] Brown's argumentation raises several related problems that bear mention. There are two reasons Brown makes his assertion that the term, "Son of God," carries the same meaning as the Messiah. The first is his assumption that in the first-century Jewish context, the Son of God did not include the meaning of deity in its primary reference to the Messiah so that he connects the Son of God in the biblical account only to the Messianic meaning without pointing to any notion of deity.[161] Relying on recent studies of Second Temple literature, Brown contends that other passages than that of the Son of God can still testify the deity of Jesus. His reasoning stands on an unlikely assumption that the meaning of the Son of God was the same between the Jewish view portrayed in Second Temple literature and the biblical view of the New Testament. He offers little evidence in support of this assumption, and his assertion becomes an implausible option within an evangelical biblical theological framework.[162]

---

158 Brown, "Why Muslims Are Repelled," 428. Travis agrees with Brown by quoting his work: "Often in Scripture 'Son of God' is clearly an alternative term that simply means the Messiah. See Luke 1:32–33; 4:41; Mark 14:61; Matt 16:16, 20." See Travis, "Producing and Using," 75.

159 Brown, "Son of God," 41–52; Brown, "Explaining the Biblical Term," 91–96; Brown, "Translating the Biblical Term," 135–45.

160 For objections to the Muslim-friendly Bible translation, see Carlton, "Jesus, the son of God," 1–30; Horrel, "Cautions Regarding Son of God," 639–66; Abernathy, "Jesus is the Eternal," 327–94. It is useful to read the dialogue between IM critics and IM advocates on this translation issue. See Brown et al., "Muslim-Idiom Bible Translations," 87–105; Abernethy, "Translating Son of God," 176–203; Greer, "Son of God," 464–70; Dixon, "Some Questions," 911–14. One recent introduction to this issue for general readers appears in Hansen, "Son and the Crescent," 19–23.

161 Brown, "Son of God," 47–49; Brown, "Explaining the Biblical Term," 93–94; Brown, "Translating the Biblical Term," 138–41.

162 While biblical scholars still debate this topic, Brown's assumption is less likely to be accepted according to the prevalent evangelical scholarly studies. See Bauer, "Son of God," 769–75.

The other way Brown validates his assertion is by providing biblical passages (Luke 4:41; Matt 16:16, 20–21; John 1:49, 51) where the Messiah and the Son of God seem to be interchangeable.[163] Brown, for example, comments on Luke 4:41: "This passage shows that Jesus did not want his kingly identity announced publicly; it also demonstrates that 'the Son of God' and 'the Christ' were still synonymous titles."[164] His contention for the synonymous use of the two terms depends on the belief that Luke uses "the Christ" in his explanatory comment after the demon shouted by identifying Jesus as "the Son of God." Since Brown does not provide an exegetical analysis of this text, it is difficult to evaluate other aspects of his exegesis in detail, but it is clear that he does not consider other exegetical explanations before proposing his predetermined conclusion.

Matthew Carlton, in his critique of Brown's claims, provides an exegetical analysis of the same text and points out an important distinction between the two terms: "So Luke's explanatory comment, 'because they knew he was the Christ' spotlights Jesus' ministry and mission, while the declaration 'You are the Son of God' highlights His divine nature."[165] Biblical scholars agree that the term "the Son of God" emphasizes the essence of who He is in terms of His uniquely intimate relationship with God the Father, His pre-existence, and His divine nature while the term "Christ" emphasizes the ministry and mission of Jesus.[166]

Based upon two counter arguments, Brown's assertions for the synonymous use of the two terms remain unconvincing. While the term "Messiah/Christ" communicates the work of Jesus within the framework of the divine mission and the fulfillment of the prophecies, it cannot communicate profound biblical truths about Jesus, such as the eternal preexistence of the Son, the co-equality of the Son with the Father, and the uniquely intimate relationship between the Father and the Son. As a result, replacing the Son of God with the Messiah in Bible translations inevitably causes theologically reductionistic results, and thus should be avoided.

This brings the discussion to a final point. The most serious problem of the dynamic equivalence translation is the lack of objective criteria to make value judgments on variable cultural forms and factors. Even in the case of "the Son of God," IM advocates contend that different expressions are to be used depending on the context. There is no clearly delineated criterion to

---

163 Brown, "Son of God," 47–48.

164 Brown, "Son of God," 47.

165 Carlton, "Jesus, the Son of God," 22. Abernathy provides a succinct summary of the main claims of Brown et al., "Muslim-Idiom Bible Translations," and the major points of his response in "Translating 'Son of God,'" 199–201.

166 Erickson, *Word Became Flesh*, 35; Bauer, "Son of God," 772–75.

make a judgment call because this matter falls into the trap of subjectivity in the end. IM advocates must pay special attention to Nicholls' emphatic statement that "dynamic equivalence principle is necessarily subjective," and that the formal correspondence principles of Scripture should be used as an important basis for making right value judgments on all cultural and religious factors.[167] Their attempt to use dynamic equivalence translations in regards to the replacement of familial terms is dangerous and unacceptable because it substantially distorts the biblical truth of Jesus Christ.

## Common Ground versus Point of Contact

IM advocates heavily rely on a common ground approach in their ministry to Muslims. Based upon the underlying assumption that there exist many similarities and common features between Islam and Christianity, they emphasize finding common ground and de-emphasize their differences. Many parallel features are used in IM writings, such as the parallel between the early Jewish believers and Muslim Insiders, Allah and Yahweh as a monotheistic God, many portrayals of Jesus in the Qur'an and in the Bible, etc.

The most fundamental presupposition of IM advocates is that Islam and biblical truth have commonality in their theologies. Travis, for example, indicates that "perhaps the single greatest hindrance to seeing Muslims come to faith in Christ is not a theological one (i.e. accepting Jesus as Lord) but rather one of culture and religious identity (i.e. having to leave the community of Islam)."[168] He assumes that a hindrance due to theological differences plays a less important role in preventing Muslims from coming to faith in Christ than a hindrance due to cultural and religious identity. Woodberry also believes that Muslim pillars have a common heritage and features for the communication of the Gospel to Muslims and in the life of Muslim Insiders. Consequently, it is argued that Muslim Insiders can freely use the Islamic religious practices they used to observe even after coming to faith in Christ.

One of the main distinctions between the common ground and the point of contact approaches to cross-cultural communication is the extent to which one remains in the initial contact point. Both approaches start on

---

167 Nicholls, *Contextualization*, 66.

168 Travis, "Must All Muslims," 414. Brown agrees with Travis when he comments about Muslims' perception of the Bible: "In all these cases, the Muslims were not reacting to the theological content of the Gospel, but to the occurrence of a literal translation of the terms 'Son of God' and 'sons/children of God.'" See Brown, "Why Muslims Are Repelled," 425–26.

a similar or common factor between Christianity and Islam. However, the point of contact approach does not remain long in the Islamic ground, and moves to the ground of biblical truth because proclaiming and teaching biblical truth is the ultimate goal in evangelizing to Muslims. The length of time in which the common ground approach remains within the Islamic framework, on the other hand, is more extensive. This approach also employs as many common ground factors as possible to communicate biblical truth while staying in the Islamic ground.[169] IM advocates encourage Muslim Insiders to remain in their Muslim communities unless they are expelled out of their communities. In the meantime, Muslim Insiders have to reinterpret some of the incompatible Islamic theological teachings in order to maintain the integrity of biblical truth.

The common ground approach of IM advocates has several problems. First, the fundamental presupposition that there exist many common features between Islam and biblical truth is questionable. This presupposition clearly advances beyond the biblical evidence. Many theological terms in the Qur'an and in the Bible have different meanings within each theological system even though they look similar. They should not be taken as common ground factors simply because of their seeming similarities. As both Kraemer and Nida strongly argue, one should be able to see an insurmountable gap in their meanings once they compare and contrast them within each individual theological system.[170] Contrary to Travis' evaluation, the greatest hindrance to seeing Muslims come to faith in Christ is fundamentally theological. This has been widely acknowledged historically, and it is still so today.

While emphasizing the common ground approach, IM advocates often overlook the importance of the apostolic proclamation of the Gospel to Muslims. Both the biblical evidence in the early church and the historical evidence from church history testify that the Gospel advanced into the nations through bold apostolic proclamation and many times through confrontation. IM advocates have largely underestimated the value of confrontation in ministries to Muslims.[171] However, there is hardly any doubt that proclamation and confrontation were the most apparent and typical approach of the early church in preaching the Gospel.

The common ground approach of the IM seems likely to induce syncretism among Muslim Insiders, because they continue to remain within the Muslim communities and observe Islamic religious practices. Some

---

169 Nida, *Message and Mission*, 214.
170 Kraemer, *Christian Message*," 130–41; Nida, *Message and Mission*, 214.
171 Kraft, "My Distaste," 139–44.

common terms and notions are freely used without making careful distinction because of the naïve assumption that they are common between the two religions. Allah in the Qur'an and in Islam has many different essential natures than the God of the Bible. When Muslim Insiders assume that both are the same God, there is a good chance they will become victims to theological syncretism because of the theological confusion they experience.

IM advocates may pay attention to Hesselgrave's caution concerning the importance of emphasizing differences in an effective cross-cultural communication. This means missionaries need to explain critical differences of seemingly similar terms and notions between Islam and Christianity by evaluating them within individual theological system they belong to. The Apostle Paul's use of the pagan poets and noncanonical sources must be understood as a model for point of contact rather than common ground. A point of contact is simply a bridge through which a messenger passes to deliver a message, not a common ground where he remains. Though point of contact may initially look as an approval of similarities, it actually emphasizes essential differences between the two sides. It is better to call it as "point of departure" or "point of contrast."[172]

Furthermore, IM advocates overlook the uniqueness of biblical truth when they overemphasize common ground. While they establish a strong basis for common ground, they easily dismiss critically important biblical truth that the integrity of the Gospel may be endangered. Talman provides an example when he argues for the need of reformulating Christology:

> We ourselves must first of all recognize that the sonship of Jesus is fundamentally a Messianic concept, not the primary proof of his deity. If our doctrine of Christ is centered around the Word (Jn. 1:1, 14), it builds on common ground (Jesus in the Qur'an is the "word of Allah") and communicates much more meaningfully and accurately than does the title "Son of God." Also, if we set aside our theological formulation of the "hypostatic union" between Christ's two natures in favor of a product of theological speculation from the history of Islam, we may find greater acceptance by the Muslim to this enigma. . . . I believe that a theology for Muslims should be more theocentric than Christocentric in its perspective, emphasizing Jesus' functional subordination as Messiah and Servant ('abd Allah), instead of his ontological equality.[173]

---

172 Poston, "Evaluating 'A Common Word,'" 62–68; Nida, *Message and Mission*, 214.

173 Talman, "Comprehensive Contextualization," 10.

He argues for a de-Hellenization of Christian doctrinal formulation for the sake of an effective communication to Muslims by reformulating Western Hellenized doctrines.[174] In doing so, he sacrifices absolute biblical truth and relativizes historical church doctrines for the sake of establishing common ground to obtain the favor of Muslims. In fact, it is inevitable for IM advocates to deemphasize historical Christian doctrines because the theological stance of Muslim Insiders or of IM advocates cannot be compatible with the historic doctrines of the church. Talman makes yet another profound error when he uses a wrong dichotomy between a theocentric and a Christocentric theology. Both are the indivisible whole in Christian theology. What he proposes by emphasizing the functional subordination instead of the ontological equality of Christ is closer to a heretical teaching of Arianism in the early church.[175] This view, termed as functional Christology, distorts the biblical Christology which entails both the ontological equality and the functional subordination. Erickson surmises, "Any Christology to be fully adequate must address and integrate ontological and functional matters" of Christ.[176]

## CONCLUSION

The IM as a contextualization model has complicated dimensions, which inevitably lead to many debatable issues. The five perspectives of the analytical framework have proved to be a useful tool for critically evaluating these issues from a comprehensive and, yet, consistent foundation. This chapter reveals that there are foundational problems in the IM, the starting point of which is the revelational epistemology. This fundamental issue is not normally dealt with in a contextualization discussion, but this chapter proves that it is an important part. IM advocates hold a problematic revelational epistemology that their view of Scripture departs from an orthodox evangelical position.

Since most of the perspectives are interrelated with one another, the first foundational problem in the epistemology causes further problems in other aspects, especially in the theological and hermeneutical features of the IM. It is pointed out that IM advocates stand on the neo-orthodox theological orientation and employ hermeneutical circle as a primary method of interpreting Scripture. They place great emphasis on the role of the human

---

174 Talman, "Comprehensive Contextualization," 9–10.

175 Millard Erickson provides an excellent summary and critique of this functional Christology in *Christian Theology*, 693–703.

176 Erickson, *Christian Theology*, 703.

cultural conditioning both in their theologizing process and in their hermeneutical method. The authority of Scripture is undermined by the overemphasis of human culture and theological relativism becomes an inevitable result in the theological framework of IM advocates. From an anthropological perspective, the major problem stems from a high view of culture contradicting a biblical view of culture. It also introduces an unbiblical theology of religions in the IM so that Islam is uncritically viewed in a positive light without a sound biblical theological evaluation and that many Islamic religious practices are considered to be neutral components of a Muslim culture. Several critical problems are identified in the IM contextualization model from a communication perspective because some pragmatic proposals of IM advocates do not stand on a sound biblical and theological ground.

As a result of this critical evaluation, it is proved that the IM stands upon a biblically unacceptable epistemology and a neo-orthodox theological orientation, which influence IM theology of missions. It is concluded that the two major claims of IM advocates, maintaining Muslim identity and remaining within the Islamic religious community by observing Muslim religious practices, do not find their biblical and theological supports and that the IM is a questionable contextualization model among Muslims.

# 6

# Conclusion

THIS STUDY DEMONSTRATED THAT the IM could not be approved as a biblically authentic and culturally relevant contextualization model among Muslims. The IM stands on the central assertion that Muslims can follow Christ within the Islamic community as Insiders by maintaining a dual identity as Muslim followers of Jesus and by continuing to practice Islamic cultural and religious practices. Two main critical evaluations were employed to evaluate the IM as a contextualization model. First, from a biblical perspective, it was demonstrated that the IM could not pass the test of biblical validation because key assertions and biblical claims of IM advocates stood upon exegetically flawed interpretations of key biblical passages. Second, when a comprehensive analytical framework incorporating the five perspectives was applied to the IM, many of its features turned out to have deviated from evangelical parameters of contextualization. The roots affect the fruits. Since the IM has unhealthy roots in its theology of missions, it is likely to induce syncretistic results in its ministries to Muslims.

## SUMMARY OF FINDINGS

The overview of historical developments of Muslim evangelism in chapter 2 sheds lights on the nature of the IM from a historical perspective. One significant trend observed in historical developments of Muslim evangelism is a shift from theologically oriented ministry models (the confrontational and traditional-theological models) to cultural and religious context-oriented models (the dialogical and contextual model). The shift entailed an increasing emphasis on cultural and religious factors in human contexts for the sake of relevance and a correspondingly decreasing focus on the theological distinctiveness of biblical faith for the sake of biblical authenticity.[1] It was indicated that such de-theologizing trends in contextualization have become a serious concern for the evangelical community. Comparing and contrasting four major models of Muslim evangelism helped identify critical issues and features of ministries to Muslims. They were also taken into consideration in the formulation of an analytical framework for Muslim contextualization. The IM was identified as a radical form of a contextual model which borrowed many factors from the dialogical and the contextualization model.

Chapter 3 established a comprehensive analytical framework by defining evangelical parameters in the five dimensions of contextualization: epistemological, theological, hermeneutical, anthropological, and communicational. Since contextualization is a multidimensional phenomenon, this framework is proved to be an objective and comprehensive tool to evaluate underlying presuppositions and theoretical notions of ministry models to Muslims from an evangelical perspective. After this framework was used to evaluate the missiological model of Kraft, it was demonstrated that his model significantly departed from orthodox evangelical positions in all five dimensions. This result is important because his missiological thinking has influenced that of IM advocates and thus shaped the IM theology of missions.

Chapter 4 evaluated the biblical interpretations of IM advocates to see if the IM could pass the test of biblical validation by asking two central questions: "Is it biblically permitted for Muslim Insiders to maintain religious identity as Muslim? Is it biblically permissible for them to participate in Islamic religious practices while following Christ?" This chapter demonstrated that the biblical interpretations of IM advocates did not employ a sound exegetical method and that their exegetical conclusions were seriously flawed. While IM advocates rely on a certain limited number of biblical passages for the biblical validation, they hardly consider clearly exclusivist passages (e.g. John 14:6; Acts 4:12; the Epistle to the Hebrews) and the overarching biblical theological stance of exclusivism. They are lacking a solid biblical theological analysis in their biblical interpretations and missiological approach.

---

1 As contextualization has become popularized among evangelical missionaries and missiologists, extensive use of social sciences has replaced biblical and theological discussions in missiology. Edward Rommen laments this trend by referring to it as the "de-theologizing of missiology," which undermines the scriptural authority and theological foundation in missiology. See Rommen, "De-Theologizing of Missiology," 1–4.

Chapter 5 employed the analytical framework developed in chapter 3 to the IM to evaluate its validity by utilizing evangelical parameters in each perspective. The origin of all the problematic features of the IM starts with instrumentalist epistemology which denies the normative, objective propositional truth of the Gospel. This epistemology elevates human experiences and new encounters in cultural contexts to an extent that they play a deciding role for interpreting the meaning of biblical revelation. Consequently, the authority of Scripture is substantially minimized, and the Bible is taken as a casebook which can be used to answer contemporary contextual issues through an analogical interpretive method. This epistemology is certainly inadequate to accommodate a biblical worldview and is largely in conflict with the truth of biblical revelation which is objective, normative, and propositional truth. The authority of Scripture should be the starting point of contextualization and the primary guiding principle of missiological thinking. IM advocates deviate from such a crucial evangelical foundation simply because they uphold an inadequate, unbiblical instrumentalist epistemology.

From a theological perspective, some IM advocates embrace a neo-orthodox theological orientation as they elevate human experiences in cultural contexts to an important factor in determining the meaning of biblical revelation and in formulating contextual theologies. Theology is relativized and every theology is claimed to be contextual in essence. Since they do not accept the existence of a normative theology, all historic creeds and orthodox Christian doctrines are understood to be contextually defined expressions of biblical truth and thus do not hold universal values for churches in different contexts. Muslim Insiders are encouraged to develop their own creedal expressions apart from historic creeds, which IM advocates refer to as self-theologizing.

This study argued why an orthodox theological orientation is an essential foundation of any biblical contextualization model in regards to its respect for scriptural authority and historic Christianity. Since the apostolic proclamation of the Gospel has been the major driving force in history in making disciples of all nations under the Great Commission, the biblical paradigm identifies the meaning of contextualization as apostolic and its method as didactic. This biblical notion significantly differs from the neo-orthodox position which identifies the meaning of contextualization as prophetic and its method as dialectic. Within an orthodox evangelical understanding, it is accepted that there is a normative biblical theology which is neither culturally conditioned nor contextually defined. Such a single unified biblical theology based upon God's redemptive history can provide a unifying platform to formulate diverse theological expressions of biblical truth in human contexts.

From a hermeneutical perspective, IM advocates employ a hermeneutical circle as the foundational method which is logically connected to their neo-orthodox orientation. IM advocates do not accept the notion of an objective meaning of biblical text because every person is culturally conditioned and thus subjective in his perception of truth. The starting point of the hermeneutical circle is human cultural context, not Scripture. Their primary hermeneutical method is analogical reasoning which heavily relies on similarities and commonalities between biblical precedents and contemporary contexts. This approach led IM advocates to flawed exegetical conclusions and to unbiblical assertions in the process of validating the IM.

The hermeneutical approach of IM advocates significantly differs from the grammatical-historical hermeneutical method because the latter starts with Scripture to search for authorial intent as the objective meaning of biblical texts. The grammatical-historical hermeneutics has been the backbone of biblical evangelicalism which has held the Body of Christ in unity both synchronically, across culturally variegated human contexts, and diachronically, throughout history. IM advocates overlooked such an important hermeneutical approach and violated its fundamental principles in their biblical interpretations. The evidently unbiblical conclusions of IM advocates are to be rejected because of their unsound hermeneutical method in the process of contextualization.

From an anthropological perspective, IM advocates borrow many concepts and assumptions from functionalist anthropology so that unbiblical presuppositions infiltrate their missiological thinking. They hold a high view of culture because it is not examined from a biblical and theological perspective. Since they consider religion as a subsystem of human culture, they hold a high view of religion and a skewed view of Islam. Consequently, their theology of culture and religion deviates from evangelical parameters, and many unsubstantiated proposals and assertions concerning Islam have been promoted in the IM.

The underlying assumptions concerning Islam and the Qur'an in the IM cannot be supported biblically and theologically because the IM advocates hold a flawed theology of religions. The continuity assumption between Islam and biblical revelation, the assertion for the extensive use of the Qur'an in Muslim evangelism, the Christocentric hermeneutics of the Qur'an are just a few fruits of their flawed theology of religions. While evangelical scholars are challenged to develop a biblical theology of religions, IM advocates have moved away from evangelical parameters in this dimension.

From a communicational perspective, the IM promotes practical ministry proposals and assertions by incorporating several facets of modern communication theories. The fundamental flaw, however, comes from their postmodern presupposition of instrumentalist epistemology in which meaning is claimed to be found in persons. Meaning is determined by receptors in communication, and there is little objective meaning in facts, events, or even in the Bible. Based upon this theory, IM advocates employ the receptor-oriented communication principle in the IM and essentially deny objective meaning of the biblical text. Since they think that meaning is separable from form, they contend for reinterpreting old forms or inserting new meanings in old cultural and religious forms. One representative corollary is the dynamic equivalence theory which they apply to Bible translation and extend to general cultural and religious forms. IM advocates promote the common ground approach which is significantly different from a biblical notion of the point of contact approach.

These assertions based on postmodern communication theories significantly depart from evangelical parameters. Biblically speaking, meaning is found in Scripture and in the created world. Although human perception may be partial and subjective, this should not negate the objective meaning of biblical truth. Since one cannot simplistically separate meaning from form, especially when it comes to cultural and religious components, the extensive application of the dynamic equivalence theory that IM advocates actively promote can induce deleterious consequences. For example, it is shown that the familial terms in the Bible cannot be replaced by dynamically equivalent terms because there is a danger of losing the rich biblical and theological meanings and distorting the essence of the Gospel in the process.

The cumulative evidence derived from the five perspectives leads to the conclusion that the IM theology of missions significantly deviates from an evangelical model of contextualization and that the IM cannot be accepted as a biblically authentic and culturally relevant evangelical approach to Muslim evangelism. Unbiblical presuppositions and problematic theoretical notions take roots in the missiological foundation of IM advocates and thus in the IM. It is, therefore, concluded that the IM cannot be an acceptable biblical contextualization model of the evangelical community although it has the benefit of creating evangelistic momentum within the Islamic community when new believers live as living witnesses through existing social networks.

## THE INSIDER MOVEMENT AND SYNCRETISM

An important question in the IM discussion involves whether or not the IM is viable to induce syncretism and whether it has produced syncretistic results in its ministries to Muslims. If syncretism is defined as "the replacement or dilution of the essential truths of the gospel through the incorporation of non-Christian elements,"[2] it seems that the IM opens a door for such syncretism by intentionally allowing Muslim Insiders to mix religious elements of two different religions and synthesize them into something which is neither biblical Christianity nor traditional Islam. It is significant to note that syncretistic results are fundamentally caused by its "overemphasis on contexts and underemphasis on Scripture."[3] This study demonstrates that the IM is such a contextualization model of this imbalanced approach that is likely to induce syncretistic results. Norman Geisler is correct in his criticism concerning the IM: "The radical contextualization [the IM] is not a hedge against syncretism; it is a cause of it."[4] At the least, it can be said that the IM as a radical contextualization model among Muslims does not have sufficient corrective mechanism to prevent syncretistic results in ministries to Muslims.

## AREAS FOR FURTHER RESEARCH

This study highlights several areas for further research. First, a comprehensive IM theology of missions is lacking. This is probably the most urgent task of IM advocates in the near future in their service to a wider evangelical missiological community. So far, many of the discussions reflected in the writings of IM advocates and IM critics have remained partial in terms of their topics and depth. Sometimes debates have remained ad hoc or reactionary while scholars of both sides have unfortunately deployed straw man arguments. This study has made a significant contribution to the IM discussion by demonstrating the usefulness of an analytical framework which IM advocates might consider using in their endeavor to develop a comprehensive IM theology of missions.

The most serious debate on the IM discussion centers on the issues related to theology of religions (Islam). Several scholars have recognized the insufficiency of the traditional three-fold categorization and underscored

---

2. Moreau, "Syncretism," 924.
3. Ott et al., *Encountering Theology*, 276.
4. Geisler, "Response to Paul G. Hiebert," 142.

the urgent need to develop other biblical theological alternatives.[5] The evangelical community has not been completely satisfied with the present understanding and desires to develop a more satisfactory biblical theology of other religions to answer all the challenging questions from a contemporary society.

Islamic context casts a completely different set of challenges and questions in the IM debate, mainly because of the seemingly similar terms and commonly shared factors between Christianity and Islam. Depending on one's presuppositions based on his theology of religions, many different views of Islam and a variety of ministry proposals can be suggested. Although the contemporary approach to religions is predominantly influenced by a comparative religions approach, the evangelical community should commence with Scripture as the supreme bulwark, both in establishing a biblical theology of religions (Islam) and in evaluating various ministry proposals, such as the use of the Qur'an or Islamic religious forms for expressing biblical truth. Further developments in formulating a sound evangelical theology of religions will certainly help to solve the complicated issues of the IM.

This study has a limitation in that it has not incorporated field research. Further research on the IM can incorporate a strategic evaluation in order to see how actual field circumstances and ministry approaches bring about ministry results. Some people do not recognize a subtle, yet very crucial distinction between a descriptive phenomenon, in terms of what is happening among Muslim nations, and a prescriptive strategic proposal, in terms of allowing Muslim Insiders to remain within the Islamic community and continue to participate in Islamic religious practices. This thin line makes an enormous difference in ministries to Muslims because converting the IM into a prescriptive mission strategy entails the dangerous distortion of the biblical truth of the Gospel and is likely to induce syncretistic results. On the other hand, when one takes the descriptive phenomenon of Muslims' following Christ within Islam, missionaries and Christian churches should perhaps ask a different set of questions such as, "How do we understand this phenomenon? How should evangelical missionaries respond to these supposed followers of Jesus? How should missionaries guide them in a biblically authentic and culturally relevant manner?"

---

5 For example, see the following works of two evangelical scholars: Tennent, *Theology in the Context*; and McDermott, *Can Evangelicals Learn*.

## CLOSING REMARKS

IM advocates and field missionaries using the IM as a contextualization approach have genuine passion for the Lord and deep compassion for the lost among Muslim nations. They endeavor to understand the minds and souls of Muslims while respecting the piety of Muslims in their own religious pursuit of encountering the true God. They are willing to suffer for the Lord and sympathize with Muslim Insiders who experience persecutions and martyrdom (Heb 10:32–34). In spite of their genuine heart and passion for the Gospel, however, their efforts are likely to induce syncretism in their ministries to Muslims, which will surely have an eternal consequence. It is, therefore, important for IM advocates to reexamine their underlying assumptions, theoretical underpinnings, and the biblical interpretations of key passages in their formulation of the IM. One most important step in this process is to buttress the biblical framework of the IM theology of missions by increasing the interaction with evangelical biblical scholarship and consolidating their hermeneutical and theological methods. Moreover, a more careful reevaluation of historic Christianity may help IM advocates to identify unchanging components of biblical truths throughout church history. IM advocates can hardly doubt the fact that God has worked in the historic Christian church throughout church history while they desire to emphasize God who is at work among Muslim nations in the contemporary human contexts.

This study reveals the importance of returning to biblical authority, not only for the content of the Gospel, but also for the missiological praxis. It is only through restoring such biblical supremacy that the evangelical community can have a firm ground to evaluate the complicated contemporary missiological issues that are reflected in the case of the IM. Hesselgrave adequately underscores this crucial point:

> The future of mission depends upon what conservatives make, not only of the authority, but also of the function of Scripture. Christian mission must be undergirded with biblical authority but it must be guided by biblical theology. The most hopeful future for mission and missiology depends on the "re-missionizing of theology" on the one hand, and the "re-theologizing of missiology" on the other.[6]

---

6 Hesselgrave, "Third Millennium Missiology," 589.

# Appendix

## Comparison of Muslim Evangelism Models

THIS APPENDIX PROVIDES A comparative snapshot of Muslim evangelism models that are introduced in chapter 2. It highlights similarities and differences between models by using twelve analytical grids. The Insider Movement is placed in the fifth column as "Radical Contextual Model" to show how it is related to other Muslim evangelism models. This appendix is prepared by the author on the basis of the discussion in chapter 2.

| | Confrontational Model | Traditional-Theological Model | Dialogical Model | Contextual Model | Radical Contextual Model |
|---|---|---|---|---|---|
| Historical Period | From 19th and early 20th century to the present | From the early 20th century to the present | From 1950s and 1960s to the present | From 1970s to the present | From 1980s to the present |
| Major Proponents | Henry Martyn<br>Karl Pfander<br>W. St. Clair Tisdall<br>Jay Smith<br>John Gilchrist<br>Nabeel Qureshi | Samuel Zwemer<br>Sam Schlorff<br>Martin Goldsmith<br>Norman Geisler<br>Many contemporary evangelical missionaries | Temple Gairdner<br>Kenneth Cragg<br>Ray Register<br>Fouad Accad<br>Henry Martyn Institute | Phil Parshall<br>Timothy C. Tennent<br>Many contemporary evangelical missionaries | John Travis<br>Charles Kraft<br>Kevin Haggins<br>Rebecca Lewis<br>Herbert Hoefer<br>Dudley Woodberry |
| Evangelism | Confrontational<br>Emotion–free theological arguments<br>Polemics<br>Apologetics<br>Rational reasoning | Conversation based on theological differences<br>Discouraging confrontations<br>Rational reasoning with didactic emphasis | Focusing on theological & religious commonness<br>Mutual respect and personal dialogue<br>Peaceful witness | Points of contact through adopting Islamic cultural elements and cautiously adopting religious elements<br>Common religious factors as bridges, not as common grounds | Radical adoption of Islamic cultural & religious elements<br>Self-identity as Muslim<br>Practicing Islamic rituals<br>Searching for "common grounds" to use for inserting biblical meanings |

| | Confrontational Model | Traditional-Theological Model | Dialogical Model | Contextual Model | Radical Contextual Model |
|---|---|---|---|---|---|
| Use of the Qur'an | Negative use (to attack or reveal contradictions) Positive use (to defend Christian truths) | No use of the Qur'an or minimal use under an inevitable case | Positive use to affirm Christian truths Christian interpretation of the Qur'an | Willing to use selective contents of the Qur'an to defend Christian truths | Positive use to affirm Christian truths Christian interpretation of the Qur'an Willing to accept selective qur'anic hermeneutics |
| Attitude to Islam | Mostly negative, but some exceptions (viewing Islam as a monotheistic reformation against idolatrous polytheistic Arabs) | Some sympathy as a religion or for religious devotion Reject its continuity with Christianity Emphasis on theological differences and distinctiveness | Positive appreciation as a religious reform Some positive aspects of Islam appreciated Islam as a religion incapable of fulfilling human needs | Positive appreciation as a religious reform Some positive cultural aspects appreciated Islam as a religion incapable of fulfilling human needs | Positive aspects as a religion Positive appreciation of the good aspects of Islam Reinterpretation of Islamic religious forms in view of biblical revelation Continuity assumed |
| Prophethood of Muhammad | Mostly reject him Some acknowledge him as a religious reformer or a political leader | Reject his prophethood Theologically he misunderstood the Christian teachings | Objective recognition as a religious reformer with monotheism to Arabs | Hesitant to accept his prophethood | Willing to accept his prophethood as a reformer and messenger Asking if "Muhammad is among prophets?" |

|  | Confrontational Model | Traditional-Theological Model | Dialogical Model | Contextual Model | Radical Contextual Model |
|---|---|---|---|---|---|
| Converts | Extraction by converts' own rejection of Islam & by persecution<br>Expulsion inevitable<br>Separation from Islamic community recommended | Extraction by their own rejection of Islam & persecution<br>Expulsion<br>Total rejection of Islamic practices<br>Separation from Islamic community | Extraction from persecution, expulsion, but not by their own will<br>Separation from Islam religiously, but not culturally<br>Identified as "follower of Isa" or "Christians" | Remaining within Islamic community as long as possible, but may be expelled in the long run<br>Some alternative identification recommended ("follower of Isa," not "Christian") | Remaining within Islamic community as Insiders<br>Identified as "Messianic Muslims or the follower of Isa"<br>Muslims consider them to be "strange Muslims" |
| Worship & Church on C-spectrum | C1–C2 model<br>Mostly foreign forms<br>Western style church | C2–C3 model<br>Foreign forms & some indigenous cultural forms<br>Much like western style church | C3–C4 model<br>More indigenous by adopting Islamic cultural & religious forms<br>More indigenous church<br>"MBBs" church | C4 model<br>More indigenous by adopting Islamic cultural & religious forms<br>Mostly indigenous church, "MBBs" church | C5 model<br>Most Islamic cultural & religious forms kept<br>Radically indigenous<br>"Muslim believers" church |

| | Confrontational Model | Traditional-Theological Model | Dialogical Model | Contextual Model | Radical Contextual Model |
|---|---|---|---|---|---|
| Contribution to Muslim Evangelization | Apologetical materials for missionary training<br>Public proclamation via open debates | Orthodox theological teaching for missionaries and MBBs<br>Crucial for discipleship | Peaceful interfaith dialogue in public platform<br>Hope for political-religious toleration to Christianity | More fruitful results than the traditional model<br>Contextualized church planting<br>Creative adoption of indigenous life & reforming traditional models | Encouraging new believers to remain within their socioreligious network for evangelistic momentum |
| Theology of Religions: Continuity | Total discontinuity<br>Theologically wrong | Total discontinuity<br>Theologically wrong<br>Biblical theology of religions (Islam) | Some possible continuity<br>Fulfillment theory | Discontinuity with cultural accommodation<br>Biblical theology of religions (Islam) | Willing to accept continuity<br>Anthropological understanding of religions (Islam) |
| View of Culture | A low view of Islamic culture | No special attention to culture | A high view of Muslim culture | Focus on a biblical view of culture | A high view of Islamic culture and religion |
| Theological Orientation | Conservative orthodox | Conservative orthodox | Orthodox or Neo-orthodox | Conservative Orthodox | Neo-orthodox |

(**Source: Author's own**)

# Bibliography

Abdul-Haqq, Abdiyah Akbar. *Sharing Your Faith with a Muslim*. Minneapolis: Bethany Fellowship, 1980.
Abernathy, David. "Jesus Is the Eternal Son of God." *SFM* 6 (2010) 327–94.
———. "Translating 'Son of God' in Missionary Bible Translation: A Critique of 'Muslim-Idiom Bible Translations: Claims and Facts,' by Rick Brown, John Penny, and Leith Gray." *SFM* 6 (2010) 176–203.
Accad, Fouad E. *Building Bridges: Christianity and Islam*. Colorado Springs: NavPress, 1997.
———. *Have You Ever Read the Seven Muslim-Christian Principles?* Limassol, Cyprus: Ar-Rabitah, 1978.
———. "The Qur'an: A Bridge to Christian Faith." *Missiology* 4 (1976) 331–42.
Accad, Martin. "Towards a Theology of Islam: A Response to Harley Talman's 'Is Muhammad Also Among the Prophets?'" *IJFM* 31 (2014) 191–93.
The Al Kalima Editorial Committee. "A Response to Jay smith's Criticisms of Common Ground and of 'The True Meaning of the Gospel.'" *SFM* 5 (2009) 15–20.
Aland, Barbara, et al. *The Greek New Testament*. 4th ed. rev. United Bible Societies. Stuttgart, Germany: Biblia-Druck, 1983.
Ali, Abdullah Yusuf. *The Holy Qur'an: Translation and Commentary*. 2nd ed. Indianapolis: American Publication Trust, 1977.
Allen, Bob. "Baptist Seminary President Labels IMB Mission Strategy 'Heresy.'" *Associated Baptist Press*, February 10, 2010. http://www.abpnews.com/content/view/4830/53/.
Allen, Joe Morris, III. "An Evaluation of the Christology of the Camel Training Manual." MA Thesis, Dallas Theological Seminary, 2007.
Anderson, John. "The Missionary Approach to Islam: Christian or 'Cultic.'" *Missiology* 4 (1976) 285–300.
Asad, Abdul. "Rethinking the Insider Movement Debate: Global Historical Insights Toward an Appropriate Translational Model of C5." *SFM* 5 (2009) 133–59.
Baeq, Daniel Shinjong. "Contextualizing Religious Form and Meaning: A Missiological Interpretation of Naaman's Petitions (2 Kings 5:15–19)." *IJFM* 27 (2010) 197–207.
Barnes, Phillip. "Missiology Meets Cultural Anthropology: The Life and Legacy of Paul G. Hiebert." PhD diss., Southern Baptist Theological Seminary, 2011.
Barth, Karl. *Church Dogmatics*. Vol. 2. Edited by G. W. Bromiley and T. F. Torrence. Translated by T. H. L. Parker et al. Edinburgh: T. & T. Clark, 1957.

Bauer, David R. "Son of God." In *Dictionary and the Gospels*, edited by Joel B. Green et al., 769–75. Downers Grove, IL: IVP, 1992.

Bauer, Walter, Frederick William Danker, William F. Arndt, and F. Wilbur Gingrich. *A Greek-English Lexicon of the New Testament and Other Early Christian Literature*. 3rd ed. Chicago: University of Chicago Press, 2000.

Bebbington, David. *Evangelicalism in Modern Britain: A History from the 1730s to the 1980s*. London: Unwin Hyman, 1989.

Bennett, Clinton. "The Legacy of Karl Gottlieb Pfander." *IBMR* 20 (1996) 76–81.

Bevans, Stephen. *Models of Contextual Theology*. Maryknoll, NY: Orbis, 1992.

Blomberg, Craig L. "The Christian and the Law of Moses." In *Witness to the Gospel: The Theology of Acts*, edited by I. Howard Marshall and David Peterson, 397–416. Grand Rapids: William B. Eerdmans, 1998.

Blount, Doug, and Joseph Wooddell. *Baptist Faith and Message 2000: Critical Issues in America's Largest Protestant Denomination*. Lanham, MD: Rowman & Littlefield, 2007.

Bock, Darrel. *Acts*. Baker Exegetical Commentary on the New Testament. Grand Rapids: Baker, 2007.

Braswell, George W. "The Encounter of Christianity and Islam: The Missionary Theology of Kenneth Cragg." *Perspectives in Religious Studies* 8 (1981) 117–27.

Bridges, Erich. "Of Jesus' Mosques and 'Muslim Christians.'" *The Commission* (August 1997) 49.

Brogden, Dick. "Inside Out: Probing Presuppositions among Insider Movements." *IJFM* 27 (2010) 33–40.

Brown, Rick. "Biblical Muslims." *IJFM* 24 (2007) 65–74.

———. "Brother Jacob and Master Isaac: How One Insider Movement Began." *IJFM* 24 (2007) 41–42.

———. "Contextualization without Syncretism." *IJFM* 23 (2006) 127–33.

———. "Explaining the Biblical Term 'Son(s) of God' in Muslim Contexts: Part I." *IJFM* 22 (2005) 91–96.

———. "Translating the Biblical Term 'Son(s) of God' in Muslim Contexts: Part II." *IJFM* 22 (2005) 135–45.

———. "The 'Son of God': Understanding the Messianic Titles of Jesus." *IJFM* 17 (2000) 41–52.

———. "What Must One Believe about Jesus for Salvation?" *IJFM* 17 (2000) 13–21.

———. "Why Muslims Are Repelled by the Term 'Son of God?'" *EMQ* 43 (2007) 422–29.

Brown, Rick, et al. "Movements and Contextualization: Is There Really a Correlation?" *IJFM* 26 (2009) 211–23.

Brown, Rick, et al. "Muslim-Idiom Bible Translations: Claims and Facts." *SFM* 5 (2009) 87–105.

Bruce, F. F. *The Acts of the Apostles: Greek Text with Introduction and Commentary*. Grand Rapids: Eerdmans, 1990.

Buswell, James O., III. "Contextualization: Theory, Tradition, and Method." In *Theology and Mission: Papers and Responses Prepared for the Consultation on Theology and Missions, Trinity Evangelical Divinity School, School of World Mission and Evangelism, March 22–25, 1976*, edited by David J. Hesselgrave, 87–111. Grand Rapids: Baker, 1978.

Caldwell, Stuart (note: pseudonym of Kevin Higgins). "Jesus in Samaria: A Paradigm for Church Planting among Muslims." *IJFM* 17 (2000) 25-31.

Carlton, Matthew. "Jesus, the Son of God: Biblical Meaning, Muslim Understanding, and Implications for Translation and Biblical Literacy." *SFM* 7 (2011) 1-30.

Carson, D. A. *The Cross and Christian Ministry: An Exposition of Passages from 1 Corinthians*. Grand Rapids: InterVarsity, 1993.

———. *The Gagging of God: Christianity Confronts Pluralism*. Grand Rapids: Zondervan, 1996.

———. "The Limits of Dynamic Equivalence in Bible Translation." *Evangelical Review of Theology* 9 (1985) 200-13.

———. "Response to Paul Hiebert's 'Sets and Structures: A Study of Church Patterns.'" In *New Horizons in World Mission: Evangelicals and the Christian Mission in the 1980s*, edited by David J. Hesselgrave, 231-32. Grand Rapids: Baker, 1979.

———. "A Sketch of the Factors Determining Current Hermeneutical Debate in Cross-Cultural Context." In *Biblical Interpretation and the Church: Text and Context*, edited by D. A. Carson, 11-29. Exeter, UK: Paternoster, 1984.

Cate, Patrick O. "Each Other's Scripture: The Muslims' Views of the Bible and the Christians' Views of the Qur'an." PhD diss., Hartford Seminary, 1974.

———. "Islamic Values and the Gospel." *BibSac* 155 (1998) 355-70.

Chandler, Paul Gordon. *Pilgrims of Christ on the Muslim Road: Exploring a New Path Between Two Faiths*. Lanham, MD: Cowley, 2007.

Christian Literature Society for India, ed. *Papers for Thoughtful Muslims*. No. 1-4. London and Madras: Christian Literature Society for India, 1900.

Cloer, Clayton P. "Samuel Zwemer: A Model of Muslim Contextualization." PhD diss., Mid-America Baptist Theological Seminary, 2000.

Coe, Shoki, and Aharon Sapsezian. *Ministry in Context: The Third Mandate Programme of the Theological Education Fund (1970-77)*. Bromley, England: Theological Education Fund, 1972.

Cogan, Mordechai, and Hayim Tadmor. *II Kings*. The Anchor Bible. Garden City, NY: Doubleday, 1988.

Cohn, Robert L., et al. *2 Kings*. Collegeville, MN: Liturgical, 2000.

Coleman, Doug. "A Theological Analysis of the Insider Movement Paradigm from Four Perspectives: Theology of Religions, Revelation, Soteriology, and Ecclesiology." PhD diss., Southeastern Baptist Theological Seminary, 2011.

———. *A Theological Analysis of the Insider Movement Paradigm: Theology of Religions, Revelation, Soteriology and Ecclesiology*. Pasadena, CA: William Carey Library, 2010.

Coleman, Marc. "A Seventh-day Adventist Approach to Islam." MA Thesis, University of the Free State, 2004.

Colgate, Jack. "Bible Storying and Oral Use of the Scriptures." In *From Seed to Fruit: Global Trends, Fruitful Practices, and Emerging Issues among Muslims*, edited by Dudley Woodberry, 219-31. Pasadena, CA: William Carey Library, 2008.

Committee of Evangelical Missionaries to Islam. *Report of Conference of Missionaries to Islam*. Chicago: Trinity Seminary, 1960.

Conn, Harvie M. *Eternal Word and Changing World: Theology, Anthropology, and Mission in Trialogue*. Grand Rapids: Zondervan, 1984.

———. "The Muslim Convert and His Culture." In *The Gospel and Islam: A 1978 Compendium*, edited by Don M. McCurry, 97-113. Monrovia, CA: MARC, 1979.

Cook, Matthew, et al., eds. *Local Theology for the Global Church*. Pasadena, CA: William Carey Library, 2010.

Coote, Robert, and John Stott. *Down to Earth: Studies in Christianity and Culture*. Grand Rapids: Eerdmans, 1980.

Corwin, Gary. "A Humble Appeal to C5/Insider Movement Muslim Ministry Advocates to Consider Ten Questions." *IJFM* 24 (2007) 5–21.

Corwin, Gary, and Ralph Winter. "Reviewing September–October *Mission Frontiers*: A Conversation about Insider Movements." *MF* 28 (January–February 2006) 17–20.

Cosgrove, Charles H. *Appealing to Scripture in Moral Debate: Five Hermeneutical Rules*. Grand Rapids: Eerdmans, 2002.

Cragg, Kenneth. *The Call of the Minaret*. 2nd ed., rev. and enl. Maryknoll, NY: Orbis, 1985.

———. *Sandals at the Mosque: Christian Presence amid Islam*. New York: Oxford University Press, 1959.

Cumming, Joseph. "Muslim Followers of Jesus?" *CT* 53 (December 2009) 32–35.

Dale, Godfrey. *The Contrast between Christianity and Muhammadanism*. London: Universities' Mission to Central Africa, 1928.

De Kuiper, Arie, and Barclay M. Newman Jr. "Jesus, Son of God—A Translation Problem." *The Bible Translator* 28 (1977) 432–38.

Decker, Frank. "When 'Christian' Does Not Translate." *MF* (September–October 2008) 8.

Deedat, Ahmed. "Christ in Islam." http://www.jamaat.net/cis/ChristInIslam.html.

Demarest, Bruce A., and Richard J. Harpel. "Don Richardson's 'Redemptive Analogies' and the Biblical Idea of Revelation." *BibSac* 146 (1989) 330–40.

Deneui, Paul. "A Typology of Approaches to Thai Folk Buddhists." In *Appropriate Christianity*, edited by Charles H. Kraft, 415–36. Pasadena, CA: William Carey Library, 2005.

Dixon, Roger. "Moving On From the C1–C6 Spectrum." *SFM* 5 (2009) 3–19.

———. "Some Questions about Bradford Greer's Principles of Exegesis." *SFM* 6 (2010) 911–14.

Douglas, James D., ed. *Let the Earth Hear His Voice: International Congress on World Evangelization Lausanne, Switzerland*. Minneapolis: World Wide Publications, 1975.

Dutch, Bernard. "Should Muslims Become Christians?" *IJFM* 17 (2000) 15–24.

D'Souza, Diane. "Evangelism, Dialogue, Reconciliation: A Case Study of the Growth and Transformation of the Henry Martyn Institute." *MW* 91 (2001) 155–84.

Eenigenburg, Don. "The Pros and Cons of Islamicized Contextualization." *EMQ* 33 (1997) 310–15.

Erickson, Millard. *Christian Theology*. Grand Rapids: Baker, 1985.

———. *God in Three Persons: A Contemporary Interpretation of the Trinity*. Grand Rapids: Baker, 1995.

———. *The Word Became Flesh*. Grand Rapids: Baker, 1991.

Fairman, Walter. "The Approach to Moslems." *MW* 16 (1926) 272–76.

Fee, Gordon. *The First Epistle to the Corinthians*. Grand Rapids: Eerdmans, 1987.

———. "Paul and the Trinity: The Experience of Christ and the Spirit for Paul's Understanding of God." In *The Trinity: An Interdisciplinary Symposium on the Trinity*, edited by Stephen Davis et al., 46–72. Oxford: Oxford University Press, 1999.

Fee, Gordon D., and Douglas Stuart. *How to Read the Bible for All Its Worth: A Guide to Understanding the Bible*. 2nd ed. Grand Rapids: Zondervan, 1993.

Fitzmyer, Joseph A. *First Corinthians*. The Anchor Yale Bible. New Haven: Yale University Press, 2008.

Fleming, Bruce. *Contextualization of Theology: An Evangelical Assessment*. Pasadena, CA: William Carey Library, 1980.

Flemming, Dean. *Contextualization in the New Testament: Patterns for Theology and Mission*. Downers Grove, IL: InterVarsity, 2005.

Garland, David E. *1 Corinthians*. Baker Exegetical Commentary on the New Testament. Grand Rapids: Baker, 2003.

Geisler, Norman. "A Response to Paul G. Hiebert." In *Mission Shift: Global Mission Issues in the Third Millennium*, edited by David J. Hesselgrave and Ed Stetzer, 129–43. Nashville: B&H Academic, 2010.

Geisler, Norman L., and Abdul Saleeb. *Answering Islam: The Crescent in Light of the Cross*. Grand Rapids: Baker, 2002.

Gilchrist, John. *The Christian Witness to the Muslims*. Benoni, South Africa: Jesus to the Muslims, 1988.

———. *Muhammad and the Religion of Islam*. Durban, South Africa: Jesus to the Muslims, 1986.

———. *The Qur'an: The Scripture of Islam*. Mondeor, South Africa: Muslim Evangelicalism Resource Centre, 1995.

Giles, Kevin. *Jesus and the Father: Modern Evangelicals Reinvent the Doctrine of Trinity*. Grand Rapids: Zondervan, 2006.

Gilliland, Dean S. "Context Is Critical in 'Islampur Case.'" *EMQ* 45 (1998) 415–17.

———. "Contextual Theology as Incarnational Mission." In *The Word Among Us: Contextualizing Theology for Mission Today*, edited by Dean S. Gilliland, 9–31. Eugene, OR: Wipf and Stock, 1989.

———. "Modeling the Incarnation for Muslim People: A Response to Sam Schlorff." *Missiology* 28 (2000) 329–38.

———. *The Word among Us: Contextualizing Theology for Mission Today*. Dallas: Word, 1989.

Glasser, Arthur. "Is Friendly Dialogue Enough?" *Missiology* 4 (1976) 259–66.

Goldsmith, Martin. "Community and Controversy: Key Causes of Muslim Resistance." *Missiology* 4 (1976) 317–23.

———. *Islam and Christian Witness: Sharing the Faith with Muslims*. Downers Grove, IL: InterVarsity, 1982.

Graham, Don. "IMB Trustees Adopt Guidelines for Gospel Contextualization." *Baptist Press*, November 15, 2005. http://imb.org/main/news/details.asp?StoryID=6197.

Greer, Bradford. "Review of *A Theological Analysis of the Insider Movement Paradigm from Four Perspectives: Theology of Religions, Revelation, Soteriology and Ecclesiology*, by Doug Coleman." *IJFM* 28 (2011) 204–9.

———. "'Son of God' in Biblical Perspective: A Contrast to David Abernathy's Articles." *SFM* 6 (2010) 464–70;

Greeson, Kevin. *The Camel: How Muslims Are Coming to Faith in Christ*. Arkadelphia, AR: WIGTake Resources, 2007.

———. *Camel Training Manual*. Bangalore, India: WIGTake Resources, 2004.

Gross, Edward N. *Is Charles Kraft an Evangelical? A Critique of Christianity in Culture*. Elkins Park, PA: Christian Bacon, 1985.

Grudem, Wayne. *Systematic Theology: An Introduction to Biblical Doctrine.* Grand Rapids: Zondervan, 1994.

Gustafson, James M. "The Place of Scripture in Christian Ethics: A Methodological Study." *Interpretation* 24 (1970) 430–55.

Hana, Mark. *Crucial Questions in Christian Apologetics.* Grand Rapids: Baker, 1978.

Hansen, Collin. "The Son and the Crescent." *CT* (February 2011) 19–23.

Heldenbrand, Richard. "Missions to Muslims: Cutting the Nerve?" *EMQ* 18 (1982) 134–39.

Henry, Carl. "Bible, Inspiration of." In *Evangelical Dictionary of Theology*, edited by Walter A. Elwell, 159–63. 2nd ed. Grand Rapids: Baker, 2001.

———. "The Cultural Relativizing of Revelation." *Trinity Journal* 1 (1980) 153–64.

Hesselgrave, David J. "Christian Communication and Religious Pluralism: Capitalizing on Differences." *Missiology* 18 (1990) 131–38.

———. *Communicating Christ Cross-Culturally: An Introduction to Missionary Communication.* Grand Rapids: Zondervan, 1991.

———. *Paradigms in Conflict: 10 Key Questions in Christian Missions Today.* Grand Rapids: Kregel, 2005.

———. *Scripture and Strategy: The Use of the Bible in Postmodern Church and Mission.* Pasadena, CA: William Carey Library, 1994.

———. "Third Millennium Missiology and the Use of Egyptian Gold." *JETS* 42 (1999) 577–90.

Hesselgrave, David J., and Edward Rommen. *Contextualization: Meanings, Methods, and Models.* Grand Rapids: Baker, 1989.

Hiebert, Paul G. *Anthropological Reflections on Missiological Issues.* Grand Rapids: Baker, 1994.

———. "Critical Contextualization." *IBMR* 11 (1987) 104–12.

———. "Form and Meaning in the Contextualization of the Gospel." In *The Word among Us: Contextualizing Theology for Mission Today*, edited by Dean Gilliland, 101–20. Dallas: Word, 1989.

———. *Missiological Implications of Epistemological Shifts: Affirming Truth in a Modern/Postmodern World.* Harrisburg, PA: Trinity Press International, 1999.

———. "Missions and Anthropology: A Love/Hate Relationship." *Missiology* 6 (1978) 165–80.

Higgins, Kevin. "Acts 15 and Insiders Movements among Muslims: Questions, Process, and Conclusions." *IJFM* 24 (2007) 29–40.

———. "Beyond Christianity: Insider Movements and the Place of the Bible and the Body of Christ in New Movements to Jesus." *MF* (July–August 2010) 12–13.

———. "Identity, Integrity and Insider Movements: A Brief Paper Inspired by Timothy C. Tennent's Critique of C-5 Thinking." *IJFM* 23 (2006) 117–23.

———. "Inside What? Church, Culture, Religion and Insider Movements in Biblical Perspective." *SFM* 5 (2009) 74–91.

———. "The Key to Insider Movements: The 'Devoted's' of Acts." *IJFM* 21 (2004) 155–65.

———. "Speaking the Truth about Insider Movements: Addressing the Criticisms of Bill Nikides and 'Phil' Relative to the Article 'Inside What?'" *SFM* 5 (2009) 61–86.

Hobbs, T. R. *2 Kings.* Word Biblical Commentary 13. Waco, TX: Word, 1985.

Hoefer, Herbert. "Muslim-Friendly Christian Worship." *EMQ* 45 (2009) 48–53.

———. "Proclaiming a 'Theologyless' Christ." *IJFM* 22 (2005) 97–101.

———. "Response to Gary Corwin from the Hindu Context." *IJFM* 24 (2007) 21.
Horrel, J. Scott. "Cautions Regarding 'Son of God' in Muslim-Idiom Translations of the Bible: Seeking Sensible Balance." *SFM* 6 (2010) 639–66.
House, Paul. *1, 2 Kings*. The New American Commentary 8. Nashville: Broadman & Holman, 1995.
Houssney, Georges. *Engaging Islam*. Boulder, CO: Treeline, 2010.
Howell, Don N. "Mission in Paul's Epistles: Genesis, Pattern, and Dynamics." In *Missions in the New Testament: An Evangelical Approach*, edited by William J. Larkin and Joel F. Williams, 63–91. Maryknoll, NY: Orbis, 1998.
Hwang, Wonjoo. "A Concern about the Recent Trends in Contextualization Discussions: A Lack or Absence of a Biblical-Theological Emphasis." *Korea Missions Quarterly* (2016) 197–225.
———. "Does the NT Quotation of Non-Canonical Sources Validate the Use of the Qur'an in Christian Witness to Muslim?" *Journal of Arab and Islamic World Studies* 2 (2015) 197–241.
———. "An Evaluation of a Muslim Contextualization Model: Insiders Movements (C5)." Paper presented at the annual southwest regional meeting of Evangelical Missiological Society, Houston, TX, March 28–29, 2008.
———. "Historical Development of Muslim Evangelism." Paper presented at the annual southwest regional meeting of Evangelical Missiological Society, Dallas, TX, March 27–28, 2009.
———. "Is the Muslim Insider Movement an Acceptable Contextualization Model? A Biblical and Theological Evaluation." Paper presented at the annual meeting of Evangelical Theological Society, San Francisco, CA, November 16–18, 2011.
Hyatt, Erik. "Christian Witness in Muslim Settings." *EMQ* 45 (2009) 84–92.
International Council on Biblical Inerrancy. "The Chicago Statement on Biblical Inerrancy." http://www.etsjets.org/files/documents/Chicago_Statement.pdf.
Jameson, Richard, and Nick Scalevich. "First-Century Jews and Twentieth-Century Muslims." *IJFM* 17 (2000) 33–39.
Johnson, Alan F. *1 Corinthians*. The IVP New Testament Commentary. Downers Grove, IL: InterVarsity, 2004.
Jones, Lewis Bevan. *The People of the Mosque*. London: Student Christian Movement, 1932.
Kaiser, Walter C. "Holy Pagans: Reality or Myth?" In *Faith Comes by Hearing: A Response to Inclusivism*, edited by Christopher W. Morgan and Robert A. Peterson, 124–42. Downers Grove, IL: IVP, 2008.
Kato, Byang H. "The Gospel, Cultural Context and Religious Syncretism." In *Let the Earth Hear His Voice: International Congress on World Evangelization Lausanne, Switzerland*, edited by J. D. Douglas, 1216–23. Minneapolis: World Wide Publications, 1975.
Keil, C. F., and Franz Delitzsch. *Commentary on the Old Testament: 1 Kings–2 Chronicles*. Vol. 3. Peabody, MA: Hendrickson, 2005.
Kerr, David. "Personal Encounters with Muslims and Their Faith." *Missiology* 4 (1976) 325–30.
Khair-Ullah, F. S. "Linguistic Hang-ups in Communicating with Muslims." *Missiology* 4 (1976) 301–16.

Kim, Caleb Chul-Soo, et al. "Relevant Responses to Folk Muslims." In *From Seed to Fruit: Global Trends, Fruitful Practices, and Emerging Issues among Muslims*, edited by Dudley Woodberry, 265–78. Pasadena, CA: William Carey Library, 2008.

Knitter, Paul F. *Theologies of Religions*. Maryknoll, NY: Orbis, 2002.

Köhler, Ludwig, and Walter Baumgartner. *The Hebrew and Aramaic Lexicon of the Old Testament*. Leiden: E. J. Brill, 2001.

Kraemer, Hendrick. *The Christian Message in a Non-Christian World*. London: Edinburgh House, 1938.

Kraft, Charles H. *Christianity in Culture*. Maryknoll, NY: Orbis, 1979.

———. *Christianity in Culture: A Study in Biblical Theologizing in Cross-Cultural Perspective*. 2nd ed. Maryknoll, NY: Orbis, 2005.

———. *Communication Theory for Christian Witness*. Rev. ed. Maryknoll, NY: Orbis, 1991.

———. "Contextualization of Essential Christianity: Three Points." *EMQ* 48 (2012) 80–86.

———. "The Contextualization of Theology." *EMQ* 14 (1978) 31–36.

———. "My Distaste for the Combative Approach." *EMQ* 18 (1982) 139–42.

———. "Dynamic Equivalence Churches in Muslim Society." In *The Gospel and Islam: A 1978 Compendium*, edited by Don McCurry, 114–28. Monrovia, CA: MACR, 1979.

———. "Pursuing Faith, Not Religion: Liberating Quest for Contextualization." *MF* 27 (September–October 2005) 9–11.

———. *Worldview for Christian Witness*. Pasadena, CA: William Carey Library, 2008.

———, ed. *Appropriate Christianity*. Pasadena, CA: William Carey Library, 2005.

Kraft, Charles H., et al. *Paradigm Shifts in Christian Witness: Insights from Anthropology, Communication, and Spiritual Power: Essays in Honor of Charles H. Kraft*. Maryknoll, NY: Orbis, 2008.

Larkin, William J., Jr. *Acts*. The IVP New Testament Commentary Series. Downers Grove, IL: InterVarsity, 1995.

———. "The Contribution of the Gospels and Acts to a Biblical Theology of Religions." In *Christianity and the Religions*, edited by Edward Rommen and Harold Netland, 72–91. Pasadena, CA: William Carey Library, 1995.

———. *Culture and Biblical Hermeneutics: Interpreting and Applying the Authoritative Word in a Relativistic Age*. Grand Rapids: Baker, 1988.

The Lausanne Movement. "The Lausanne Covenant." https://www.lausanne.org/content/covenant/lausanne-covenant.

Lee, Samuel. *Controversial Tracts on Christianity and Mohammedanism*. Cambridge: J. Smith, 1824.

Lenski, R. C. H. *The Interpretation of St. Paul's First and Second Epistles to the Corinthians*. Minneapolis: Augsburg, 1963.

Lewis, Rebecca. "Insider Movements: Honoring God-Given Identity and Community." *IJFM* 26 (2009) 16–19.

———. "The Integrity of the Gospel and Insider Movements." *IJFM* 27 (2010) 41–48.

———. "Promoting Movements to Christ within Natural Communities." *IJFM* 24 (2007) 75–76.

———. "Sharing the Gospel through Open Networks." *MF* 28 (January–February 2006) 22–23.

Lewis, Tim, and Rebecca Lewis. "Planting Churches: Learning the Hard Way." *MF* 31 (January–February 2009) 16–18.
Lingel, Joshua, et al., eds. *Chrislam: How Missionaries Are Promoting an Islamized Gospel*. Garden Grove, CA: i2 Ministries, 2011.
Lingel, Joshua. "Islamizing the Bible: Insider Movements and Scripture Translation." In *Chrislam: How Missionaries Are Promoting Islamized Gospel*, edited by Joshua Lingel et al., 156–72. Garden Grove, CA: i2 Ministries, 2011.
Longenecker, Richard N. "Acts." In vol. 9 of *The Expositor's Bible Commentary*, edited by Frank E. Gaebeliein, 205–573. Grand Rapids: Zondervan, 1981.
Luzbetak, Louis J. *The Church and Cultures*. Pasadena, CA: William Carey Library, 1970.
Malefijt, Annemarie de Xaal. *Religion and Culture: An Introduction to the Anthropology of Religion*. New York: McMillan, 1968.
Marlowe, Michael. "Against the Theology of 'Dynamic Equivalence.'" http://www.bible-researcher.com/dynamic-equivalence.html.
Massey, Joshua. "God's Amazing Diversity in Drawing Muslims to Christ." *IJFM* 17 (2000) 5–14.
———. "His Ways Are Not Our Ways." *EMQ* 35 (1999) 188–97.
———. "Living Like Jesus, A Torah-Observant Jew: Delighting in God's Law for Incarnational Witness to Muslims." *IJFM* 21 (2004) 13–22, 55–71.
———. "Misunderstanding C5 and the Infinite Translatability of Christ." *EMQ* Unabridged Online Edition (2004) 1–18. http://bgc.gospelcom.net/emis/ pdfs/ Misunderstanding_ C5.pdf.
———. "Misunderstanding C5: His Ways Are Not Our Orthodoxy." *EMQ* (2004) 296–304.
———. "Planting the Church Underground in Muslim Context." *IJFM* 13 (1996) 139–53.
McCurry, Don M. "Cross-Cultural Models for Muslim Evangelism." *Missiology* 4 (1976) 267–83.
McCurry, Don M., ed. *The Gospel and Islam: A 1978 Compendium*. Monrovia, CA: MARC, 1979.
McDermott, Gerald R. *Can Evangelicals Learn from World Religions? Jesus, Revelation and Religious Traditions*. Downers Grove, IL: InterVarsity, 2000.
McDowell, Bruce A., and Anees Zaka. *Muslims and Christians at the Table: Promoting Biblical Understanding among North American Muslims*. Phillipsburg, NJ: P&R, 1999.
Mohler, R. Albert, Jr. "Confessional Evangelicalism." In *Four Views on the Spectrum of Evangelicalism*, edited by Kevin T. Bauder et al., 68–96. Grand Rapids: Zondervan, 2011.
Moreau, Scott. *Contextualization in World Missions: Mapping and Assessing Evangelical Models*. Grand Rapids: Kregel, 2012.
———. "Evangelical Models of Contextualization." In *Local Theology for the Global Church*, edited by Matthew Cook et al., 165–93. Pasadena, CA: William Carey Library, 2010.
———. "Syncretism." In *Evangelical Dictionary of World Missions*, edited by Scott Moreau, 924–25. Grand Rapids: Baker, 2000.

Morgan, Christopher W. "Inclusivism and Exclusivism." In *Faith Comes by Hearing: A Response to Inclusivism*, edited by Christopher W. Morgan and Robert A. Peterson, 17–39. Downers Grove, IL: IVP, 2008.

Morgan, Christopher W., and Robert A. Peterson. *Faith Comes by Hearing: A Response to Inclusivism*. Downers Grove, IL: IVP, 2008.

Mott, John R. *The Outlook in the Moslem World*. London: Edinburgh House, 1924.

Muir, Sir William. *The Coran: Its Composition and Teaching, and the Testimony It Bears to the Holy Scriptures*. London: SPCK, 1878.

———. "The Koran Examined." In *The Witness of the Koran to the Christian Scriptures: Papers for Thoughtful Muslims*, no. 2, 12–43. London and Madras: Christian Literature Society for India, 1900.

———. *Mahomet and Islam*. London: Religious Tract Society, 1887.

———. *The Mohammedan Controversy and Other Indian Articles*. Edinburgh: T. & T. Clark, 1897.

———. *The Rise and Decline of Islam*. London: Religious Tract Society, 1883.

Musk, Bill. "Honour and Shame." *Evangelical Review of Theology* 20 (1996) 156–67.

Nash. Ron. *Is Jesus the Only Savior*. Grand Rapids: Zondervan, 1982.

Netland, Harold. *Dissonant Voices*. Grand Rapids: Eerdmans, 1991.

———. *Encountering Religious Pluralism*. Downers Grove, IL: InterVarsity, 2001.

———. "Evaluating Truth Claims across Boundaries." In *The Relationship between Epistemology, Hermeneutics, Biblical Theology and Contextualization: Understanding Truth*, edited by Douglas W. Kennard, 72–92. Lewiston, NY: Edwin Mellen, 1999.

Nicholls, Bruce. *Contextualization: A Theology of Gospel and Culture*. Vancouver: Regent College, 1995.

———. "Theological Education and Evangelization." In *Let the Earth Hear His Voice: International Congress on World Evangelization Lausanne, Switzerland*, edited by J. D. Douglas, 634–45. Minneapolis: World Wide Publications, 1975.

Nichols, Laurie Fortunak, and Gary Corwin, eds. *Envisioning Effective Ministry: Evangelism in a Muslim Context*. Wheaton, IL: EMIS, 2010.

Nickel, Gordon D. *Peaceable Witness among Muslims*. Scottdale, PA: Herald, 1999.

Nida, Eugene A. "Intelligibility and Acceptability in Bible Translating." *The Bible Translator* 39 (1988) 301–08.

———. *Message and Mission: The Communication of the Christian Faith*. New York: Harper & Brothers, 1960.

Niebuhr, H. Richard. *Christ and Culture*. New York: Harper & Brothers, 1951.

Nikides, Bill. "Evaluating 'Insider Movements': C5 (Messianic Muslims)." *SFM* 4 (2006) 1–15.

———. "A Response to Kevin Higgins' 'Inside What? Church, Culture, Religion and Insider Movements in Biblical Perspective.'" *SFM* 5 (2009) 92–113.

Oden, Thomas C. "Without Excuse: Classic Christian Exegesis of General Revelation." *JETS* 41 (1998) 55–68.

Okholm, Dennis L., and Timothy R. Phillips, eds. *Four Views on Salvation in a Pluralistic World*. Grand Rapids: Zondervan, 1996.

Osborne, Grant R. *The Hermeneutical Spiral: A Comprehensive Introduction to Biblical Interpretation*. Downers Grove, IL: InterVarsity, 1991.

Ott, Craig, and Harold A. Netland, eds. *Globalizing Theology: Belief and Practice in an Era of World Christianity*. Grand Rapids: Baker Academic, 2006.

Ott, Craig, et al., eds. *Encountering Theology of Missions: Biblical Foundations, Historical Developments, and Contemporary Issues*. Grand Rapids: Baker, 2010.
Packer, James I. "The Gospel: Its Content and Communication: A Theological Perspective." In *Down to Earth: Studies in Christianity and Culture*, edited by Robert Coote and John Stott, 97–114. Grand Rapids, William Eerdmans, 1980.
Padilla, C. Rene. "Hermeneutics and Culture: A Theological Perspective." In *Down to Earth: Studies in Christianity and Culture*, edited by Robert Coote and John Stott, 63–94. Grand Rapids: Eerdmans, 1980.
Parshall, Phil. *The Cross and the Crescent: Understanding the Muslim Heart and Mind*. Waynesboro, GA: Gabriel, 2002.
———. "Danger! New Directions in Contextualization." *EMQ* 34 (1998) 404–6, 409–10.
———. "Evangelizing Muslims: Are There Ways?" *CT* (January 1979) 28–29.
———. "Lessons Learned in Contextualization." In *Muslims and Christians on the Emmaus Road*, edited by Dudley Woodberry, 251–65. Monrovia, CA: MARC, 1989.
———. *Muslim Evangelism: Contemporary Approaches to Contextualization*. Waynesboro, GA: Gabriel, 2003.
———. *New Paths in Muslim Evangelism*. Grand Rapids: Baker, 1980.
Peters, George W. "Issues Confronting Evangelical Missions." In *Evangelical Missions Tomorrow*, edited by Wade T. Coggins and E. L. Frizen Jr., 156–71. South Pasadena, CA: William Carey Library, 1977.
———. "An Overview of Missions to Muslims." In *The Gospel and Islam: A 1978 Compendium*, edited by Don M. McCurry, 390–404. Monrovia, CA: MARC, 1979.
Peterson, Brian K. "The Possibility of a Hindu Christ-Follower: Hans Staffner's Proposal for the Dual Identity of Disciples of Christ within High Caste Hindu Communities." *IJFM* 24 (2007) 87–97.
Peterson, David. "The Worship of the New Community." In *Witness to the Gospel: The Theology of Acts*, edited by I. Howard Marshall and David Peterson, 373–95. Grand Rapids: William B. Eerdmans, 1998.
The Pew Forum and Research Center on Religion and Public Life. "Mapping the Global Muslim Population: A Report on the Size and Distribution of the World's Muslim Population." Washington, DC: Pew Research Center, 2009. http://www.pewforum.org/2009/10/07/mapping-the-global-muslim-population/.
Pfander, Karl G. *Balance of Truth*. Edited by W. St. Clair Tisdall. Rev. and enl. ed. Villach, Austria: 1986.
Phil. "A Response to Kevin Higgins' 'Inside What? Church, Culture, Religion and Insider Movements in Biblical Perspective.'" *SFM* 5 (2009) 114–26.
Philip, Johnson C., and Saneesh Cherian. "Introduction to Integrated Christian Apologetics." http://d.scribd.com/docs/273vjofcj9ev3dpy8epp.pdf.
Pinnock, Clark. "Toward an Evangelical Theology of Religions." *JETS* 33 (1990) 359–68.
———. *A Wideness in God's Mercy: The Finality of Jesus Christ in a World of Religions*. Grand Rapids: Zondervan, 1992.
Piper, John. "Minimizing the Bible? Seeker-Driven Pastors and Radical Contextualization in Missions." *MF* (January–February 2006) 16–17.
Polhill, John B. *Acts*. The New American Commentary, vol. 26. Nashville, TN: Broadman, 1992.

Poston, Larry. "Evaluating 'A Common Word': The Problem of 'Points of Contact.'" *EMQ* 46 (2010) 62–68.
Provan, Ian W. *1 and 2 Kings*. New International Biblical Commentary. Peabody, MA: Hendrickson, 1995.
Qureshi, Nabeel. *Answering Jihad: A Better Way Forward*. Grand Rapids: Zondervan, 2016.
———. *No God But One: Allah or Jesus? A Former Muslim Investigates the Evidence for Islam and Christianity*. Grand Rapids: Zondervan, 2016.
———. *Seeking Allah, Finding Jesus: A Devout Muslim Encounters Christianity*. Grand Rapids: Zondervan, 2014.
Register, Ray G. *Dialogue and Interfaith Witness with Muslims*. Kingsport, TN: Moody, 1979.
Rheenen, Gailyn Van, ed. *Contextualization and Syncretism: Navigating Cultural Currents*. Pasadena, CA: William Carey Library, 2006.
Richardson, Don. *Eternity in Their Hearts*. Ventura, CA: Regal, 1984.
———. *Peace Child*. Glendale, CA: Regal, 1981.
Rickards, Donald R. *The Contextualization of the Gospel in the World of Islam*. Lynchburg, VA: Liberty Baptist Seminary, 1984.
———. "The Development of New Tools to Aid in Muslim Evangelism." In *The Gospel and Islam: A 1978 Compendium*, edited by Don M. McCurry, 429–41. Monrovia, CA: MARC, 1979.
Ridgway, John. "Insider Movements in the Gospels and Acts." *IJFM* 24 (2007) 77–86.
Robertson, Archibald, and Alfred Plummer. *A Critical and Exegetical Commentary on the First Epistle of St. Paul to the Corinthians*. Edinburgh: T. & T. Clark, 1914.
Rommen, Edward. "The De-Theologizing of Missiology." *Trinity World Forum* 19 (1993) 1–4.
Rommen, Edward, and Harold Netland, eds. *Christianity and the Religions: A Biblical Theology of World Religions*. Evangelical Missiological Society Series 2. Pasadena, CA: William Carey Library, 1995.
Sanders, John. "Inclusivism." In *What About Those Who Have Never Heard?: Three Views on the Destiny of the Unevangelized*, edited by Gabriel J. Fackre et al., 21–55. Downers Grove, IL: InterVarsity, 1995.
———. *No Other Name: An Investigation into the Destiny of the Unevangelized*. Grand Rapids: Eerdmans, 1992.
Savelle, Charles H. "A Reexamination of the Prohibitions in Acts 15." *BibSac* 161 (2004) 449–68.
Schlorff, Samuel. "The Hermeneutical Crisis in Muslim Evangelization." *EMQ* 16 (1980) 143–51.
———. *Missiological Models in Ministry to Muslims*. Upper Darby, PA: Middle East Resources, 2006.
———. "The Missionary Use of the Qur'an: A Historical and Theological Study of the Contextualization of the Gospel." ThM Thesis, Westminster Theological Seminary, 1984.
———. "Muslim Ideology and Christian Apologetics." *Missiology* 21 (1993) 173–85.
———. "Theological and Apologetical Dimensions of Muslim Evangelization." *WTJ* 42 (1980) 335–66.
———. "The Translational Model for Mission in Resistant Muslim Society: A Critique and an Alternative." *Missiology* 28 (2000) 305–28.

Schnucker, R. V. "Neo-orthodoxy, History." In *Evangelical Dictionary of Theology*, edited by Walter A. Elwell, 819–21. Grand Rapids: Baker, 1984.
Schreiter, Thomas. *Constructing Local Theologies*. Maryknoll, NY: Orbis, 1985.
Sharkey, Heather J. "Arabic Antimissionary Treaties: Muslim Responses to Christian Evangelism in the Modern Middle East." *IBMR* 28 (2004) 98–104.
Shaw, R. Daniel. *Transculturation: The Cultural Factor in Translation and Other Communication Tasks*. Pasadena, CA: William Carey, 1988.
Shumaker, Richard, ed. *Report of Conference on Media in Islamic Culture*. Clearwater, FL: International Christian Broadcasters, 1974.
Simnowitz, Adam. "How Insider Movements Affect Ministry: Personal Reflections." In *Chrislam: How Missionaries Are Promoting Islamized Gospel*, edited by Joshua Lingel et al., 199–226. Garden Grove, CA: i2 Ministries, 2011.
Smith, Jay. "Courage in Our Convictions: Debating Muslims, New Life for an Old Method?" *EMQ* 34 (1998) 28–35.
Soards, Marion L. *1 Corinthians*. New International Biblical Commentary 7. Peabody, MA: Hendrickson, 1999.
Spradley, James P. *Participant Observation*. New York: Holt, Rinehart and Winston, 1980.
Steele, William. "The Insider Movement as a Strategy for Evangelizing Muslims." *SFM* 5 (2009) 127–32.
Stein, Robert H. *Luke*. The New American Commentary 24. Nashville: Broadman, 1992.
Strange, Daniel. "General Revelation: Sufficient or Insufficient?" In *Faith Comes by Hearing: A Response to Inclusivism*, edited by Christopher W. Morgan and Robert A. Peterson, 40–77. Downers Grove, IL: IVP, 2008.
Strauss, Steve. "Creeds, Confessions, and Global Theologizing: A Case Study in Comparative Christologies." In *Globalizing Theology: Belief and Practice in an Era of World Christianity*, edited by Craig Ott and Herold A. Netland, 140–56. Grand Rapids: Baker, 2006.
Taber, Charles R. *The World Is Too Much with Us*. Macon, GA: Mercer University Press, 1991.
Talman, Harley. "Comprehensive Contextualization: Islam, Once a Hopeless Frontier, Now?" *IJFM* 21 (2004) 6–12.
———. "Is Muhammad Also Among the Prophets?" *IJFM* 31 (2014) 169–90.
Tennent, Timothy. "The Challenge of Churchless Christianity: An Evangelical Assessment." *IBMR* 29 (2005) 171–77.
———. "Christian Encounter with Other Religions." In *Encountering Theology of Missions: Biblical Foundations, Historical Developments, and Contemporary Issues*, edited by Craig Ott et al., 292–316. Grand Rapids: Baker, 2010.
———. "Followers of Jesus (Isa) in Islamic Mosques: A Closer Examination of C-5 'High Spectrum' Contextualization." *IJFM* 23 (2006) 101–15.
———. *Invitation to World Missions: A Trinitarian Missiology for the Twenty-First Century*. Grand Rapids: Kregel, 2009.
———. *Theology in the Context of World Christianity*. Grand Rapids: Zondervan, 2007.
Terry, John Mark. "Approaches to the Evangelization of Muslims." *EMQ* 32 (1996) 168–73.
Thiselton, Anthony. *The First Epistle to the Corinthians*. The New International Greek Testament Commentary. Grand Rapids: Eerdmans, 2000.

Timmons, Tim. "Christianity Isn't the Way—Jesus Is." *IJFM* 25 (2008) 157–60.
Tisdall, W. St. Clair. *Christian Reply to Muslim Objections*. Villach, Austria: Light of Life, 1980. A Reprint of *A Manual of the Leading Muhammedan Objections to Christianity*. London: SPCK, 1904.
———. *The Original Sources of the Qur'an*. London: SPCK, 1905.
———. *The Religion of the Crescent*. London: SPCK, 1895.
Travis, John. "The C1 to C6 Spectrum: A Practical Tool for Defining Six Types of 'Christ-Centered Communities' ('C') Found in the Muslim Context." *EMQ* 34 (1998) 407–08.
———. "Messianic Muslim Followers of Isa: A Closer Look at C5 Believers and Congregations." *IJFM* 17 (2000) 55–59.
———. "Must All Muslims Leave 'Islam' to Follow Jesus?" *EMQ* 34 (1998) 411–15.
———. "Producing and Using Meaningful Translations of the Taurat, Zabur, and Injil." *IJFM* 23 (2006) 73–77.
———. "Response to Timothy C. Tennent's Article." *IJFM* 23 (2006) 124–25.
Travis, John, and Anna Travis. "Appropriate Approaches in Muslim Contexts." In *Appropriate Christianity*, edited by Charles H. Kraft, 397–414. Pasadena, CA: William Carey Library, 2005.
———. "Contextualization among Muslims, Hindus, and Buddhists." *MF* (September–October 2005) 12–15.
———. "Factors Affecting the Identity that Jesus Followers Choose." In *From Seed to Fruit: Global Trends, Fruitful Practices, and Emerging Issues among Muslims*, edited by Dudley Woodberry, 193–205. Pasadena, CA: William Carey Library, 2008.
———. "Maximizing the Bible! Glimpses from Our Context." *MF* (January–February 2006) 21–22.
Travis, John, and Dudley Woodberry. "When God's Kingdom Grows Like Yeast: Frequently-Asked Questions about Jesus Movements within Muslim Communities." *MF* 32 (2010) 24–30.
Travis, John, et al. "Four Responses to Timothy C. Tennent's Followers of Jesus (Isa) in Islamic Mosques: A Closer Examination of C-5." *IJFM* 23 (2006) 124–26.
Wallace, Daniel B. *Greek Grammar Beyond the Basics: An Exegetical Syntax of the New Testament*. Grand Rapids: Zondervan, 1996.
Wan, Enoch. "A Critique of Charles Kraft's Use/Misuse of Communication and Social Sciences in Biblical Interpretation and Missiological Formulation." In *Missiology and Social Sciences: Contributions, Cautions and Conclusions*, edited by Edward Rommen and Gary Corwin, 121–64. EMS Series 4. Pasadena, CA: William Carey Library, 1996.
———. "A Critique of Functional Missionary Anthropology." *His Dominion* 8 (1982) 18–22.
Warfield, B. B. *The Inspiration and Authority of the Bible*. London: Marshall Morgan and Scott, 1951.
Waterman, L. D. "Do the Roots Affect the Fruits?" *IJFM* 24 (2007) 57–63.
Watt, W. Montgomery. *Islam and Christianity Today: A Contribution to Dialogue*. Boston: Routledge & Kegan Paul, 1983.
Werff, Lyle Vander. *Christian Mission to Muslims: The Record*. South Pasadena, CA: William Carey Library, 1977.
Wilder, John. "Some Reflections on Possibilities for People Movements among Muslims." *Missiology* 5 (1977) 301–20.

Williams, Mark. "Aspects of High-Spectrum Contextualization in Ministries to Muslims." *JAM* 5 (2003) 75–91.
Wilson, J. Christy. *The Christian Message to Islam*. New York: Revell, 1950.
———. "Moslem Converts." *MW* 34 (1944) 171–84.
———. "Presenting Christ to Moslems." *MW* 25 (1935) 336–46.
Witherington, Ben, III. *The Acts of the Apostles: A Socio-Rhetorical Commentary*. Grand Rapids: Eerdmans, 1998.
Wolfe, J. Henry. "Insider Movements: An Assessment of the Viability of Retaining Socio-Religious Insider Identity in High-Religious Contexts." PhD diss., Southern Baptist Theological Seminary, 2011.
Woodberry, Dudley. "Can We Dialogue with Islam? What 38 Muslim Scholars Said to the Pope in a Little-Known Open Letter." *CT* 51 (January 2007) 108–9.
———. "Contextualization among Muslims: Reusing Common Pillars." *IJFM* 13 (1996) 171–86.
———. "To the Muslim I Became a Muslim." *IJFM* 24 (2007) 23–28.
———, ed. *From Seed to Fruit: Global Trends, Fruitful Practices, and Emerging Issues among Muslims*. Pasadena, CA: William Carey Library, 2008.
———, ed. *Muslims and Christians on the Emmaus Road: Crucial Issues in Witness among Muslims*. Monrovia, CA: MARC, 1989.
Woodberry, Dudley, et al. "Why Muslims Follow Jesus: The Results of a Recent Survey of Converts from Islam." *CT* 51 (October 2007) 80–85.
Woods, Scott. "Biblical Look at C5 Muslim Evangelism." *EMQ* 39 (2003) 188–195.
Youssef, Michael. *Making Christ Known to Muslims*. Atlanta: Haggai Institute, 1980.
Zaka, Anees. "Church without Walls: North American Ministry Promoting Understanding." *Urban Mission* 15 (1998) 47–54.
Zwemer, Samuel. *Arabia: The Cradle of Islam*. 4th ed. rev. New York: Fleming H. Revell, 1900.
———. "The Chasm." *MW* 9 (1919) 111–16.
———. *The Cross Above the Crescent*. Grand Rapids: Zondervan, 1941.
———. "The Diversity of Islam in India." *MW* 2 (1928) 111–23.
———. *Evangelism Today: Message Not Method*. New York: Fleming H. Revell, 1954.
———. "Karl Gottlieb Pfander." *MW* 31 (1941) 217–26.
———. *The Law of Apostasy in Islam*. London: Marshall Brothers, 1924.
———. *The Moslem Christ*. New York: American Tract Society, 1912.
———. *Studies in Popular Islam*. New York: Macmillan, 1939.

www.ingramcontent.com/pod-product-compliance
Lightning Source LLC
Chambersburg PA
CBHW051056230426

43667CB00013B/2314